THE OUTPUT-ORIENTED MANAGER

The Output-Oriented Manager

Bill Reddin, PhD

Gower

Published by
Gower Publishing Company Limited,
Gower House,
Croft Road,
Aldershot,
Hants GU11 3HR,
England

British Library Cataloguing-in-Publication Data

Reddin, Bill, *1930–*
    The output-oriented manager.
    1. Companies. Managers. Effectiveness.
    Improvement
    I.   Title
    658.4'0714

ISBN 0 566 02711 9

Printed and bound in Great Britain by
Biddles Ltd, Guildford and King's Lynn

This book is dedicated to the memory of
Henri Fayol on whose principle
'responsibility must be commensurate
with authority' this book is based.

Contents

PART IV CASE STUDIES

PART V END PIECES

Preface

The book is in five parts: the principles, the application, the benefits, case studies and end pieces. The chapters on principles examine the nature of outputs, how measurement areas must be matched to outputs, and why outputs must be matched to authority. The applications section concentrates on how to apply the principles. It contains many ideas on how to introduce the concept to your colleagues and your superior – that is, to the team of which you are a member – how to apply it on a one-to-one basis in a meeting with your superior, and how to apply it on a team basis with your subordinate team members. All these events lead to much sharper role clarification. When the role is clearly defined, and only then, one moves to objectives and obtaining resources to match objectives and then on to planning. The third part specifies the benefits to be obtained by being an output-oriented manager. Part four presents case studies.

Several of the case studies and some of the examples have appeared in other books I have written over the last 25 years. If a case study or an example makes the point well there seems little need to make changes just for the sake of it.

Some readers will be CEOs of large or small organizations, some will be the top person of a division or other type of major unit, some will be the top person of a particular smaller unit; most will be managers who feel that they could improve their managerial effectiveness and so become output-oriented managers.

This book is designed to help you become more effective. It will help you by showing how to create a special 'mind set' in all of those who report to you and those who report to them. This mind set concerns outputs rather than inputs.

You may find that this book will simply organize your existing knowledge. You may well say, 'I knew all of this, really, but it was not organized in quite this fashion and now I know what I knew.' This is a frequent comment made when the ideas are given in seminar form. There is surely nothing wrong with this kind of comment. It is easy to make things in management difficult; it is hard to make them simple and still right. The only problem with common sense in management is that it is not very common. What this book may do for you is to clarify what you already knew. It will make your knowledge more coherent so you can do a better job at acting on what you know.

The book is designed to be read sequentially. Unless one understands precisely what an output is then much less use can be made of later chapters. The ideas have been used by, literally, hundreds of thousands of managers. All of them were encouraged to challenge the concepts to see if they fitted their own work settings. In response to some consistent comments in the early years, aspects of outputs, measurements and authority have been refined and are reflected here. It demonstrates the practice of many managers over many years and incorporates their suggestions for improvements.

The objective of this book is to help make managers more effective through providing a crisp understanding of their job, in output terms. I first made outputs a central theme in *Effective Management by Objectives* (McGraw-Hill, 1971). It linked management by objectives with outputs and organization development. The book was found to be useful. It stayed in print for fifteen years, went through numerous printings and was translated into many languages. Since then I have worked with this idea in many companies and have refined it and its practice. Seventeen years later, this book represents the best I have learned from myself and others in applying the ideas of that earlier book.

When I introduced the idea of 'second-generation MBO' I gave great emphasis to introducing management by objectives through the team, basing management by objectives on outputs and using the concept of effectiveness as the central value. Of course, I was not the first to use the concept of 'outputs'. However, I was the first to introduce it explicitly into the definition of managerial effectiveness used here. I am sometimes asked, 'How does your concept of output differ from the concept of key result areas?' My answer is simple. 'If you define key result areas exactly as I define outputs and if you arrive at key result areas exactly as I arrive at outputs then they are the same. If you use a different method, they are different.'

The book is meant to be eminently practical for the individual manager to study alone and then to apply in the work situation. As role clarification of the individual position depends very much on the clarity of surrounding roles, this book has to take a team approach. So, while any manager will benefit a great deal by reading it alone, the application has to be with those others immediately surrounding the position occupied. After reading it, a manager should be able to make at least a rough draft of the outputs of the position and how these outputs should be measured. Then the manager should meet the work team consisting of colleagues and the top member of the team, then with the top member alone, and finally with all of the immediate subordinates. This method will lead directly to a far higher output orientation.

This book is designed to create more output-oriented managers. It accomplishes this by providing the manager with all the tools necessary to get a much clearer idea of the job to be done. A recurring problem with organizations is low role clarification. This book gives coherent guidelines on how to overcome this completely. Another problem with organizations is a low connection across roles even when there is high role clarification. There can be high role clarification but no one talks to anyone else. Experienced managers will recognize this problem and know how it leads to low effectiveness.

I do urge those in advisory positions to resist the temptation to build yet another company manual based on this book. This does little except make the staff person temporarily look like something of a hero – and keeps the photocopier running. This book constitutes a sound company manual as it is. Managers deserve to have *this* book placed in their hands, not a potted version of it written by someone not in a line role.

Effectiveness is the central issue in management. It is a manager's job to be effective. It is the only job. The manager may be a managing director, plant manager, research and development manager, government officer, or military general – the central issue is always the same. There is an enormous confusion about effectiveness. Some writers go so far as to claim that it cannot be measured. Some managers measure themselves by what they do rather than what they achieve. Some people think that effectiveness has something to do with 'trying hard'. Effectiveness is not efficiency. Effectiveness is doing the right things, not doing things right.

The prime purpose of any managerial action is to improve managerial effectiveness. It is in the name of this endeavour that one decides on, initiates and pursues one particular course of action over another. For profit-making concerns this amounts to the principle of profit-maximization at the managerial level. There are those who ask about social values and ask what role managers should have in preserving these. The answer is, of course, that a sound way to protect a culture against outside cultural influence is through the individual firm's economic success due to the effectiveness of its individual managers.

One of the central problems in organizational life, leading to lower managerial effectiveness, is lack of clarity about what the job really is. Some jobs, in particular those in production and sales, can be quite clear, but it is my distinct experience that even this is not necessarily true. Jobs at the top of organizations and middle management generally often suffer from low job clarity. Sometimes the job is not understood, sometimes two people are responsible for the same thing, sometimes no one is responsible for some things. At times, in badly designed organizations, people are given responsibility but have no authority. This is a particularly good way to increase conflict and lower effectiveness.

There is more said in this book about authority than in any other management book I know. The reason it is emphasized here is that it is absolutely impossible to determine the outputs of a position unless one knows the authority vested in it. If a brand manager cannot change price then the manager cannot be responsible for profit. The position is that of brand planner. If a regional bank manager cannot close down a branch that manager cannot be responsible for total branch profits. That is obvious when you think about it but it is amazing how many banks do *not* think about it. Without authority being known, it is impossible to determine the true outputs of the job.

In applying outputs this book emphasizes meetings. It is by talking with others you work with that not only your own job but also the jobs of all the others can be more sharply defined. This is not a paperwork exercise, it is a human exercise. It consists of people talking about their work and how their jobs can relate better to each other.

Output orientation is not a one-sided concept, it is a value we can embrace and use. Whatever our personal values, objectives, moral philosophy or political orientation, output orientation is a lifeline. It says: 'Use resources productively, waste less, and make work enjoyable and worthwhile.' The question is not 'Should I be nice to people?' or 'What rules should be followed?', but 'What does it take to be output-oriented here?' We are not talking about the work ethic – and clearly not about the welfare ethic – we are talking about the *output* ethic. It says nothing about 'more power to the workers' or 'screw the workers down'. It does not argue for higher profit. It simply says, 'Measure managers by the extent to which they achieve the output requirements of their positions'.

I am gloriously optimistic about the possibility of sharply increasing output orientation for the individual and for the organization as a whole, with this leading directly to improved individual and organization effectiveness. Readers will quickly recognize that part of their problem is overcoming resistance to throwing out some existing poor systems and poor concepts. It is a relatively easy matter to bring in new concepts if the poor ones are not there to begin with.

While the bulk of the book focuses on the individual manager and improving the individual manager's effectiveness there are many direct links given to the organization as a whole. Chapter 11 in particular discusses how the concepts of outputs can be used as the conceptual base of many other systems in the organization, ranging from the appraisal system to the management information system.

The theme running through this book is that a single description of a job can have many purposes. Some confused writers actually propose one kind of job description for job specification (the kind of person and skills needed for the job), another one for job evaluation (how much is the job worth), yet another one for management by objectives . . . and sometimes even yet another one for appraisal!

Then, even worse, one can find management information systems being designed by those with access to the mainframe but with little access to managers. The only way to design a management information system is by creating job effectiveness description first, and seeing what measurement areas the managers need in order to be effective in their jobs. That's the way.

This book demonstrates that the Job Effectiveness Description can serve all of these purposes equally and well and thus put the concept of effectiveness at the centre of many organization systems.

The sad truth is that many, if not most, organizations are littered with paper purporting to describe aspects of jobs which have no value whatsoever. I have seen job descriptions thirty pages long. I have also seen three-page job descriptions which were equally useless. Short ones, often written by outside consultants for the wrong reasons, emphasize status, number supervised, academic qualifications required, and things like that. They do not get to the main point: what is the contribution of this job to the organization? In short, what are the job outputs? All readers would be advised to burn their existing job description before starting to work through it. If you are timid, burn a photocopy.

This book is not about increasing profit. It is about increasing effectiveness. Some organizations exist to provide service to clients. Some organizations exist to keep costs low. There is nothing in this book that does not apply to government, the military, volunteer organizations, health organizations, educational systems, and the churches. If a position exists it must exist for a reason and this reason is best expressed in output terms. There is no place these days for managers or administrators – or whatever they are called – who actually believe that their work is such that their contribution is not measurable. What they must be told, as kindly as possible, is: 'If you cannot measure the outputs of your work, then simply forget your work because no one will ever know about its effect anyway.'

I have quite deliberately not given much attention to the methods of identifying outputs for production and sales systems. The reason is that it is much too easy. The examples given, in the main, are the ones presumed to be more difficult and drawn from universities and governments and those apparently vague middle-management jobs.

I have been highly selective in the case studies chosen. One is from a small firm where the CEO decided to go it alone without any outside help. The results were dramatic. Another, quite different, case study involves a firm of 35,000 people. Introducing output orientation in a firm of that size takes a great deal of effort but they decided it was worth while and did it. And, after all, it *was* worth it: their profits, already considered high, quadrupled in four years. IBM and many other large firms use the ideas precisely as explained in this book. They drew their conceptual foundations directly from my earlier works as can be seen in the identical terminology, methods and examples used. The case study in Chapter 15 will help you think about your organization, or your part of the organization, rather more diagnostically in terms of its strengths and weaknesses and what needs to be changed in order for output orientation to be increased.

This book is the second of a trilogy. The other two books are *The Output-Oriented Organization* and *Pay for Outputs*. The obvious overlap across the three is the concept of outputs, and the chapters dealing with outputs are virtually repeated in each. The *Output-Oriented Organization* very much reflects the title in that it looks at the organization as a whole rather than, as here, the individual positions in it. That book is best used by those who are heads of units in organizations. *Pay for Outputs* proposes a new method of payment for potential effectiveness and payment for actual effectiveness. Payment for potential effectiveness means paying for what the job is worth compared to other jobs and is usually based upon a job evaluation technique. There are many of these. None of them, however, relentlessly pursues the concept of outputs. My book carries job evaluation further than usual in that it also links payment to the actual outputs achieved. That is, what the managers actually achieve. This is sometimes called incentive pay. Readers who are comfortable with any one of these three books should find as much comfort in the other two.

Much in this book has been derived from the Managerial Effectiveness Seminar described in Chapter 10. This seminar has been conducted for over twenty years in over twenty countries in many companies, large and small. By any standards, the seminar is highly useful. It not only gives formal training in outputs and applying these to neutral objects such as case studies but, for more than half of the seminar, applies the concept of outputs and managerial styles and effectiveness generally to the individual and to the job the individual is in. Those thinking of driving the organization to a greater output orientation should look at this seminar which is conducted on an in-company basis and is also available publicly in many countries.

The structure of this book spells out what I think the limiting factor on effectiveness really is. It is not brains, knowledge, intent, motivation or lack of external persuasion. It starts with knowing precisely what the job is. In technical terms this is called role clarity. All of us must understand the position we occupy if we are going to be effective in it.

We all need a much sharper concept of the function of managerial effectiveness in society. It it apparent to me that productive organizations are designed by society to produce added value. That is, the inputs are less than the outputs in terms of social economic value expressed in some way or another. There is a logical conclusion: managers have a social duty to be more effective.

W.J. Reddin, PhD
Station Road,
Motspur Park
Surrey KT3 6JH
UK

My thanks to . . .

I would like to thank many people.

John Fry and Valerie Richardson were very helpful, as usual, in producing the right kind of documentation I wanted in the right form at the right time – all the way to sending this book to the publisher.

Angela Wood used the magic of the word processor, Joan Wilson helped a great deal with earlier drafts, and Val Barrett with the later ones. Claudia Maconick was very helpful in the editing process.

In particular I wish to acknowledge the cooperation and support of those companies who used this approach to organization change. In particular, to thank them for advancing these ideas, making them even more practical and being willing to share their information and experiences. I am deeply indebted to them. They are:

Arthur Young
Atlas Air
Bowater Scott
Ethiopian Airlines
Falconbridge Nickel Mines
Ford Motor Company
IBM Corporation
International Computers Limited
John Player & Son
Johnson Wax
Metal Box
Moosehead Breweries
New Brunswick Electric Power Commission
Pedigree Petfood
Siemens
Westinghouse
Westpac Banking Corporation

My thanks go also to Ross O'Brien and the other four members of the OD Team at Westpac – Keith Barber, Ian Colley, Bryn Harris and William Paget – for contributing several valuable ideas.

W.J.R.

Acknowledgements

I should like to express my thanks and acknowledgements to the following publishers and individuals for their courtesy in permitting quotations from the following copyrighted works:

McGraw-Hill Book Company Limited (UK) for permission to adapt the exhibit 'Basic Style Differences', from W.J. Reddin, *How To Make Your Managerial Style More Effective*; and for permission to use the chapter 'How To Improve Your Managerial Effectiveness Through Training', from the same text.

Colin Ward, Managing Director, Atlas Air Australia Pty for permission to quote from his letter and talk on 'Change In An Air Conditioning Firm'.

The Financial Review for permission to quote from an article by Richard Hefy, 'Atlas Reconditions The Attitude to Success'.

Westpac Banking Corporation for permission to use extracts from their internal document 'Managing For Results – The Westpac Management System'.

Bob White, CEO of Westpac Banking Corporation, for permission to quote from his talk to a meeting of the International Monetary Conference in Boston, USA.

IBM Australia Limited for permission to use their internal documents 'Performance Planning Counselling and Evaluation' and 'Performance Planning For Individuals and Teams'.

The Delegation matrix in the above IBM documents was designed by Gery Harlos of Harlos Australia Pty Ltd.

W.J.R.

PART I
The Principles

Introduction

This book is designed as a handbook to help individual managers become more effective. This is accomplished by verifying the principles on which high outputs are based, giving straightforward guides to action, providing clear concrete action steps, and giving illustrative case studies.

The precise principles on which output-oriented management are based, include outputs, measurement and authority. The output-oriented manager needs: clarity about the outputs of the position; precise measurement areas for all of the outputs; and a clear match of authority to these outputs. If the authority is unavailable, then the outputs must change. Part I deals with these issues.

1 What are your outputs?

The manager has the task of creating a true whole that is larger than the sum of its parts, a productive entity that turns out more than the sum of the resources put into it.

Peter F. Drucker

The business of life is to go forward.

Samuel Johnson

There is only one realistic and unambiguous definition of managerial effectiveness. Effectiveness is the extent to which a manager achieves the output requirements of the position. Seen this way, the concept of managerial effectiveness becomes the central issue in management. It is the manager's job to be effective. It is the only job. Once this definition is accepted and understood it can lead directly to changes in personnel policy and fundamental changes in management development practices, and in the philosophy leading to output orientations.

Managers occupy positions. The positions have inputs or duties associated with them. The manager performs these. The most important thing though is to achieve the outputs. Exhibit 1.1 shows the difference between the inputs, what the manager does, the position in which the manager is, and the outputs, what a manager achieves.

To understand what managerial effectiveness is, it is necessary to distinguish the three terms: managerial effectiveness, apparent effectiveness and personal effectiveness.

CONCEPTS OF MANAGERIAL EFFECTIVENESS

Managerial effectiveness

Managerial effectiveness is not an aspect of personality; it is not something a manager has. To see it this way is nothing more or less

4

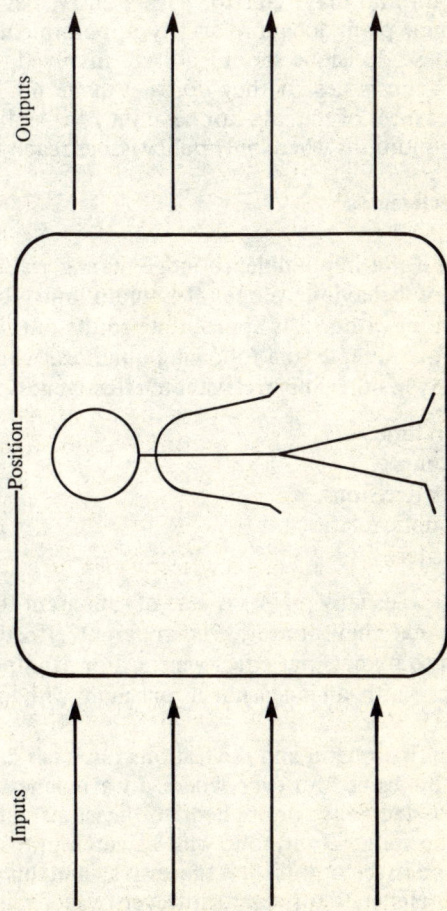

Managers occupy positions. The positions have inputs, or duties, associated with them.
The manager does these. The key point is, however, to achieve the outputs.

Exhibits 1.1   The outputs are the thing

than a return to the now discarded trait theory of leadership which suggested that more effective leaders have special qualities not possessed by less effective leaders. Effectiveness is best seen as something a manager produces from a situation by managing it appropriately. In current terminology it represents output, not input. The manager must think in terms of performance, not personality. It is not so much what managers do, but what they achieve. The following is an extreme example:

> The managers' true worth to their companies may sometimes be measured by the amount of time they could remain dead in their offices without anyone noticing. The longer the time the more likely it is that they make long-run policy decisions rather than short-run administrative decisions. The key decisions in a company are long-run and may refer to market entry, new-product introduction, new-plant location or key appointments. The persons making these decisions should not get involved, as can happen, with short-run issues. If they do, they have not decided on the output measures of the job, nor have they the skill or opportunity to create conditions where only policy issues reach them.

Apparent effectiveness

It is difficult, if not impossible, to judge managerial effectiveness by observation of behaviour alone. Behaviour must be evaluated in terms of whether or not it is appropriate to the output requirements of the job. For example, the following qualities, while important in some jobs, may in others be irrelevant to effectiveness:

> usually is on time,
> answers promptly,
> makes quick decisions,
> is good at public relations,
> is a good writer.

These qualities usually give an air of apparent effectiveness in whatever context they appear. But apparent effectiveness may or may not lead to managerial effectiveness. For example, consider the case of Charles Smith, an independent consultant with four employees.

> He was the first one in and the last one out each day. He virtually ran everything and ran everywhere. In a business which usually makes low demands for immediate decisions, he always made them on the spot. 'Do it now' was his catch phrase. He was very intelligent, active, optimistic, aggressive, and his job input was enormous. His staff turnover, however, was 100 per cent in one

year, and he sometimes signed contracts which he had no chance of fulfilling.

If his business failed, the casual observer might well say, 'It wasn't because of Charlie', thus showing the confusion that exists over the important differences between apparent effectiveness and managerial effectiveness.

Conventional job descriptions often lead to an emphasis on what could be called *managerial efficiency*: the ratio of output to input. The problem is that if both input and output are low, efficiency could still be 100 per cent. In fact, a manager or department could easily be 100 per cent efficient and 0 per cent effective. Efficient managers are easily identified. They prefer to:

do things right	rather than	do right things
solve problems	rather than	produce creative alternatives
safeguard resources	rather than	optimize resource utilization
discharge duties	rather than	obtain results

Conventional job descriptions lead to the apparent effectiveness of the behaviour as listed in the left-hand column; a job effectiveness description which emphasized managerial effectiveness would lead to performance as listed in the column on the right.

Conventional job descriptions and management audits are usually on the internal efficiency of an organizational system rather than on its external effectiveness or its outputs. It is a simple matter to greatly increase internal efficiency at the same time by the same procedures.

The distinction between managerial effectiveness and apparent effectiveness can be further illustrated by what happens when an over energetic new manager brings what appears to be chaos to an organization but the situation clearly begins to improve. Unless outputs are the focus of attention, the result can be serious distortion about what is really going on.

Personal effectiveness

Poorly defined job outputs can also lead to what might be called personal effectiveness, that is, the satisfying of personal objectives rather than the objectives of the organization. This is particularly likely to occur with ambitious people in an organization having only a few closely defined management output measures. Meetings with these people are riddled with hidden agendas which operate below the surface and lead to poor decision–making. To illustrate:

In a three-day meeting to set corporate objectives for a consumer goods firm, one of the four divisional managers initiated a series of proposals for reorganization and argued for them forcibly.

While all had some merit, it emerged, as they were outlined, that most would not lead to greatly improved team effectiveness. Other team members saw quickly that all these proposals were aimed, to some extent unconsciously, at improving the manager's power and prestige.

This issue was confronted for several hours and the team members, many of whom had previously had intentions similar to those proposed, finally decided to turn their attention away from improving their personal effectiveness to improving their managerial effectiveness and, therefore, their total team effectiveness. The top management structure was modified but in keeping with market, consumer, competitive and organization needs; not with personal needs.

There is nothing wrong with either personal effectiveness or apparent effectiveness. We all like to succeed in our own terms and we all like to appear effective. The problem arises when either condition is confused with managerial effectiveness. In a well-designed firm, all three kinds of effectiveness could occur simultaneously for a particular manager. This would mean that managers who are in fact effective look as if they are (apparent effectiveness), and are rewarded for it (personal effectiveness).

THE DEADLY SIN OF INPUTS

The first step in helping managers to be more effective is to help them see their job in output terms. To keep the concept of effectiveness in mind, we can refer to these outputs as effectiveness areas, but they can have a variety of other names. The problem is that too many jobs are described in terms of inputs, not outputs, in terms of input areas and not in terms of effectiveness areas.

Some managers have narrow views of their jobs. What they do they may do well, but they leave an enormous amount undone. Some managers let the in-basket define the nature of their potential contribution and the clock its limit. Some managers might view their contribution as simply that of managing a going concern and keeping it on an even keel, while others might see the same job as incorporating large components of subordinate development and creative problem-solving. Still others might see their position primarily as a linking pin connecting with other parts of the firm, and thus might take a wider view of their responsibilities.

Conventional job descriptions

The source of much of the problem which surrounds effectiveness is found in the way job descriptions are written. Lengthy job descriptions or crash programmes to write or update them usually have little actual usefulness. As C. Northcote Parkinson has pointed out, the last act of a dying organization is to issue a revised and greatly enlarged rule-book. This observation may hold as well for crash programmes to write job descriptions.

Many, if not most, managerial jobs are defined in terms of their input and behaviour requirements by such phrases as: 'administers' . . . 'maintains' . . . 'organizes' . . . 'plans' . . . 'schedules'. Naturally enough, managers never refer to job descriptions like these; once made, they are not very useful as an operating guide. They are often proposed initially by those who want to use a seemingly scientific technique to justify a widespread change in salary differentials or a change in the organization's structure. They are often a negative influence, as they focus on input and behaviour, the less important aspect of the manager's job.

The most common error in writing effectiveness areas is in producing input areas instead. An input area is an incorrect statement of an effectiveness area which is based on activities or input rather than results or outputs.

The best thing that can be said about such job descriptions is that they encourage creative writing, they lead to the increased sale of paper, and they often keep consultants off the streets. Obviously, they directly encourage managers to exaggerate the importance of their job and the wide range of duties entailed. It is no wonder that they are rarely used to improve managerial effectiveness, and in fact contribute to lowering managerial effectiveness – unless they are not looked at at all, which is usually the case. Such descriptions are often produced as a basis for a job evaluation scheme which may itself be based on inputs. Thus inputs are linked into rewards and this, naturally enough, can help drive an organization to death's door.

Some job description schemes are, in fact, based only on input descriptions. Here one finds such objectives as 'Answer letters within two days' or 'Have all reports in on time'. All of these sound like important objectives, and all are measurable. The problem is that, while they may be important, all are really inputs and, for most positions, have nothing to do with why the position was created.

What is your potential contribution?

Once managers have decided they want to become effective, they should first consider how they could contribute more, or more effectively, than they are doing at present. Specialists seldom take contributions into account. They often see themselves simply as a knowledge bank: 'I am not paid for what I do but for what I know.' Such a view can and does insulate the specialist from the firm, the professor from the student and the university from society. Job descriptions rarely take account of contributions and if followed too closely may discourage contributions from being made. Too often, job descriptions look downward not outward. They concentrate on activities a manager must perform and not the method by which effectiveness may be increased. Contributions can seldom be expressed, or seen, in terms of maintenance of a system. Where possible, contribution should be expressed through effectiveness areas in terms of growth, profitability and innovation.

INPUTS GONE WILD

Here are the proposed effectiveness areas, though called by another name, of three staff positions. These, together with the areas for other positions, were published and widely distributed by a consulting firm to demonstrate the type of work they did. They demonstrated it only too well.

Training Officer
- For administering the training of all personnel in operator or technical or managerial skills.
- For formulating training methods.
- For maintaining training records.
- For advising on methods of meeting statutory requirements.
- For reviewing all developments in training techniques and for applying them when suitable to the Company's requirements.

Security Officer
- For maintaining a fire watch and security team.
- For carrying out periodic searches to combat pilfering.
- For advising on the methods or procedures to combat industrial espionage.
- For liaison with the police in cases of prosecution for security offences.

Safety Officer
- For ensuring that the Company meets statutory requirements for the safety of personnel.
- For carrying out safety checks on any equipment or operation and advising the management of the department on the action required to eliminate any hazards.
- For providing safety training and promoting safety consciousness.

Believe it or not, a firm in the United States published the following objectives as models, published in turn by the American Management Association.

Personnel Manager
- Fix responsibility: to fix responsibility for each function.
- Delegate authority commensurate with responsibility: to delegate authority and accountability commensurate with responsibility, and to recognize that the three are inseparable.
- Follow organizational lines: individuals shall not circumvent the lines of authority.
- Give each employee one administrative supervisor: to give each employee only one administrative supervisor.
- Recognize the individual: to handle all Company–employee relationships with understanding, honesty, and courtesy, recognizing the employee's individuality and dignity.
- Outside interests: to respect the rights of employees to engage in activities outside of their employment, which may be private or public in nature and (shall) in no way conflict with or reflect unfavourably upon the Company and/or its corporate image, nor encroach upon the rights of the Company to the full services of its employees.

It would appear that the training officer was not responsible for changing behaviour, the security officer was not responsible for fire or thefts, and the safety officer was not responsible for safety levels, while the personnel manager had such a mixed-up set of inputs that the manager was either very busy or had nothing to do.

The senior public servant
A senior public servant said he was using outputs. He said that one of his effectiveness areas was 'letter answering' and that the associated objective was to answer all letters within two days. Here was a perfect example of an emphasis on inputs, not outputs, on apparent effectiveness, not managerial effectiveness. He was asked the key question, 'Why do you want to answer all letters within two days?',

and he replied, 'To improve our service to clients.' He was asked again, 'Why?' and still again 'Why?' until he ended up with seeing his job linked to increasing national income. One could say that his real job was to increase national income, but here we are going off the other end of the output scale as this public servant obviously had no control over many decisions affecting national income. His real effectiveness areas were somewhere in between.

The training officer

While many initial attempts to set effectiveness areas turn out instead to be a list of activities, many attempts can go in the other direction so that everyone appears to think they are heading a profit centre. Of any proposed effectiveness areas the question should be asked, 'Why is this being done?' or 'Why is this important?' For example, training managers might go through this kind of process. They are first asked what their most important area is. To which they might reply, 'To design a management development programme.' When asked, 'Why?', they reply, 'To put on courses for managers.' When again asked, 'Why?' they reply, 'To improve the quality of managerial decisions.' To yet another 'Why?', the reply is, 'To improve profit performance.' The correct areas for these training managers would probably be 'to increase managerial skill in problem-solving'. It cannot be 'to improve the quality of managerial decisions' or 'to improve profit performance' as these are both influenced by many factors over which the training managers have no control. They have no relevant authority.

The inputs of teachers

A government official said that a set of nineteen professional duties had been decided, which must form part of any new contracts of employment for all teachers there. While you may not agree with all of them, they do give, overall, a lucid example of important inputs. Collectively they can be used to make the point that inputs are important, too. However, what one still would have liked is a list of outputs to go along with these. Let us hope that the teachers do not consider their real job to consist of this list.

- Plan, prepare and review personal teaching methods and work programmes.
- Teach and ensure the discipline and safety of assigned timetabled classes.
- Set, mark and record pupils' work.
- Promote the general progress and welfare of a class of pupils and provide initial guidance or counselling on educational, social and career matters.

- Assess and record pupils' personal and social needs, development progress and attainment, and provide oral or written assessments.
- Contribute to and participate in formal performance appraisal and review, and in service training.
- Advise and cooperate with colleagues on teaching programmes and methods.
- Cooperate with specialist agencies and outside bodies.
- Ensure the safety and good order of pupils by sharing supervision of pupils arriving at or leaving school, and whenever they are authorized to be on school premises, except the midday break.
- Consult and liaise with parents and attend meetings arranged for that purpose.
- Participate in staff meetings and activities.
- Share the responsibility for covering for absent colleagues.
- Share in organizational and administrative tasks flowing from teaching duties.
- Take part in arrangements for presenting pupils for public examinations.
- Contribute to the appointment and professional development and assessment of junior colleagues, including new entrants to teaching.
- Coordinate the work of other teachers.
- Supervise ancillary staff.
- Order and allocate appropriate equipment and materials.
- Carry out such other related duties and responsibilities which may be allocated by head teacher.
- But what are the outputs of teachers?

Is your job described in terms of managerial effectiveness?

The work a manager is expected to accomplish, or the behaviour or outputs expected, may be described in one of two ways:

1. Conventional job description – focus on input behaviour of position.
2. Job effectiveness description – focus on outputs of position and including measurement areas and authority.

The use of the conventional job description is likely to inhibit the improvement of managerial effectiveness. The use of the job effectiveness description can only enhance it as it is based on outputs.

FROM INPUTS TO OUTPUTS

Most inputs can be converted to outputs if the position is needed at all. Some examples of inputs converted to outputs are the following:

maintain machines	to	machine availability
coach subordinates	to	subordinates effectiveness
church attendance	to	religious values
farmer education	to	high-value crop acreages
speed reading	to	speed learning
calls made	to	sales made
changing attitude	to	changing behaviour

One should beware of such areas as communication, relationships, liaison, coordination and staffing: these areas usually suggest inputs.

The following are actual examples of improved effectiveness areas, showing both first and second attempts at establishing them. The first attempt was most often produced as private work without consultation. The second attempt shows how these first attempts were improved after a small group discussion. These before–after changes are typical. They demonstrate what an imperfect view many, or even most, managers have of their jobs, and how easy it is to change it, given the appropriate method and conditions. None of the second attempts is claimed to be perfect for the job in question, and in any case this would be impossible to determine without much more information. The point is that the second attempt is self-evidently better than the first.

Manager of government employment agency

Government officials are often perceived as being buried under paperwork and losing sight of their real job in output terms. Prior to an effective implementation of output orientation this condition is in fact prevalent. The manager of a regional government employment agency produced what amounted to a simple set of inputs at the first attempt. This manager had been exposed to a departmental outputs programme and on such a narrow view of the job had based numerical 'objectives'.

First attempt	*Second attempt*
1 Promotion of service	7 Unemployment decrease
2 Control of staff	8 Labour force upgrading
3 Capability of staff	9 Manpower forecasting
4 Availability of staff	
5 Research	
6 Planning	

About the only effectiveness area of the first attempt which was maintained was 5 (Research) but worded as 9 (Manpower forecasting), which is still somewhat on the input side but acceptable.

University director of physical education

A newly appointed university director of physical education with a staff of about ten produced the following as first and second attempts.

First attempt		*Second attempt*	
1	Character-building	7	Utilization of facilities
2	Health	8	Readinesss of facilities
3	Sports activity	9	Quality of facilities
4	Maintenance	10	Programme innovation rate
5	Staffing	11	Growth of facilities
6	Future programmes		

This director came to see that there could be only partial influence on areas 1 (character-building) and 2 (health) and that there was no practical measuring device for the former (character-building) that 3 (sports activity) and 4 (maintenance) were best expressed as 7 (utilization of facilities) and 8 (readiness of facilities), and that 5 (staffing) was an input and that 6 (future programmes) could be more clearly worded as 10 (programme innovation rate). Unlike some such directors, this director had some responsibility for fund raising and it was thought appropriate to include 11 (growth of facilities).

Chairman of the board

A full-time chairman of the board of a 6000-employee company produced these two sets of effectiveness areas:

First attempt:		*Second attempt:*	
1	Improve value of board	7	Board decision quality
2	Assure good executive meetings	8	National corporate image
3	Provide useful counsel to company officers	9	Corporate strategy
4	Maintain effective remuneration and personnel policies for senior executives		
5	Develop good high-level corporate image and public relations		
6	Initiate sound long-range planning		

The realization that the second set of areas was really the chairman's job led to many changes, particularly in time allocation. Number 1 (improve value of board) and number 2 (assure good executive meetings) could be replaced by number 7 (board decision quality), that 3 (provide useful counsel to company officers) was meddling, and that 4 (maintain effective remuneration and personnel policies for senior executives) should be given to the CEO, 5 (develop good high-level corporate image and public relations) was the chairman's job, but on a national scale, as expressed in 8 (national corporate image), and that 6 (initiate sound long-range planning) was best replaced by 9 (corporate strategy).

CEO of a food processing company

The CEO of a 5000-employee food processing company initially produced a set of thirteen effectiveness areas. They included:

First attempt		*Second attempt*	
1	Profitability	14	Profitability
2	Planning	15	Planning
3	Top team quality	16	Reputation in industry
4	Profit growth	17	Company climate
5	Reputation growth	18	Customer–top
6	Gowth momentum		management relations
7	Trade relations		
8	Industry relations		
9	Government relations		
10	Board and employee relations		
11	Capital employment		
12	Return on investment		
13	Management succession plan		

This CEO decided to retain number 1 (profitability) and number 2 (planning) as numbers 14 (profitability) and 15 (planning). Area 3 (top team quality) was seen as being too general; 4 (profit growth) could be included as a sub-objective of 14 (profitability) by using a longer timespan; 5 (reputation growth) was changed to 16 (reputation in industry) – this was kept as this marketing-oriented CEO spent much time on customer and industry visits; 6 (growth momentum) moved to 14 (profitability); 7 (trade relations) moved to part of 16 (reputation in industry); and 8 (industry relations) became more specific as 18 (customer-top management relations); 9 (government relations) was identified as the executive vice president's area exclusively; 10 (board and employee relations) was changed to 17 (company climate); 11 (capital employment) and 12 (return on investment) were given to the deputy CEO of finance; and 13 (management succession plan) was seen as an area belonging to the deputy CEO of personnel.

Deputy CEO-marketing

A deputy CEO-marketing produced these as the first and second attempts, and only relatively minor changes were made.

First attempt		*Second attempt*	
1	Sales	7	Sales
2	Revenue	8	National sales force
3	New product introduction	9	Sales costs
4	Coordinate sales organization in two countries	10	Gross margins
		11	Market penetration
5	Development of national sales force	12	Create other country sales organization
6	Market penetration	13	New product sales

Area 1 (sales) was left unchanged; 2 (revenue) was refined to both 9 (sales costs) and 10 (gross margins); 3 (new product introduction) was made more on the output side by changing it to 13 (new product sales); 4 (coordinate sales organizations in two countries) was completely incorrect, and 12 (create other country sales organization) focused on what the manager should really do; area 6 (market penetration) was left in as 11.

When outputs look like inputs

An actual output can look rather like an input. For most line managers such expressions as planning, scheduling and budgeting are inputs. They show the means to achieve an output. A planner however might well have planning as an output. Someone with no authority about a particular area will make recommendations that are accepted and which later lead to improvement, as an output. When many jobs impinge on one programme so that no one person has any substantial authority over any part of it, the true output of some parts may well be, to complete aspects of the programme.

ACTION STEPS

1. Review your current job description and indicate for each item on it whether the item is an input, an output or something in between.

2. Then make list of what you see now as the effectiveness areas for your position. You will be refining and improving that list as you work through the book.

GLOSSARY

Apparent effectiveness: The extent to which a manager gives the appearance of being effective.

Conventional job description: A written statement emphasizing the input requirements of a particular managerial position.

EAs: See *Effectiveness areas*.

Effectiveness areas (EAs):   General output requirements of a management position.

Inputs: What a manager does, or is to do, rather than what a manager achieves by doing it.

Job description: See *Conventional job description*.

Managerial effectiveness: The extent to which a manager achieves the output requirements of the position.

Outputs: What managers achieve, or are to achieve, rather than what they do.

Personal effectiveness: The extent to which managers achieve their own private objectives.

2 Outputs applied

The great end of life is not knowledge but action.

Thomas Huxley

The objective of this chapter is to provide a number of ideas concerning how to make managerial effectiveness operational. The ideas include suggestions for effectiveness areas by various functions, sets of effectiveness areas by position, the typical errors in effectiveness areas, guides for testing effectiveness areas and the job effectiveness description.

FUNCTIONAL AREAS RELATED TO EFFECTIVENESS AREAS

As an aid to managers who wish to think about their effectiveness areas, here are sets of effectiveness areas usually associated with specific functions. There is a great deal of overlap however, and several of those listed under 'production' for instance would apply equally to other functions. The functions covered are:

Production
Material
Marketing
Personnel
Finance – Accounting
Supply

Production effectiveness areas

Production effectiveness areas may include:

Quality
Quantity
Timing
Scrap
Rejects

Inventory
Labour costs
Material costs
Safety
Machinery utilization

and the associated material effectiveness areas which may include some of the following.

Material effectiveness areas

Material effectiveness areas may include:

Unit cost reductions
Unit cost handling
Rejects
Inventory level
Inventory ratio
Model change time

The management of manufacturing processes, generally, is assisted greatly by output orientation.

Marketing effectiveness areas

Marketing effectiveness areas may include:

Sales
Margins
Costs
New markets
New customers
Marketing strategy
Market research
Marketing plans
Market penetration
Distribution

While all functional areas are suitable for outputs implementation, there is little doubt that marketing is one of the easiest functional areas in which to draft effectiveness areas.

Personnel effectiveness areas

Personnel effectiveness areas may include:

Selection
Management succession
Wage and salary equity
Personnel policy
Management information
Union–management relations
Contract terms
Safety
Behaviour change
Training

One issue that has to be clarified with labour effectiveness areas is just whose responsibility they are. There is sometimes some confusion about whether certain of the labour effectiveness areas are the responsibility of the personnel department or whether that department's role is limited to simply collecting the data and providing advice. The answer depends on who really approves the appropriate policies and who really controls the reward and punishment system associated with the policy implementation.

Finance – accounting effectiveness areas

Finance – accounting effectiveness areas may include:

Cost of capital
Capital availability
Statutory information
Management information
Data processing
Accounts receivable
Cost effectiveness
Annual report
Audit
Disbursements

Supply effectiveness areas

Supply effectiveness areas may include:

Acquisition cost
Processing cost
Production cost
Distribution cost

Number
Average size
Damage claims
Customer complaints
Missed delivery dates
Back-order level

Supply effectiveness areas are of interest to both marketing and distribution. The first four effectiveness areas listed form a set, and it is often very useful to identify and separate these four cost elements. An extensive list of effectiveness areas is provided in Appendix A.

ILLUSTRATIVE SETS OF EFFECTIVENESS AREAS

Here is a further aid to you as you begin to think about your effectiveness areas.

Sets of effectiveness areas are given for many different positions, grouped broadly by functional area, position in the organization, or type of organization. One thing can be said with certainty about them. It is highly unlikely that any will fit a particular position perfectly. While most are actual examples, companies differ enormously in what they mean by a particular position title. In addition, the titles of subordinate positions are not given and, most important, the locus of the real authority is not specified. Managers should use these only as a starting point in thinking about their job.

These examples are grouped as follows:

CEO
Knowledge workers
Consultants
Government
Production
Engineering
Finance, accounting and audit
Public relations
Marketing and sales

Effectiveness areas – CEO

The effectiveness areas of a CEO position are highly flexible. They differ from one firm to another and from one position to another, and they change over the length of time during which the CEO grows into the job and comes to trust the subordinates more or builds the organization around a preferred style.

This CEO of a large firm had a grandiose view of his job. He saw himself very much as a strategist.

CEO A
  Corporate strategy
  Company organization
  Management objectives
  Management development
  Employment of capital
  Return on capital

The CEO of a smaller firm of 700 employees, with little senior management as subordinates, saw the position's effectiveness areas as:

CEO B
  Yield on capital
  Commodity profitability
  Growth of established lines
  Administrative costs
  Product innovation
  Long-term planning
  Organization flexibility
  Management succession
  Trade relations
  Government relations

In a larger firm or one with additional senior management, many of these areas would go to a subordinate.

The CEO of a small selling agent was naturally much more marketing and sales-oriented:

CEO of a Selling Agent
  Profit on capital employed
  Profit on sales
  Sales with capital employed
  Sales-to-stock ratio
  Costs of sales
  Sales-to-promotion ratio
  Market leadership
  New markets

The top position administratively, in a university of 2000 students had these as effectiveness areas:

University Vice President – Administrative
    Provisions of basic services
    Student faculty ratio
    Space utilization system
    Cost per student
    Administrative percentage
    Academic budget allocation formula
    Organization structure
    Financial information

This person had a great deal of authority but did not get involved directly in areas of teaching or curriculum.

Effectiveness areas – knowledge workers

There are two kinds of statements which fit a variety of knowledge workers who have no power. One is for staff specialists in general and the other is for faculty members. This disarmingly simple set is capable of measurement if the associated objectives are worded correctly.

Staff specialist – General
    Consulted in area of competence
    Advice accepted
    Advice acceptance leads to improvement

The three areas in turn state that the specialist must be competent and that part of the job is to see that that is so. The second area puts responsibility upon the specialist, to be consulted, not the manager. Too many staff specialists, like some university professors, see themselves as an information reservoir with no responsibility to provide a tapping facility, which is usually sorely needed. Staff specialists, more then managers, have the opportunity so to develop a relationship that their advice is sought when appropriate. Industry has no place for the staff specialists who do not themselves create consultative conditions. The job must also include a degree of advice acceptance and of improvement leading from this. This example is considered in more detail on pp. **100** and **101**.

Another kind of knowledge worker is the university lecturer. While academics are often uncomfortable about the whole notion of academic effectiveness, these are the effectiveness areas:

Faculty member
    Knowledge storage

Knowledge retrieval
Knowledge distribution
Knowledge expansion

This set would include 90–100 per cent of every faculty member's job. Some faculty members like to add 'student relations' not recognizing that this is an input to the broader purposes of the university.

A research and development manager's set of effectiveness areas might be:

Research and Development Manager
New product innovation
Existing product development
Patent protection
Corporate innovative reputation

It would be likely that the first two items would be broken down into several objectives, while the last one, in some firms, would not be considered important.

Effectiveness areas – consultants

Business consultants are usually knowledge workers who operate on a contract basis. A general set of effectiveness areas for a consultant is:

Consultant
Time utilization
Meet contract terms
Client effectiveness

While the manager of the consultant might have these:

Branch Manager – Consulting firm
Profit
Sales
Business mix
Quality of service
Costs
Sales expansion
Consultant quality

Effectiveness areas – government

Positions in government pose no inherent problem for outputs implementation. The difficulty arises when the position has no real authority and the incumbent is really a clerk, or when the incumbent is so busy compiling reports on what is being done that little else is accomplished.

A government trade commissioner had a time-weighted set of objectives. They asked him to spend 15 per cent of his time on marketing and 85 per cent of his time on reporting and administration. Sad but true.

The director of a national government communication centre had these as effectiveness areas:

Director – National Government Communication Centre
   Messages handled
   Transmission delay
   Security
   Error rate
   Peak-load facility

There was no control over the message input, but the director could influence staff size over time.

A CEO of a government agricultural unit had these as effectiveness areas:

CEO of Government Agricultural Unit
   Agriculture development
   Agriculture productivity
   Public relations crisis management
   Return on budget
   Legislation innovation

They reveal an imaginative view of the job. All the associated objectives were measurable and related directly to the authority in the position.

The single employee of a farm loan board had these effectiveness areas:

Farm Loan Board Manager
   Loan losses
   Loan arrears
   Loan outstandings
   Legislation innovations

Loan leverage
Private-lending availability

These again show, in the last three areas, a broad view of the job. The last area is particularly significant. Part of the job was to eliminate the need for it.

The crop director of a region also had an easily measurable set of outputs:

Crop Director
Tobacco acreage
Crop insurance coverage
Noxious weeds
Soil and feed sample requests
Seed production
Research output
Pesticide residue
Land use planning
Farmer knowledge

Effectiveness areas – production

Production, together with marketing, tends to be the easiest function for which to form effectiveness areas, and objectives and statements of them abound in the literature.

The effectiveness areas can vary very much from position to position, however, depending on such things as whether or not:

Continuous-flow process is used
Plant has autonomy over policy, especially personnel
Structure at the top is flat or tall
Models change frequently

A mill superintendent had this set of effectiveness areas:

Logging Mill Superintendent
Production level
Production cost
Production quality
Labour safety

While a plant manager in another firm had this set:

Plant Manager
Production level

Production cost
Production quality
Labour safety
Inventory control
Machine and space utilization
Delivery times

Notice that the plant manager had the complete set of the logging mill superintendent plus three additional areas. The mill superintendent had one simple process, having no responsibility for supply, and the logs took a fixed time to process. The plant manager, on the other hand, had twenty different products to produce and responsibility for a raw material supply, and could delay producing some products to maximize machine and space utilization.

The effectiveness areas for quality control depend much on whether the position involved is simply advisory or not. If a quality control manager has fairly broad authority, the effectiveness areas could be:

Quality Control Manager
  Quality standards
  Quality level
  Quality control cost
  Quality control methods

If there was little authority the effectiveness areas would reflect that the job was to detect and report deviations quickly and accurately at low cost.

Some jobs are not recognized as basically production. The example is that of a manager of a management information system. The effectiveness areas of that job can be very similar to that of a production manager – because the job is production. A set of effectiveness areas could be:

Manager of Management Information System
  Production level
  Delivery times
  Cost level
  Quality level
  Machine utilization

Effectiveness areas – engineering

A power system engineering manager had these effectiveness areas:

Power System Engineering Manager
Design of power systems
Protection of power systems
Design of generation plant
Construction of generation plant
Design of transmission system
Construction of transmission system
Operation of thermal plant

And a mechanical engineering manager had these:

Mechanical Engineering Manager
Plant installations
Design of manufactured equipment
Machinery specifications

Effectiveness areas – finance, accounting and audit

Accountants can have serious problems in defining their effectiveness areas. Their training has essentially been in data collection and storage. Some of them think their job is done when books or figures are neat, well stored and accurately counted. But this is not their real job. Their real job, of course, is facilitating information retrieval, not facilitating information storage.

A typical set of effectiveness areas for an accountant is:

Accountant
Management information
Statutory information
Forecasting
Control

Notice that the first and second effectiveness areas are designed to separate clearly the responsibility imposed by government legislation and that imposed by firm profitability.

A financial manager had this set of effectiveness areas:

Financial manager
Capital inflow
Finance of acquisitions
Legal aspects of acquisitions
Cost of capital
Internal financial information
Underwriter relationships
Government financial relationships

Notice the absence of overlap between the two sets of effectiveness areas.

An audit manager might have these effectiveness areas:

Audit Manager
   Quality of work
   Cost recovery
   Staff utilization
   Client relations
   Practice development

Effectiveness areas – public relations

As with many such staff jobs the important question to ask about the position of public relations director is: Who really has the power? It may be that the managing director approves all press notices, that no public relations policy exists, and that the public relations director simply responds to the in-basket rather than exercising initiative over policy or programmes. The public relations person may be a clerk.

One public relations manager of an airline had this set of effectiveness areas:

Public Relations Manager
   Corporate information availability
   Corporate image
   Column inches obtained
   Public relations crisis management

The last item was a particularly important measure. When a plane crashes, what is and what is not done or 'managed' in the next twenty-four hours can be crucial to the airline.

Effectiveness areas – marketing and sales

A US sales manager of a large Canadian firm had these as effectiveness areas:

Manager – US Sales
   Profit
   Sales
   Accounts receivable
   Inventory turnover

Image
Marketing strategy
New-product sales
New-product proposals

The profit and sales areas are usually present in marketing and sales positions. Accounts receivable was important owing to the few very large accounts involved and the very short cycle from raw material purchase to product. Inventory turnover was important owing to the short shelf-life of the product. Image was in because the company had previously entered and withdrawn from the United States market three times and had left behind poor trade relations. This manager proposed to spend 25 per cent of time on this area and to contract for a quarterly survey among all major customers. New product sales was separated from sales simply to give it more importance, while new product proposals was put in owing to the newness of the market.

A marketing manager in manufacturing had these effectiveness areas:

Marketing Manager
Revenue
Margins
Sales policies
Distribution
Product innovation
Legislation
Manpower development
Consumer product image
Market intelligence

A basic set which applies to most marketing managers is:

Marketing Manager
Brand strategy
Advertising strategy
Market penetration policy
Market margin

A complete set of effectiveness areas for the position of sales manager could be:

Sales manager
Sales policies

Sales levels
Sales costs
Line profitability

ERRORS IN EFFECTIVENESS AREAS

The most typical errors in creating effectiveness areas arise from confusing an effectiveness area with one or more of the following:

An input area
A worry area
Another's area
A non-measurable area
A time area

The deadly sin of inputs has already been discussed so let us now consider each of the others.

Worry area

A common error is in identifying worry areas. A worry area is an effectiveness area managers show as their own because they do not expect another manager, whose responsibility it really is, to deal with it effectively without intervention. In organizations which have grown rapidly and which have weak management development programmes the top people often propose several worry areas among their effectiveness areas. The underlying problems may be one or more of these:

- Lack of delegation
- Subordinate incompetence
- Confusion over where decision is actually made

At a meeting between the general manager in a public utility and all subordinates, the general manager proposed 'labour relations' as an effectiveness area for the position, but so did the personnel director for that position. The consultant pointed out, 'If two people are responsible for the same thing, one of them is not needed – and the thing would not be done well anyway.' This duplication of an effectiveness area prompted a lengthy discussion on the lack of true delegation of the CEO in certain areas. The area was eventually given to the personnel director, and many underlying issues were subsequently resolved.

If outputs are put in without the identification and modification of problems such as worry areas it simply freezes what may already be a poorly designed organization structure.

Another's area

A third error in writing effectiveness areas is called 'another's area'. This is an effectiveness area managers show as their own over which they have no control. This is distinct from a worry area in that it arises from a confusion of where the power lies rather than from a distrust of competence or interest. Such confusion can often arise if the power of the staff, or lack of it, is not clearly defined. In one firm this issue arose sharply over quality control. As it was worked out, the effectiveness areas concerning it were assigned as:

● Establish standards (Development Director)
● Information on conditions (Quality Control Inspector)
● Implementation (Production Director)

All of these deal with quality control, but all are completely different.

Decisions associated with successful products tend to move upward as those managers associated with the sound decisions get promoted. This is particularly true in marketing-oriented firms. As a temporary measure this is appropriate, as new subordinate competence may not be fully developed and a poor decision may be too much risk to take. In one firm the key decisions, concerning price and advertising percentage of a highly successful product, stayed with the person who was promoted from brand manager to marketing director. This means that the new manager was really a brand planner. This gives rise to such linked positions as the following four:

● Marketing Director
● Brand Manager
● Brand Planner
● Salesperson

All suggest different effectiveness areas, and a sound outputs implementation could clarify exactly what each is responsible for so that the 'another's area' problem does not arise.

Non-measurable area

The fourth error in writing effectiveness areas is the 'non-measurable area', which is an effectiveness area whose associated objective is not measurable. Whether or not the associated objective is measurable cannot always be determined simply from the wording of the area or measurement method itself and would have to be obtained instead from the proposed objective.

While the measurement problem can usually be solved with imagination, the cost of the measurement problem may remain. Measurement of the impact of training on behaviour necessitates many phone calls or questionnaires, and preferably a field survey. The outputs of a public relations position are hard to measure without a formal survey of some kind. In cases like this, one has to ask whether the area is important enough to have even a rough measurement of its effectiveness. If not, then eliminate the area. If so, then allocate 10 per cent of the total appropriate budget to measurement. There is too much conventional wisdom that a particular activity is a 'good thing'. Measurement is the only way to test it.

A difficult thing for some managers to accept about output orientation is, 'If you cannot measure it, forget it, because no one will know anyway.' Accurate measurement is central to the philosophy of outputs. Without measurement, outputs cannot be implemented. Some managers initially see their jobs as having vague, pervasive and very long-term effects and claim that it is impossible to measure their performance by normal methods. If, when managers learn about outputs, they still say their contribution is not measurable, then they:

- are in a position that is not needed;
  or
- have no authority to do their job;
  or
- are avoiding responsibility.

As a simple example, good relations are often proposed as an effectiveness area. This is not measurable except by highly subjective methods. A sales manager who once proposed it said later that it was not only non-measurable but an input as well, and that it was seen that the effectiveness in this area could be equally well measured by short- and long-term sales.

Time area

A time area represents an item on which a manager spends a great deal of time but which is not an effectiveness areas. These almost always reflect a poor organization design where responsibilities are diffuse, a job that is too small, or a top person who is doing something simply because it is liked.

Time areas can be identified quickly, first by making a time budget, which consists of allocating a time percentage to each proposed effectiveness area, and then by asking how important the area is to the overall output of the position.

HOW TO SELECT EFFECTIVENESS AREAS

Here is a simple list of questions for managers to ask themselves. They should then be able to develop an initial list of effectiveness areas to test on their superior and their co-workers. There is much overlap in the list. All that the questions really ask is: What is the job? But they ask it in different ways. Some managers find that ideas are triggered when the question is asked in one way and some when it is given another way:

- What is the position's unique contribution?
- Why is the position needed at all?
- What would change if the position was eliminated?
- What changes if I am highly effective in the position?
- How would I know, with no one telling me, when I am performing effectively?
- Where does asking 'Why?' lead?
- What authority does the position really have?
- What can the position most easily improve?
- What does the job description and the organization manual say?
- What is the biggest external change made that affected the position?
- How do I spend my time? How would I like to spend it?
- What would I be most likely to concentrate on over two or three years if I wanted the greatest improvement in my unit?
  In my superior's unit? In the organization as a whole?

Do effectiveness areas cover the whole job?

One of the more interesting differences of approach of writers of MBO books is in the percentage of the job that they believe should be covered by effectiveness areas. One writer claims: 'The key results analysis probably covers only the 15 per cent of total tasks which are vital and leaves great discretion in the others.' Advocates of output orientation, on the other hand, believe that effectiveness areas, and therefore objectives, must cover 100 per cent of the job.

How many effectiveness areas?

The number of effectiveness areas each manager has depends more on how they see their job than on what the job is. It is quite possible for two people in identical positions to have a different number of areas. A few managers report that they work effectively with up to fifteen effectiveness areas, while others work effectively with only one, though usually with many associated objectives. While the number of effectiveness areas must always depend on each manager, a range of three to seven or eight is normal.

Is one effectiveness area enough?

It is true that many jobs can be described adequately by one effectiveness area. A CEO may well say that the job is profit and that is it. A financial manager may see the job as reporting financial information and nothing else. The CEO, though, when asked to apply measurement areas to that one effectiveness area will probably list half a dozen. These measurement areas can quite adequately become the effectiveness areas. After all a measurement area is nothing more or less than a refinement of an effectiveness area. In much the same way the financial manager might well list as measurement areas such things as: cost, time, acceptability and accuracy. These to start with are the measurement areas but they should be converted to effectiveness areas. The main problem with having only one or two effectiveness areas is that planning can become difficult.

Rules for wording effectiveness areas

There are three simple rules to follow when wording effectiveness areas. They are:

1 Use from one to four words.
2 Avoid directional indicators such as 'increase', 'maximize', 'satisfy'.
3 Avoid any quantities or timings.

These three rules help to ensure that effectiveness areas are not confused with measurement areas or objectives, and that organization design rather than corporate planning is the focus.

Ten guides for testing effectiveness areas

When effectiveness areas are identified, they should satisfy these tests which check on the adequacy of the effectiveness areas both individually and collectively. Each effectiveness area should:

1. represent output, not input;
2. lead to associated objectives which are measurable;
3. be an important part of the position; and
4. be within the actual limits of authority and responsibility.

Effectiveness areas as a whole should:

5. represent 100 per cent of the outputs of the position, and
6. not be so numerous as to avoid dealing with the essence of the job or so few as to make planning difficult.

Effectiveness areas, with respect to the associated positions should:

7. avoid overlaps,
8. avoid underlaps,
9. align vertically and
10. align horizontally.

Flexibility of effectiveness areas

Managers at the top of any organization unit usually have some flexibility in the choice of the effectiveness areas they decide to associate with their own position. This freedom is very marked when they have the ability to create a subordinate and can assign part of their own work to the subordinate. Under these conditions effectiveness areas are fully flexible; they can make them what they want to be. They could, for instance, become an 'outside' person with an emphasis on liaison with other organization units or customers. The newly created subordinate could be the 'inside' person concerned with managing the unit. The reverse situation is equally feasible. This demonstrates clearly that, within broad limits, managers who can create a subordinate and can design their subordinates' effectiveness areas have a very wide range of different areas which they can associate with their own job.

It is impossible to look at the effectiveness areas for a particular position in isolation. Such areas are best seen as sets of areas which link several positions together. It is quite possible, then, that if the set of areas for one position changes a great deal, sets of areas for other positions may change as well; and they should. When setting areas, then, the question is not 'What are they?' but 'What could they best be?' Clearly, outputs are intimately related to organization design and organization flexibility.

It would be an unusual manager who could draft a perfect set of effectiveness areas simply after reading this chapter. Some assistance is always useful and is usually required. First, the manager should draft and re-draft the effectiveness areas as best possible, then discuss the statement of them with co-workers, superior and in-company specialist (if one is available). The more common errors in drafting effectiveness areas can be avoided by studying the examples of such errors earlier in the chapter.

A plant manager after three years on the job may well decide to change the effectiveness areas established three years earlier, and may have trained one or more subordinates to assume some of them.

The important thing is that effectiveness areas should not simply be applied to an existing organization design and then considered to be relatively permanent. Instead, the assigning of effectiveness areas should be used as a basis for inducing organization flexibility and seeing that it is maintained.

Effectiveness areas usually are subject to change when: a new manager is appointed, co-workers change, a manager grows in skill, power and decision levels move, management by objectives is implemented, or any major organization change occurs.

MAKING MANAGERIAL EFFECTIVENESS OPERATIONAL

Managerial effectiveness may be made operational in the organization as a whole by linking it to personnel and other policies. Such linking amounts to imposing the value of managerial effectiveness on the operation of the organization. Managerial effectiveness should be linked directly to organization philosophy, induction training and managerial development. In this way it becomes the organization central value induced by both managerial and organization development. Effectiveness areas should be the basis of describing jobs and of linking one job to another, that is, system design. Measurement areas form a basis for job specifications – what kind of manager is required?; manager selection – is this the person we want?; training plans – how do we obtain desired behaviour?; and job evaluation – how much should we pay? Objectives form the basis of the link between corporate strategy and managerial appraisal. These four concepts then can provide the central theme for a philosophy of management.

- Managerial effectiveness: the extent to which a manager achieves the output requirements of the position.
- Effectiveness areas: general output requirements of a managerial position.
- Measurement areas: specific output requirements and measurement criteria of a managerial position.
- Objectives: measurement areas which are as specific, as time bounded, and as measurable as possible.

While the idea of objectives is central in output orientation, the other three ideas (managerial effectiveness, effectiveness areas, and measurement areas) are the foundations of any objectives that are set. Only with an understanding of these foundations will the objectives be sound.

Managerial effectiveness

A sound implementation of outputs must be preceded by the acceptance of managerial effectiveness as the central value or philosophy in management. Unless this is given primary importance, output-oriented management will be no more than a highly sophisticated managerial-level work study. A small, or even a large, firm can have values built in which counter the idea of managerial effectiveness. Such values may seriously interfere with or completely prevent the implementation of the output philosophy.

Effectiveness areas

The second idea – effectiveness areas – is based on the view that all managerial positions are best seen in terms of the outputs associated with them. Surprisingly few managers see their positions this way. Effectiveness areas spring primarily from the strategy of the organization as made operational by the organization structure. To a lesser but significant extent they depend on top management's views on the best locus for decision making.

Measurement areas

Measurement areas are subdivisions of effectiveness areas, which incorporate measurement criteria explicitly or implicitly. An effectiveness area of 'sales' might be conveniently broken down into one or more of these sets of measurement areas:

Existing products – existing markets; existing products – new markets; new products – existing markets; and new products – new markets.

Or – unit sales by area, product, customer.

Or – sales of product A, product B, product C.

Or – sales of product A, gross margin of product A, profitability of product A.

One of these four sets of standards or some combination of them would suit most situations. The set of measurement areas chosen is that which best covers the total job in output terms.

Measurement areas are the subject of Chapter 3.

Objectives

Objectives are specific measurement areas with time limits and numerical values attached to them. Thus, for the effectiveness area 'sales', we have seen that one measurement area might be 'unit sales of product A'. The associated objective might then be 'increase sales of product A by 15,000 units for the period 1 January to 31 December.'

The concepts are related in this way:

Effectiveness Area
Product A

Measurement Areas
1. Sales increase in money units on product A
2. Gross margin increase in per cent on product A
3. Profitability increase per unit on product A.

Objectives
1. Increase sales of product A to 400,000 units during . . .
2. Increase gross margin of product A to 22 per cent by decreasing distribution cost to 11 per unit during . . .
3. Increase net profitability of product A to 6.2 per cent during. . . .

For each measurement area there is usually one objective, as shown in the example above. All this is relatively straightforward but it is almost worthless if the effectiveness areas do not represent outputs from the beginning. The objectives are the subject of Chapter 7.

The job effectiveness description

A job effectiveness description is needed which describes a managerial position almost exclusively in output terms. It contains, first, a list of the effectiveness areas of the position. Together with each of the measurement areas, managers develop a specific objective (usually annually), and measure their degree of attainment of the objective by the established measurement area also contained in the job effectiveness description. For most managers, all this can be put down on one side of one sheet of paper. The only additional content of the job effectiveness descriptions are specific statements of the authority vested in the position. These statements may refer to authority to enlarge or decrease staff, use overtime, change the product or service, rearrange work flow, or modify a production programme. In constructing these job effectiveness descriptions, great care is needed to ensure that the authority is sufficient for the specified measurement areas and the objectives derived from them. Either the authority is found, or made sufficient, or the effectiveness areas and measurement areas are passed upwards.

Job effectiveness descriptions are prepared for each managerial position and also for each unit, which include a manager and all the subordinates. Managerial objectives are thus formally linked to team objectives. Examples of job effectiveness descriptions are given in Chapter 5.

ACTION STEPS

1. Review the effectiveness areas for your position which you created based on your reading of Chapter 1. It may help you to read the section 'How to select effectiveness areas'.
2. Check your effectiveness areas against the 'Rules for wording effectiveness areas' and follow those rules.
3. Check each of these revised effectiveness areas against the guides for testing effectiveness areas.

GLOSSARY

Another's area: Effectiveness areas managers show as their own which are really those of other managers.

Effectiveness areas errors: The five effectiveness areas errors defined in this glossary are: Input, Worry, Another's, Non-measurable and Time.

Input area: An incorrect statement of an effectiveness area which is based on an activity rather than a result.

JED: See *Job effectiveness description*.

Job effectiveness description (JED):   A written statement specifying the effectiveness areas, measurement areas and authority of a particular management position.

Measurement area: How an effectiveness area is measured.

Non-measurable area: An unsuitable effectiveness area as the associated objective is not measurable.

Objectives: Effectiveness areas which are as specific, as time-bounded, and as measurable as possible. Specific output requirements of a management position.

Time area: An item on which a manager spends a great deal of time but which is not an effectiveness area.

Worry area: Effectiveness areas managers show as their own because they do not expect another manager, whose area it is, to deal with it effectively without intervention.

3 Matching measurement areas to outputs

Count what is countable, measure what is measurable, and what is not measurable, make measurable. . .

Galileo

The high output-oriented manager wants to have a sound method of measuring each effectiveness area. There are two reasons for this:

- Self-motivation
- Self-control

Self-motivation
A series of psychological experiments, on a particular topic, were conducted over a period of about twenty years. The general line of enquiry was abandoned by many researchers and universities because the results from these various experiments were uniform. The matter being investigated was the effect of knowledge of performance on performance. That is, when one knows how well one is doing does performance improve? The virtually uniform results revealed that those who had accurate knowledge of the level of the prior performance tended to perform better than those who did not have that knowledge. The experiments were conducted in a great variety of ways. As one example, two groups of subjects were asked to make as many crosses on a piece of paper as they could in a given time-period. The members of one group were individually informed on their performance level. The members of the other group were not. Those who were told did better next time. It is incontrovertible that knowledge of performance level and quality improves performance. Unfortunately, this point seems to be missed by many writers on management. They appear to think that measurement is exclusively for control or appraisal purposes. Some managers use it for these reasons only, and miss the greatest advantage of measurement which is motivation.

Knowledge of performance does not have to come from the superior. It can simply come from the internal information system. In fact there is some evidence that it is better when the information on performance is provided impersonally.

The following experience has been repeated with other kinds of groups thousands of times:

> A division manager and with subordinate managers decided to establish their effectiveness areas and develop their objectives. It was not difficult for them to see that their performance was measurable, but no data were available for doing it. This led to many changes in accounting and recording procedures, so that ultimately all of them had clearly quantified performance measures on a weekly, monthly, quarterly or annual basis. Their interest in measurement led directly to a fundamental redesign of part of the total accounting system of the company, which became centred on output measurement rather than input control.

These managers were engaged in a self-motivational process. Instinctively they knew they wanted more measurement. Perhaps they would not have said it was for self-motivational reasons but clearly that was the result. A central intent was not to control themselves and not to control and appraise others, though this would naturally occur, but for self-motivation. That must be obvious.

Self-control

Good measurement areas lead to much better self-control. Any manager wants to be able to measure results and to have a greater degree of being able to control them. If an objective cannot be measured its attainment cannot be known. If an objective cannot be subject to control, it is simply a prediction and not an objective. Output-oriented managers are quite definitely held up because of poor measurement and control systems. Control is well recognized as a key management function. The central activity in control is measurement. Without measurement there is no clear advance warning of when corrective action should be taken in order to assure the accomplishment of an objective. Measurement can provide an alarm signal well in advance of the disaster that may otherwise occur. Measurement provides an opportunity to correct off course deviation.

Are you getting the information you need?

Company information systems vary widely in sophistication, accuracy, usefulness and timeliness. Few are perfect. Some managers receive information they do not want, and they do not get the information they really need. One production manager in a cigarette firm received daily reports on the hours of sun in Kenya but did not receive direct quality control information quickly enough and in the most useful form. This kind of thing is common enough almost to be called a natural state. It can be changed, however, if managers, having set clear objectives, insist on being provided with information against which to measure their attainment.

The most important single test of any information a manager receives is its usefulness. This is determined by its relevance to a manager's own objectives, its timeliness, its accuracy and the form of its presentation. If any of these are missing or inadequate the data will be less useful or even useless. Many managers complain about the quantity of data they receive, or its absence, but too few do something about it. It is an easy matter to remove one's name from a distribution list or, failing that, to ask one's secretary to file the report on receipt. All managers should look closely at the data they themselves disseminate and ask themselves whether everyone would not be better served with much less of it in a more useful form. Low trust levels are one of the biggest causes of excess paper.

While most managers have a feast of data they do not want, they also have a famine of data they do want. This most often arises because they have not asked for it or have not been too clear on what they really want. They do not question established accounting procedures or else they believe them too difficult to change.

QUALITATIVE OBJECTIVES ARE NEVER NEEDED

Many management writers, and managers themselves, claim that some measurement must be qualitative rather than quantitative. This is a serious error. All clearly defined effectiveness areas are measurable. The error concerning the supposed need for qualitative objectives arises in writers from fuzzy thinking and often arises in managers from both fuzzy thinking and an attempt to avoid being measured.

Output-oriented managers will not agree with this statement from a Management by Objectives text:

Setting specific, quantitative objectives for many staff positions is particularly troublesome for many companies. Traditionally, the line does, the staff helps. In many firms, this distinction is being softened almost to the point of obliteration as the work of the staff function becomes more crucial to business. Still, the nature of staff work if often hard to state in measurable terms. The staff propose courses of action for the line to act upon. The staff study situations to advise the line on what to do. The specific results often depend upon what the line does and are not under the direct control of the staff specialists and managers.

So-called qualitative objectives should not be considered objectives at all but should simply be called 'activities'. For any qualitative objectives, 'Why?' should be asked and then the conversion from input activities to output objectives be made.

Conversion of qualitative to quantitive measurement areas and objectives

In the left-hand column below is a list of qualitative objectives which are used as an illustration in one popular management by objectives (MBO) book to suggest that such qualitative objectives must sometimes be used. This is incorrect. To illustrate, in the right-hand column are this author's conversions to show that such qualitative objectives are usually unnecessary.

Actual suggested qualitative objectives in standard Management by Objectives (MBO) book	Conversion to illustrate that qualitative objectives are usually found to be activities. By asking the purpose of the activities, the quantitive objectives are derived.
Conduct monthly management development sessions for superintendents in techniques of standard cost programme.	Have 50 per cent of superintendents using standard cost programming techniques on at least two projects by end of July.
Prepare a programme for patent productions.	Have no patent loopholes in our patents discovered by our own staff, independent agents, or competitors during the year.
Prepare and distribute an internal public relations manual.	Obtain an average of 75 per cent unaided recall by all non-managerial employees of 50 per cent of the key corporate activities or accomplishments of the prior month for each month next year.
Improve statistical reports to reduce time lag between production and publication dates.	Without decreasing usable content, reduce by an average of four days, the time to distribute the following reports by the end of September.

Prepare quality control manual for supervisors.	Eighty-five per cent of first line supervisors to know eight of the ten key points in company quality control practice by the end of December.
Improve appearance, packaging and design of products.	For each item in product line, design a package which will receive more consumer jury votes than any competing product by the end of November.
Undertake to ally research efforts more closely with production needs.	Have at least 80 per cent of pro- posals to production manager accepted during the year.

It is true that most of these conversions from inputs to outputs involve a broader view of one's job, a greater responsibility for the staff function, and a higher cost of measurement.

PERCEIVED DIFFICULTY IN MEASUREMENT

It is difficult for some managers to accept the philosophy that 'if you cannot measure it, forget it, because no one will know anyway.' Accurate measurement is central to good management. Some managers initially see their job as having vague, pervasive and very long-term effects and claim that it is impossible to measure their performance by normal methods. If such managers also say that they understand what managerial effectiveness really means then they are in a position that is not needed, or they have no authority to do their job, or they are avoiding responsibility.

Six perceived difficulties

There are six perceived difficulties in measurement. These are:

1 Cost of measurement
2 Length of time to measure
3 Personal evaluation of quality
4 Uncontrollable events
5 Input measurement
6 Staff positions measurement

Cost of measurement
While the measurement problem can usually be solved with imagination, the cost of measurement problem may remain. To measure the impact of a training course on behaviour necessitates at least many telephone calls or questionnaires, and preferably a field survey. The outputs of a public relations position are hard to measure without a formal survey of some kind. In these cases one has to ask whether the function is important enough to have even a rough measurement of its effectiveness. If not, then eliminate the function. If so, then allocate 10 per cent of the total appropriate budget to measurement. There is too much conventional wisdom that a particular activity is a 'good thing'. Measurement is the only way to test it. Do not confuse the problem of cost of measurement with the perceived but inaccurate observation of impossibility of measurement.

Length of time to measure
Some factors take a long time to measure. Examples include the output of a research and development function, the results of hiring a new senior manager, new product decision and a new plant location decision. Usually the further one moves up in an organization the longer the length of time for the quality of a decision to be measured accurately. It is well known that the life of some CEOs is made particularly difficult because the stock market wants their perform-ance to be measured on a quarterly basis and yet the best way to deal with foreign competitors, who may have a much longer time-frame, would be to be measured on a three to five-year basis. The problem of length of time to measure is usually overcome by setting some short-term measurement methods and some long-term measurement methods as well. A technical paper submitted could be a short-term measure. The impact of the technical paper would be a long-term measure. Both should be measured. In much the same way, the impact of a new plant or new product can be made the subject of short-term measurements such as when the decision is made and longer-term measurements involving the impact of the decision.

Personal evaluation of quality
While some things are easy to count in an objective manner their quality may not be as easy to assess. In the short term how does one assess the quality of a plan or of a company procedure manual? In the long term the quality of each can be measured fairly easily in terms of why the plan or the procedure manual was developed to begin with. In the short term the assessment of quality would have to be made by the person commissioning the report, the report users or expert judges. It is clear that the weakness of such measurement is

that it can depend very much on the personal opinion of one person. If this one person is not too interested in quality and really does not want to be bothered then a 'sufficient quality' note will be made. This is but one of many reasons why more than one person should be involved in evaluation where one has to resort to personal evaluation of quality.

Uncontrollable events
Some claim that because they have low control of events their effectiveness cannot be measured. This is completely wrong. The measurement is easy to make, what is hard to make is the decision concerning the level of the objective. No marketing manager has control of all the variables in the marketplace. The manager does not control the actions of competitors. The position though can still be measured on such things as market share. Measurement is very easy. What is not so easy, and these points need to be distinguished, is the level of the objective. That is whether the market share should change from 2.4 per cent to 2.6 per cent or by some other level. This does not hinder measurement. Apart from actions of competitors other uncontrollable events which affect the objective, not the measurement, include weather, plane crashes and restrictive legislation.

Input measurement
Sometimes inputs are subject to measurement when the associated output should be measured instead.

Staff positions measurement
Those working in positions with no power, sometimes called staff positions, sometimes assume quite incorrectly that the measurement of their job is difficult. Page 24 provides the effectiveness area for most types of staff positions with no power. There is normally some reluctance for staff positions to accept these because it can require a major change in their thinking about the job and makes their performance completely measurable. The outputs for staff positions are:

● Consulted in area of competence.
● Advice accepted.
● Advice acceptance leads to improvement.

All of these are easy to measure. Consulted in area of competence can be the subject of a count of the number of times various client systems approach the staff advisor for advice in the area of speciality. Again, what is not being discussed is how many times the advice should be sought. . . this is the level of objective not the measurement area. Advice accepted is easily measured. Advice acceptance leading to improvement is easily measured though usually only in the longer term. As the staff position is normally considered one of the most difficult for measurement and it is obvious when clear thought is applied that it can be measured easily, then surely the argument must be made that the high output manager must insist on a much higher degree of measurement in all associated positions than is perhaps the existing case.

This position is discussed in more detail on pp. 100–101.

CONVERSION OF EFFECTIVENESS AREAS TO MEASUREMENT AREAS

An effectiveness area is a general output statement associated with a position. A measurement area is a far more detailed output statement in that it incorporates the effectiveness area but also adds detail on just exactly what is meant. It is perfectly legitimate to have profit as an effectiveness area. But there are at least twenty ways to measure it. Safety could be an effectiveness area but this might be measured by the number of compensation cases, knowledge of safety practices implementation of safety practices, down time due to safety and so on. So, a measurement area is a refined effectiveness area. It incorporates all the effectiveness area has but goes into detail on exactly what is meant by the effectiveness area and, therefore, how it is to be measured.

Bases for measurement areas

Examples of the many possible bases for measurement areas are:

Past period	— x above 199-
Raw data	— units per shift
Amount of	— handling costs/time
Units processed	— x per cent of those handled
Ratios	— product 'A': total products
Units available	— x per cent of those available
Own forecast	— units
Competitors results	— per cent of market
Opinion regarding	— company image
Scales	— hi/med/lo

Market statistics	— market share
Time	— days to set-up
Cost	— per unit
Quality	— percentage scrap
Quantity	— goals scored
Frequency	— fires

Another common base may be in terms of deviation from something else. Such wording as 'within', 'not outside' and 'with ± x per cent of', may be used.

Refinement of measurement

Even when a measurement is found it may often be capable of refinement. The right-hand members of these pairs illustrate a move towards refinement of measurement:

Gross sales	versus	Contribution to overhead
Per cent increase	versus	Per cent increase adjusted for annual trend
Absolute increase	versus	Per cent increase
Lost time accident frequency	versus	Lost time accidents per 100,000 hours worked

The refined measures are generally better and are less affected by changes over which a manager may not have control. Suppose that one manager had an objective of increasing sales and another that of decreasing distribution cost. If the first was successful it is unlikely that the second would be. This could be corrected easily if instead of 'Decrease distribution cost', 'Decrease distribution cost as a percentage of sales' was substituted.

Use of per cent

Expressing one thing as a percentage of something else is often a good method of refining measurement. Here are some examples:

Past period:	per cent above 199-
Units processed:	per cent of those handled
Other's forecast:	per cent of Marketing Guide's market estimate

Competitors:	per cent of market
Market statistics:	per cent of disposable income
Utilization:	per cent utilization of space
	per cent utilization of capital
	per cent utilization of stock
	per cent utilization of machinery

EXAMPLES OF CONVERSION OF EFFECTIVENESS AREAS TO MEASUREMENT AREAS

This section will give you many ideas on how to convert effectiveness areas to measurement areas. For each of your effectiveness areas there are a few measurement areas that are highly appropriate and some that are probably less appropriate. By reviewing this section you will get all or most of the ideas you will need to select from. It is a good idea to read over the entire section even though some sub-sections may not seem to apply to you.

Profitability measurement areas

Some managers head profit centres and they can use profitability as a measure of their performance. Typical measures include:

Gross profit
Net profit
Profit as per cent of sales
Profit as per cent of capital
Rate of profit change
Profit of territory
Profit by line or department
Return of capital invested

Even this kind of measure is never perfect, but it nevertheless, is a very good one if available.

Sales measurement areas

An effective area of 'sales' might be conveniently broken down into some combination of the following:

Existing products – existing markets
Existing products – new markets

New products – existing markets
New products – new markets
Unit sales by area
Unit sales by territory
Unit sales by product
Unit sales by customer
Unit sales by new customers
Sales in money units of product A or B or C
Sales in new product X vs old product Y
Per cent market penetration
Gross margin product Z
Profitability per product
Market share
Rates of sales change
New customers

Many measures depend on competitors' actions just as they do on one's own. However, implicit in using these measures is taking these actions into account.

Material measurement areas

Material measurements are directly useful to those involved in the production process and they include:

Unit cost reductions
Unit cost handling
Scrap/waste
Rejects
Inventory level
Inventory rates
Inventory turnover
Model change time
Quality level

Many of these will be applied to individual products or product lines. A few can be applied to the total material handled.

Safety measurement areas

The need for safety is more obvious in some industries, and the incidence of accidents more associated with particular jobs. However, these measurements will cover most basic situations.

Number of compensation cases
Knowledge of safety practices
Implementation of safety practices
Absenteeism due to accidents
Down-time due to safety
Accident frequency
Accident per employee hours/days
Accident per cent decrease
Accident cost
Ratio of organization to industry accidents
Ratio of deaths from serious to minor accidents

Other measurement areas

There are, of course, many measurement areas, which would be applicable across a variety of jobs not necessarily associated with any one function. A selection of these are:

Quality:
- number of rejects
- cost of rejects
- reject ratio
- percentage scrap
- cost of waste disposal
- typing/filing errors
- customer returns
- customer complaints
- batting average

Quantity:
- units produced (hour, day, week, machine, department, plant, national)
- units sold
- commission earned
- tons moved
- gallons stored
- barrels piped
- calls made
- reports written
- books borrowed
- records pressed
- goals scored

Training:
- programmes available
- trainees graduated
- number new trainees
- trainee performance

                        – cost of training
                        – cost of training materials
                        – days of training
                        – per cent trainees passed/failed
                        – degrees/ diplomas obtained
                        – succession plans filled

Lost time:
- lost hours, days, weeks, months
- lateness
- absenteeism
- sickness
- machine down time
- material hold-ups
- first aid room visits
- training/re-training
- unfilled vacancies
- jury service
- community service
- family bereavements
- weather
- industrial action (own/other)

Employee relations:
- number of industrial actions
- grievances registered
- attitude surveys
- opinions of supervision
- suggestion scheme usage
- company social event attendance

Costs:
- budget variance
- past period comparison
- down-time
- head count variance
- ratio fixed to variable
- value of cost control proposals

Maintenance:
- money cost of machine down-time
- time delay of machine down-time
- ratio maintenance cost to production cost
- average response time to call out

Technical:
- number of R & D projects completed
- project variance against budget
- ratio project cost to organization increase in profit/sales/costs/headcount/market share

           – project money unit savings
           – time span, idea to implementation

Other ways to measure

Another approach to measurement is to ask the question. 'What is
. . . the amount of, the time of, the opinion of and the frequency of
. . .'? Here are a few examples, but the reader will have many others.

Amount of	– sales
	– units produced
	– expenses
	– material costs
	– distribution costs
	– customer complaints
	– people needed
	– vacancies
	– scrap
	– theft
	– accounts outstanding
	– dividends paid
Time of	– trouble diagnosis
	– trouble rectification
	– product design
	– order filling
	– machine resetting
	– repairs
	– installation
	– delivery factory to customer
	– training operation
	– board meetings
	– money borrowed
Opinion of	– public to company usage
	– community to waste emission
	– new employees
	– union officials
	– supervisors to management
	– accountants to engineers
	– sales to production
	– participants to seminar
	– board to government legislation
Frequency of	– strikes
	– fires

- sickness
- pay increases
- grievances
- deaths
- power failures
- freeze-ups
- resignations

SOURCES OF INFORMATION

Most firms have vast reservoirs of untapped information. Most of it will, thankfully, remain untapped. However, much useful information exists ready-made or is easily obtainable, and it is an obligation of individual managers not to do what they can but to do everything possible to tap it. The primary sources of data are:

Central accounting department
Local accounting departments
Sales record analysis
Records and reports check
Sight checks (visual inspection)
Internal surveys
External surveys
Secondary data

Central accounting department

The central accounting department is, of course, a prime source of information, but company accountants are required by law to produce reports in specific forms. They are also required by their profession to follow numerous accounting principles, such as conservatism in valuing assets. The reports so produced are a valuable historical record of a company's progress and are often most helpful in establishing long-term strategy. They are not generally useful as operating guides to the practising manager. These reports are well designed for use outside the firm, not inside it. For instance, why should managers base their actions on what the government officials or the accounting profession think are appropriate depreciation rates? It is a serious error to see performance data for managers based on bits of data collected for other purposes. Progress toward managerial objectives can seldom be measured by a simple one-day slice of the balance sheet or profit and loss account prepared for statutory purposes.

Most of the useful information central accounting departments produce is based on the key figure elements in a cost or profit centre and includes:

Sales
Cost of sales
Cost of materials
Cost of production
Cost of distribution
Budget variance
Return on capital

Unless managers are at the top of a profit or cost centre, they may find the information supplied by central accounting departments somewhat too general for them, and so they turn to local accounting departments instead.

Local accounting departments

Local accounting departments are likely to provide such information as:

Cost by specific products
Cost by specific markets
Cost of hiring new employees
Scrap level by specific products
Cost by achieving budget objectives

The procedures of local accounting departments are usually locked in fairly tightly with those of the central accounting departments. This makes it difficult to obtain changes locally without changing important parts of the larger system. Supplementary local accounting sub-systems may be introduced, but only at increased cost. Changes may be made locally but should be extensive only when the executive agrees to modify the total system of measurement and reporting – if such a change is needed at all.

Two kinds of accountants

There are two kinds of accountants, or other types of information specialists. One is interested in producing immediately useful information; the other, only in keeping records. The primary orientation of each can shape the nature of the information system of the firm. The first type, the effective accountant, is a wonder to behold, and is considered a precious gem, and deservedly so. While wanting to be useful, this type still has to wait until managers say what information they want; more important perhaps is for them to tell the accountant why they want it. Without these statements the willing information expert can do nothing. The second type is usually amenable to change, but not in the short term. Perhaps they have been driven to the position through years of witnessing misused or under-used information. This type may even be willing to change immediately but is naturally suspicious of an overnight change of heart on the part of managers fresh from an output course. They do not plan to ask employees to work months of overtime and to switch the system around simply because one director spent a day on an outputs course. In most firms, however, some information system redesign is necessary to produce the measurement data required for high output management. The total cost of measurement must be weighed against the use that will be made of the data and the expected benefits of an output programme. It is of little value to spend 7000 money units on obtaining information which, if properly used, will save less than 1000.

Sales record analysis

Sales record analysis, or that of any functional area, always has been, and still is, one of the most useful and least used sources of information on such things as:

  Order size and trend
  Customer types
  Customer distribution
  Impact of the firm's own major marketing strategies
  Impact of competitors' marketing strategies

Many marketing and sales managers could employ clerical help very effectively in mining the information that sales records contain. Most sales managers can recall trends they spotted too late or know what an analysis of the impact of a particular competitor's strategy could provide. After training, medium-grade clerical assistance can provide a wealth of such data at nominal cost. After using such data for a year or so, and after the various wrinkles are ironed out, managers often decide to computerize the sales analysis reporting system. While only sales records have been used for illustration, the general principle of analysis applies equally to production, pur-chasing, stores, personnel, and other areas.

Records and reports check

Probably the most useful but unused information is in the files. It takes but little effort to install a simple counting system to obtain such information as:

Employee turnover by division
Damage claims
Missed delivery dates
Order errors
Grievances
Labour rates
Absenteeism
Turnover

Other information is obtainable from such sources as:

Administration meetings
Correspondence files
Daily activity card
Delinquent status reports
Time diary
Appointment diary
Periodic status reports
Personnel reports

In larger firms, or those with elaborate systems, much or most of this may be generated at the moment. If not, however, it costs little to produce it.

Sight checks (visual inspection)

Sight checks are very useful providing the sampling procedure is reasonably fair and unknown in advance to those who might have reason to want to distort the data. Sight checks might be used for:

Per cent machine utilization
Per cent space utilization
System installation

Internal surveys

Internal surveys and tests are used to discover such things as:

Employee attitudes
Levels at which decisions are made
Impact of training
Actual implementation of a system
Cost of typing a letter
Reject rates

Product quality
Raw material quality
Reasons for termination

External surveys

Output-oriented management usually leads to a decision to make some surveys outside the firm. As these surveys can be expensive a serious cost/benefit analysis of the information sought is very important. The type of information most often sought includes:

Company image
Product image
Product display
Customer satisfaction
Share of market

The surveys may be made by telephone, mail, personal interview or by inspection. The typical survey respondents include: suppliers, customers, general public, news media, legislators, shareholders, competitors, customers, and many others. It is almost always wise to obtain professional assistance in survey design and analysis. No such survey should ever be initiated unless management can state clearly just what decisions it proposes to make based on the data collected. Such surveys are sometimes conducted to make management feel comfortable; a pillow would be cheaper.

Internal and external surveys are usually expensive. The problem is never measurement but the cost of measurement. If no measurement area exists and if performance would increase with it then clearly some special expenditure is justified.

Secondary data

'Secondary data' is information collected by someone else, usually for a general purpose. The best examples are economic trend summaries produced by the banks, trade associations or government statistics. Many managers keep informally abreast of such data by reading trade or general business magazines. For special projects or corporate strategy development, however, a special search for secondary data is advisable. Typical of the secondary data available is information on:

Average work-week manufacturing
New orders by industry

Industrial production
Quarterly gross national product
Building contracts
New companies formed
Industrial share indices
Retail sales
Unemployment levels
Business failures
Non-agricultural employment
Personal income
Quarterly company profits
Quarterly dividends

EFFECTIVE DATA

To be a high output manager you need to receive and distribute quantified information that is relevant, timely, accurate and in an easily usable form. Measure the information you get now, send now, and plan to get and send in the future, along these criteria:

● Relevance
● Timeliness
● Accuracy
● Presentation

The data reaching managers should be only those on which they can base decisions. If parts of the data do not affect them they should not get those parts. The poorest kinds of data are those which enable a manager only to say, 'Old Bill isn't doing too well this month.'

The data must also be available early enough for appropriate decisions to be made, if necessary. If crisis management breaks out whenever the data arrive they should have come sooner, or the wrong person is getting them. If no decisions could ever be made on the data, they could probably arrive later or not at all. The data should also come at the right frequency. Some should come daily, others monthly, and so on. Learning experiments by psychologists are virtually consistent in proving that short feedback loops improve performance. If a manager could get immediate feedback on the probable or actual effectiveness of actions, performance would improve sharply. The cost of providing these loops must be considered, of course, but so also must their potential benefits. In department stores both senior and junior managers get one-day or shorter-period feedback, and this often occurs in production management as well.

To be useful, data need not be 100 per cent accurate. They need be only accurate enough so that correct decisions are more likely to be made. To make a report 100 per cent accurate unnecessarily incurs a high cost and results in delay. For these reasons sampling techniques of measurement are becoming more and more widely used, though they have already been used for years on such things as market share and product quality.

Managers should decide not only on the data they want and when they should get them, but also on how these data should be presented. Some managers prefer graphs, some tables, and others both. Some want their data cumulative; some look after such records themselves. Some wish to use charts on their office walls, and so on. Any competent manager should be willing to support, or at least tolerate, any presentation peccadilloes as long as they help to get the data used.

The data appropriateness checklist

For every piece of routine data landing on the desk a manager should complete one column of the Data Appropriateness Checklist either YES or NO. After doing so the changes required should be initiated.

The checklist asks six questions which relate to the measurement data and should be answered yes or no:

- Do I want these data?
- Are they relevant to my position?
- Do they come in time?
- Do they come at the right frequency?
- Are they accurate enought?
- Is their presentation in the best form for me?

The use of this checklist and a follow-up on what it reveals usually results in less and better data. The form should be used to cover all written or statistical reports, minutes, carbons of letters, magazines, and virtually anything with an information content appearing in the in-tray. The manager who wishes to be effective will want a major decrease in the bulk of the information received. One newly appointed top manager using the form eliminated about 70 per cent of the information and said, 'I felt quite guilty about it at first but then I realized that I was paying other people to read them and take action on them so why should I?'

Feedback loops design

The way in which data are supplied to a subordinate is a direct reflection of organization philosophy and management style. The methods may be categorized as:

- Management by hunch
- Management by tight control
- Management by staff
- Management by exception

Management by hunch
Occurs when there are no feedback loops at all or when there are only a few very long-term ones. Management decision-making is guesswork at best, and hunch and prejudice are the primary guides to

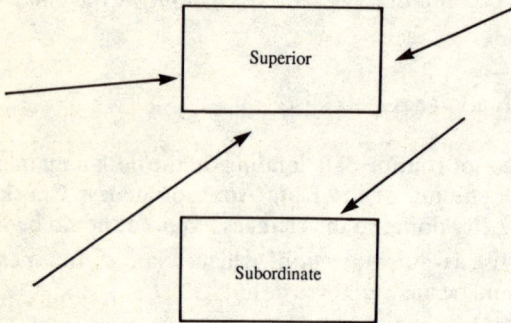

No organized feedback here.

Exhibit 3.1   Management by hunch

action. An enormous number of firms operate this way, even those with a large number of reports. The reports they get are not feedback loops on output at all, but duty activity or input reports. Thus management by hunch may be represented as in Exhibit 3.1. There is no organized feedback to either the superior or the subordinate.

Management by tight control
Occurs when information on the subordinate's performance is fed back directly to the superior through a staff unit and then only through the superior to the subordinate. A very large number of information systems are still designed this way. Notice in Exhibit 3.2 that the subordinate produces performance data, which are processed by central staff, accounting or computer staff, who then feed them to

the superior, who then passes them to the manager. This design is based on the view that it is management's job to tell subordinates

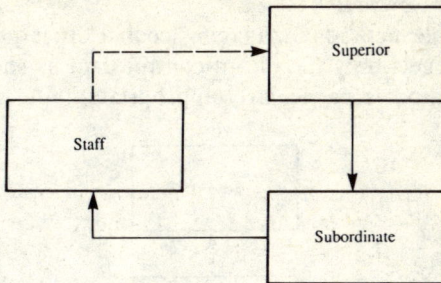

'Now this is how you are doing.'

Exhibit 3.2   Management by tight control

when they make mistakes. The underlying assumption appears to be that managers have neither the wit nor the interest to accept and act on the data themselves.

Management by staff
Occurs when the staff are given, or have assumed, too much responsibility as shown in Exhibit 3.3. It may have gone so far that the staff decide the primary measures of managerial effectiveness

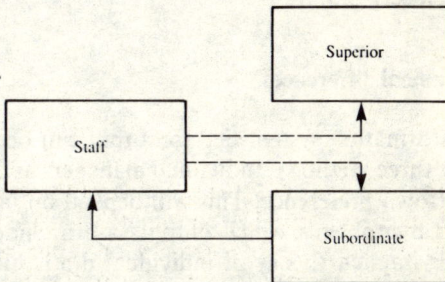

'Wait till they read this. Where shall we send it?'

Exhibit 3.3   Management by staff

and, a more serious situation, when it should be released and to whom. There is nothing more demotivating than having no control over your own performance feedback. This method should always be discouraged. It occurs most often when managers do not see system management as their job and so abdicate their responsibility.

Management by exception
Is an acceptable method of managing feedback in large organizations.
The superior gets only the out-of-control data as shown in Exhibit
3.4. This method is particularly appropriate if the superior has to

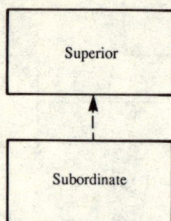

```
            ┌─────────────────┐
            │                 │
            │    Superior     │
            │                 │
            └─────────────────┘
                     ▲
                     ┊
            ┌─────────────────┐
            │                 │
            │   Subordinate   │
            │                 │
            └─────────────────┘
```

Out of control data only

Exhibit 3.4   Management by exception

coordinate several functions. In this case it must be known when one
function is out of control. It is often possible, however, to remove
this coordination function from the superior if it does exist.
Improved information systems make it possible for managers to
coordinate themselves.

Major philosophical differences

Clearly the information system tied to output can be installed using
any of the last three methods. Individual managers and organizations
will have their own preference. This will depend on how they define
the organization problems which outputs are intended to clear up
and what their implicit theory of individual motivation happens to
be.

PERSONAL FEEDBACK

Up to now this chapter has dealt with measurement in an easily
quantifiable way. This measurement provides feedback for motivation
and control purposes. Output-oriented managers are interested in
another kind of feedback which might be called personal. That is
feedback from other individuals or feedback from situations generally.

The feedback-learning cycle

Learning from feedback can be seen as a cycle continuously repeating itself. So long as the cycle is maintained, learning can continue. The two key elements in the cycle are making sound situational diagnosis and obtaining feedback on the results of the actions.

The situational-sensitivity cycle of Exhibit 3.5 has six steps. The sixth step leads into a repeating of the cycle.

1. A situational diagnosis is made.
2. The manager decides to adapt to the situation or to change it.
3. The manager takes action.
4. The manager obtains feedback on the results of the actions. Without this step, the feedback-learning cycle cannot continue. It is its weakest link since it depends on the climate the manager has created and skill in listening and observing.

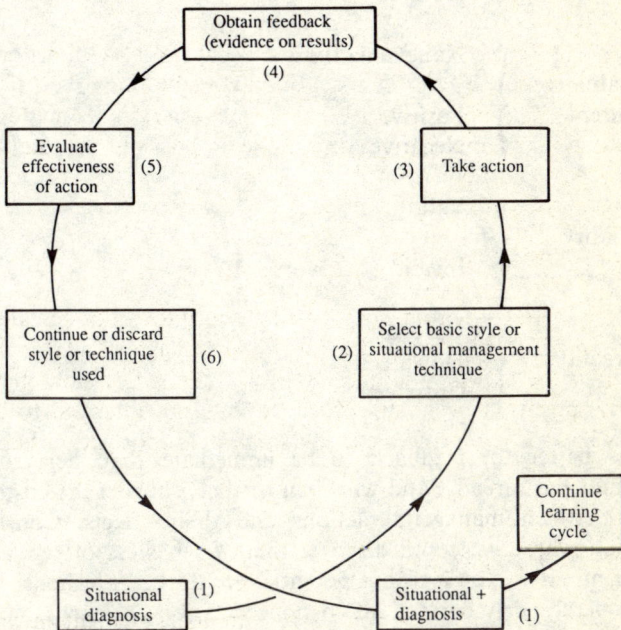

Exhibit 3.5 Situational-sensitivity cycle. Learning, like music, goes around and around.

5. The manager evaluates the effectiveness of the action. Then decides whether it led to more or less effectiveness and how much more effectiveness is possible.
6. The action taken is continued or discarded.

Learning is a continuous process. It is difficult to suggest where it starts or ends. An effective manager is constantly making a diagnosis of the situation, using style flexibility or situational management, and assessing the effectiveness of the actions so that an improvement can be made on the nature of the interventions.

Types of feedback

Feedback may be classified by its timing, evaluative content, validity and direction.

| Timing | { | Immediate |
| | | Delayed |

Evaluative content	{	Nonevaluative
		Positive
		Negative

| Validity | { | Valid |
| | | Invalid |

Direction	{	Upfeed
		Downfeed
		Crossfeed

It is better for feedback to be immediate than delayed. The computer has already, and will even further, shorten the customary delay between managerial actions and their effects. Consider a situation where we could discover the effectiveness of our actions within minutes. The learning potential would be enormous, not to mention the early corrections to poor decisions. Clearly managers should consider the timing of their existing feedback loops. How long does it take to know how a situation has changed, what it has become, or what the level of effectiveness is in it?

The best feedback is non-evaluative – that which simply 'tells it like it is'. Feedback, on which action must be taken, is less effective if feelings, positive or negative, are transmitted along with the information. For example, a subordinate is much more likely to respond to 'You did not meet your objectives', than the same statement with the often unspoken override of '. . . and I do not like you because of it.' The first is non-evaluative feedback; the second is negative feedback. The terms 'negative' and 'positive', then, refer not to the content of the feedback but to the feelings that go with it. Unless specially designed to be otherwise, mechanical feedback devices or computer printouts are completely non-evaluative. Although difficult to accomplish, managers find that the closer they come to such feedback, the easier it is for others to accept it and take action on it.

Feedback is either valid or not. Valid feedback may be negative, positive or non-evaluative, but it is always accurate.

Feedback may come from any direction in an organization. To indicate its direction, it is called upfeed, downfeed, crossfeed. Downfeed almost always occurs plentifully; crossfeed and particularly upfeed have to be planned.

AN EVALUATION OF THE QUALITY OF YOUR MANAGEMENT INFORMATION

A survey, called the organization output survey, consists of eight scales of ten items each. One of the scales is called 'effective management information'. It is designed to indicate the degree to which the management information system is seen as adequate.

Organization Output Survey

Scale: Effective Management Information

The degree to which the management information system is seen as adequate.

Item Number	Item	This organization	International norming	Difference
7	Most of the job-related information I receive comes in good time	52%	77%	-25%
9	Most of the job-related information I receive is accurate enough	62%	70%	- 8%

26	I can get most of the job-related information I need fairly easily	58%	75%	-17%
35	Most of the job-related information I receive is useful to me	100%	73%	27%
40	I receive all the job-related information I need to perform effectively	76%	85%	- 9%
50	I can use most of the job-related information I receive	88%	65%	23%
52	Much of the job-related information I am required to produce seems to be of value	92%	55%	37%
56	Most of the job-related information I get seems to reflect reality	70%	60%	10%
62	I receive the information I need in order to judge my effectiveness	62%	54%	8%
73	I receive the information I need in order to judge my subordinates' effectiveness	84%	75%	9%

In the first column is the number of the ten items of the scale. They are not numbered sequentially as the items on each scale are distributed randomly throughout the 80 items in the survey. Next is the item itself to which the manager has to answer yes or no, and the percentage of managers who said yes to each item in a particular organization which used this survey. This is explained in more detail in Chapter 15. Then are listed the international norms which give the average of managers who said yes from a large variety of companies. And then the difference. The negative differences show what the organization is poorer at than the average of other organizations, and positive differences indicate what the organization is better at. As you read this you can see that the company has some clear strengths on which to build and some clear weaknesses which it should overcome. You might think of the information system surrounding you, or in your company as a whole, against these ten items listed.

ACTION STEPS

1. Make a rough assessment of how well you now measure your effectiveness. (Zero is low, five is high.) Circle one number.

    0   1   2   3   4   5

2. Make a general review of the quality of the measurement you are now receiving on your outputs. Use one or more of the criteria mentioned in this chapter, whichever you think is most important.
3. For each of your effectiveness areas as revised develop one or more measurement areas that would be the best possible. Do not pay attention, at this point, to the difficulty of obtaining them.
4. For the measurement areas listed above decide which ones you have now or could get now easily and which ones you have to make a special plan to get.
5. Make a plan of how you will obtain your measurement areas that needs extra work by you.
6. Check out the above with one or more others who know your job.
7. How would you answer the survey items given on pp. **69–70**.

GLOSSARY

Effectiveness data: Quantified information which is relevant, timely, accurate and in an easily usable form.

Management information system (MIS): The method by which managers are provided numerical measurement to evaluate their progress towards achieving objectives.

Measurement area: How an effectiveness area is measured.

MIS: See *Management information system*

4 Matching outputs to authority

Authority is the right to give orders and the power to exact obedience.
Fayol

Life always gets harder towards the summit – the cold increases, responsibility increases.
Friedrich Nietzsche

The final step in establishing your complete role clarification is a clear statement of your authority areas. You have the outputs, you have the measurement areas, now clarify the authority. These three, and no others, are needed for your work role to be fully established. While not identified as such, up to now, the foundation of being an output-oriented manager is to know precisely what the job is. In more formal terms this is complete role clarification. This consists of a complete and agreed set of effectiveness areas, measurement areas and authority areas. The most important and lucid statement about authority was made by the French manager, and management writer, Henri Fayol. 'Responsibility must be commensurate with authority.' This means that outputs and authority must match. That is the subject of this chapter.

So, the third item on the job effectiveness description is a statement of the authority area that goes with the position. Authority refers to the type of change that can be decided by the job-holder. For example, a position may have the authority to engage or dismiss staff. If so, the authority statement includes information about limits such as: how many, which departments, and up to what levels? Similarly, an authority area concerning the modification of a production programme should give indications as to the scope of the modifications which may be instituted, for example: production speed or product quality or costs.

You cannot accept the responsibility for an output unless you have the authority to achieve the output. Clearly, effectiveness areas must be matched with the authority to achieve the objectives based on the effectiveness areas. This chapter will lead you to take another look at your effectiveness areas. When you look at your actual authority areas you may decide that your effectiveness areas exceed your authority or you may decide the opposite. The point is, your responsibility, that is outputs as represented by your effectiveness areas, must match your authority.

This chapter will give you a precise framework with which to look at your authority. You will then be able to list the things over which you have authority, and this may well lead you to revise your proposed effectiveness areas by either expanding or contracting them. It will, in all probability, lead to a meeting with your unit or your unit top member, your superior, to discuss what you are held responsible for and your view of what you see you have the authority to achieve.

This chapter is concerned with your formal authority. That is, the authority you exercise by virtue of the position you hold. While discussed, it is not concerned with your informal authority, that is, your leadership acts. The emphasis is on stating formal authority in normal, formal, business structures.

One organization's statement on matching outputs and authority
Here is what one large organization writes on the importance of matching outputs and authority.

- The matching of outputs and authority is a major problem in most large organizations including ours. For example, some of our managers used to be held responsible for profits but they did not control many of the costs.
- Many of our managers appear to be prepared to delegate outputs to their subordinates but are reluctant to delegate the necessary authority.
- It is critical that we improve our matching of outputs and authority. In future we must concentrate on each situation in which the requirement for an output is high yet the authority is inadequate. We must fix it. This will require a team effort by all managers.
- When you make your subordinates responsible for outputs you must give them adequate authority.
- Effects on our company of improving this matching will be to make our decision making more decentralized and closer to our customers. This would be consistent with our basic company objectives.
- Proving our matching of outputs and authority will lead us to reduce overlap between jobs. This will increase our productivity.

FORMAL AND INFORMAL AUTHORITY

Some cultures and some people have confused ideas about authority. Essentially, authority is what you can decide to do on your own, that is, decide without reference to another party. There are two kinds of authority: formal authority and informal authority. Formal authority involves the influence of the action of others or the utilization of things such as space, or money, which is derived from the authority vested in the position one occupies. That is, you receive the authority from the organization structure. Informal authority is influence over the actions of others or the utilization of things derived from one's personal qualities. This is sometimes called leadership. Leaders make things happen, at times, without formal authority. Obviously, both formal and informal authority are exercised together sometimes, but it is worthwhile to consider them independently to start with.

A morass of terms

Because many writers are confused about authority many terms have been coined concerning it. They present a morass. One of the objectives of this chapter is to establish the fewest and most specific terms possible. Some of the unnecessary concepts regarding authority include:

    Staff authority
    Sapiential authority
    Charismatic authority
    Moral authority
    Line authority
    Official authority
    Personal authority
    Sequential authority
    Lateral authority
    Authorization authority
    Knowledge authority

   None of these terms is necessary for you to understand your authority unequivocally. Most are overlapping and confusing. The terms in this chapter are fully sufficient. As an example from the above list, three related terms are sapiential authority, staff authority above list, three related terms are sapiential authority, staff authority and knowledge authority. These all spring from the mistaken idea pay people for what they know, unless they are university professors . . . only for what they achieve.

Some terms are useful but are duplicated. There is no need, for instance, to differentiate between power and authority. Each can be defined as:

> The influence over the actions of others or the utilization of things by the exercise of both formal authority and informal authority.

This definition is helpful only when formal authority and informal authority have been clearly distinguished as they are in this chapter.

Accountability

Some organizations find the word accountability to be useful. But the term is not needed as it can be inferred from the JED and surely it must be obvious that managers are accountable. Accountability is defined in this book as 'the requirement to achieve outputs'. The term *accountability management* is defined by Louis Allan as 'The obligation to perform responsibly and exercise authority in terms of established performance standards'. You may find one or the other of these definitions useful but the point must be made that the term is unnecessary as, with any manager interested in outputs, it is obviously inferred. Defining it becomes a trite joke.

Examples of formal authority

Here are some examples of formal authority being exercised. Some may seem to border on the frivolous. They were deliberately chosen to make it absolutely clear what, in fact, formal authority really is.

- The American President Truman deciding to remove General Douglas MacArthur.
- A manager deciding to lay off a typist.
- An umpire or referee deciding to give a penalty.
- A symphony conductor deciding to give an encore.
- A marketing manager deciding to change a price.
- A production manager deciding to institute a programme of quality control circles.
- A new CEO deciding to clear out the dead wood.

Examples of informal authority

Here are some examples of informal authority being exercised:

- An office pool supervisor convincing the typists to work an extra

half-hour a day until a back-log is eliminated.
- A production manager with a good idea about marketing, managing to convince the marketing manager that it should be introduced.
- A new CEO of a single plant in a small town convincing the town council that the land taxes should be withheld for a forthcoming period.
- A successful fund raiser.
- Two lorry drivers of a highly successful brewery convincing the marketing director that their tape of a proposed jingle would better represent the firm. As it happens, this actually occurred with a Reddin Organization client.

Clarifying some terms

At this stage it would be helpful to go over the difference in meaning in some widely used terms. They are often confused and need not be. These are:

Formal authority	vs	Informal authority
Manager	vs	Leader
Management	vs	Leadership
Responsibility	vs	Accountability

The terms may be differentiated in this way:

Formal authority
Influence over the actions of others or the utilization of things derived from the authority vested in the position one occupies.

Informal authority
Influence over the actions of others or the utilization of things derived from one's personal qualities

Manager
Someone exercising a high degree of formal authority.

Leader
Someone exercising a high degree of informal authority.

Management
The exercise of formal authority.

Leadership
The exercise of informal authority.

Responsibility
Outputs.

Accountability
The requirements to achieve outputs.

'DECIDE', THE ONLY POSSIBLE KEY FIRST WORK

Authority has to mean a right to decide about something. Therefore it is better if all authority areas start with the word 'decide'. Many schemes of authority statements are quite confusing and have key words such as approve, consult, implement, inform, agree, veto . . . and many more. None of these is needed as the key first word. The first word must always be 'decide'. As will be shown, 'decide' can have subsequent modifiers which specify the nature of the decision but 'decide' as a key word cannot be challenged.

Office cleaners decide too

As a perhaps extreme case, consider the authority areas of office cleaners and the use of the word decide. While the book emphasizes the managerial role, virtually all of it applies at all levels in an organization. The concept of the JED applies equally well at the lowest level in an organization. An office cleaner, a typist and a labourer all have outputs. They all have measurement areas and, while sometimes not recognized, they have authority as well, though obviously it is limited.

While the following statements may not appear to fit the concept of authority they all, in fact, refer to it. Clearly, the office cleaner role may have more or less authority depending upon the situation. The following is not a list of proposed authority for office cleaners but is illustrative of the possibility.

Possible authority areas for an office cleaner

- Decide equipment/use or purchase
- Decide route/sequence
- Decide amount of dosage of cleaning materials to use
- Decide start time/end time
- Decide timing of own rest breaks
- Decide when anything needs cleaning
- Decide time spent on a particular thing to be cleaned

The office cleaner working alone for a small office normally has all of these authorities. A member of an office tower cleaning gang would have fewer but still identifiable, authorities.

Well, surely the point is made. If one can prefix the authority of office cleaners always with the word 'decide' then surely it must apply to any managerial job and for that matter any other job. Agree?

LIMITS TO 'DECIDE'

Some of those involved with organization design decisions are
apprehensive about 'decide' because they think that if 'decide' is
spread around the organization what will happen is not organization
but rampant anarchy. As can be seen from the office cleaning
example the word 'decide' can be used for that position but its use
can be limited, in a very simple fashion, to decisions 'of what?' Other
ways in which 'decide' is still used but may be limited include the
ideas covered by these phrases:

● Decide within budget . . .
● Decide within ratio of . . .
● Decide if up to 20 additional . . .
● Decide then inform . . .
● Decide after consultation with . . .

If your authority involves 'consult' or 'inform'

There is no problem with authority areas that involve consult or
inform. These areas are quite legitimate as long as they are
understood – that is, as long as you have to make the ultimate
decision. If the terms 'consult' and 'inform' really mean that others
make the decision for you then you know what to do with your
effectiveness areas. Pass them along. The main thing is, please, be
clear about who is carrying the decision. There is a lot of shamming
in decision statements. Play the game if you want. It is good for
creative writing. But it is not good for role clarity and that is why you
have got this far. If you are an effective staff person, pass the book
around. Please do not pass around your potted version of it. We do
not want heroes, we want effectiveness.

If one must be consulted
Some decision statements for line managers often require that before
the line manager makes a decision some other position must be
consulted. So, in this kind of situation what is the 'decide' statement
for the position that must be consulted? Statements are normally
worded along these lines.

● Decide on which things one must be consulted.
● Decide whether to report any non consulting incident to the
   superior of the non consultee.

For the consultee position the decision statement is normally worded along these lines

● Decide after consultation with . . .

Virtually parallel wording is used for the situations where there is a requirement to inform.

● Decide on which things one must be informed.
● Decide whether to report any non-informing incident to the superior of the non-informer.

For the position that must inform, the decide statement is normally along these lines:

● Decide, then inform

It is critical to be clear on whether the informing or consulting really implies authority in the other position. Consultation should mean consultation – and only that. If, in fact, the personnel department is making all the decisions based on their authority then you are not consulting, you are asking whether you may do it. Here again you pass the effectiveness areas that are related over to them. As you can see, authority statements can be a very good way to achieve role clarity and straight lines in organizations. Sometimes who has the power is fudged. Unambiguous areas will not allow that.

Specifying positions in decide and inform statements
These are the methods that are normally used to specify particular positions in a consult and inform statement:

● Decide after consulting unit top member
● Decide after consulting other unit members of same level
● Decide after consulting a particular position
● Decide after consulting own subordinate team members
● Decide then inform unit top member
● Decide then inform other unit members of same level
● Decide then inform a particular position
● Decide then inform own subordinate team members

What if your superior has to approve your decisions?

If your superior has to approve your decisions then the associated effectiveness areas belong to your superior's position not yours. That's all. Two people cannot be responsible for the same thing. A different point entirely is if you are required to consult with your superior *before* you make the decision, but the decision is still yours. It is quite clear what happens. If your superior trusts your decision-making then the superior will allow you to continue to keep making the decisions. If your superior thinks you are rather unclear about the right decision then the decision-making will not be yours. 'Decide after consultation with a superior' means what it says. You still decide. If it happens that many of the decisions you want to discuss turn out to be changed significantly then clearly you are not making the decisions as your superior thinks you should. So it is not your effectiveness area any more. If you cannot sell your ideas upward then some of your effectiveness areas must move upward.

Decide if to request . . .

The prefix 'decide if to request . . .' may or may not be a legitimate authority area. If the longer statement is 'decide if to request permission to . . .' then the decision is not with the decision holder but rather with the person of whom the request is being made. Quite a different situation might be represented by an army field commander who has as an authority area 'decide if to request air cover for . . .'. This statement recognizes the field commander's right to request air cover but also recognizes that the position supplying the air cover may have higher priorities and may not provide it. However, when evaluating the effectiveness of the field commander the question would have to be raised whether or not the field commander exercised this element of the authority areas if in fact it was probably needed.

The extreme of decisions

The extreme of authority can only be based on the following:

● Decide own effectiveness areas
● Decide own measurement areas
● Decide own authority areas
● Decide own resources
● Decide own objectives

Those at the top of organizations are more likely to have one or more of these. If informal authority is high then more influence over these might occur. If you own the company and you are the CEO then you have control over all five. You make the decisions. If you do not own the company and you are still the CEO you may have to work things out with the shareholders' representatives you work with. The only point to be made is that these five are areas to be considered as an extreme case. For most managers none will apply at all as aspects of the system will decide most.

If you are in total control of the output variance

Control of variance is a good concept to think about when considering your outputs and authority. It refers to what authority you actually have to vary the level of an output. If you can dismiss an employee with reference to no one else, and unions or government legislation do not intervene then you clearly control 100 per cent of the variance. However, if you are the top marketing person and one of your outputs is market share you do not control 100 per cent of the variance in that output simply because you have competitors. You may in fact have only 10 per cent of the output variance under your control, perhaps even much less. The simple rule is: The position that controls most of the variance in an output in an organization has responsibility for the outputs. The variance you control may be 100 per cent or 2 per cent; the issue is whether or not anyone else in the company has more. The reality is that very few positions control 100 per cent of any variance. The position that has most control takes it as an output.

Having authority does not necessarily mean low participation

To have 100 per cent authority concerning a decision does not mean that one personally cannot decide, for a particular decision, to proceed only if all the members of the unit agree. For many decisions this will be unnecessary and the unit members would not want it. For some decisions it might be crucial to obtain team member commitment. There are only two occasions when participation should be used. One is when the decision is improved with it and the other is when the commitment to the decision is improved with it – and commitment is essential to effective implementation.

A unit top member can *decide* to make decisions in any one of these ways. This basic five-method system has been used and implemented by the Reddin Organization for more than twenty years.

(A) ONE-ONLY   In the ONE-ONLY method the unit top
                  member alone makes the decision and
                  announces it to the unit.

(B) ONE-ONE   In the ONE-ONE method the unit top member
                  obtains the suggestions of a single unit
                  member. The top member bases the decision,
                  in part, on the suggestions received from the
                  single member.

(C) ONE-TEAM   In the ONE-TEAM method the unit top
                  member obtains suggestions and ideas at one
                  time from all team members affected by the
                  decision. The top member bases the decision
                  largely on suggestions received from all team
                  members.

(D) MAJORITY   In the MAJORITY method the decision is put
                  to a vote and the majority vote decides.

(E) CONSENSUS   In the CONSENSUS method the total unit
                  shares its information, suggestions, and ideas,
                  and, as a unit reaches a decision through
                  obtaining consensus.

All of these methods are appropriate from time to time. For some
decisions the low participation ONE-ONLY method is appropriate,
and sometimes one of the other successively higher participation
methods should be used. The more effective manager would make
use of all of them.

No real value in responsibility charting

Many current attempts at defining authority involve what is called
responsibility charting. It results in a neat matrix of positions on one
axis and responsibilities on the other. The procedure is to put 'Xs' in
the various boxes. It was, and still is, used widely by those who think
they are being scientific. One terror of it is that consultants like it.
Yes, they like it because we are not talking about management but
rather about keeping things at a reasonably high intellectual level
and spending time doing little.

   Consider the following widely used and typical statement concerning authority:

   There are seven different types of authority:
   General Responsibility
      The individual who guides and directs the execution of a

function through the person to whom he has delegated operating responsibility and over whom he retains approval authority.

Operating Responsibility

The person who is directly responsible for the execution of the function.

Specific Responsibility

The person who is delegated the responsibility for a specific portion of the function.

Must be consulted

The person who, if a decision affects his area of responsibility, must be called in prior to any decision being made in order to render advice or relate information, but who does not make the decision or grant approval.

May be consulted

The person who may be called in prior to a decision being made, in order to confer, render advice, relate information, or make recommendations.

Must be notified

The person who must be notified of a decision once it is made.

Must approve

The person, other than persons holding general and operating responsibility, who must grant approval.

Do not use the above. Always use the word decide as the operating prefix. All of the above is a silly horror.

AUTHORITY CATEGORIES

There are many categories in which authority statements may be made. The two main ones are personnel and expenditure. However when looking at the detail of particular jobs it is evident that these two categories are insufficient.

The categories in which authority statements may be made include:

Equipment
Materials
Capital expenditures
Running expenditures
Payment authorization
Confidentiality
Staffing selection/type/level
Assets

Floor space
Organization structure
Work re-design
Own time
Time of others
Equipment purchase
Equipment modification
Changing standards
Salary levels
Add to or decrease personnel
External liaison
Customer contact
Innovation
Records
Pricing
Marketing
New products
General public
Government
Your own inputs
The inputs of others
Your own outputs
The outputs of others
Discretionary funds
Supply information to
Request information from
Mechanical aids/computer/word processing/typing/machinery

Examples of authority areas

Here are some examples of authority statements:
- Decide on capital expenditure . . .
- Decide all personal travel up to . . .
- Decide on all maintenance and repair costs for . . .
- Decide organization policy concerning . . .
- Decide whether to report violations from company procedures in the areas of . . .
- Decide on pricing for products . . .
- Decide on all suppliers.
- Decide how to spend budget in areas of . . .
- Decide on inventory level.
- Decide how to spend advertising budget.
- Decide how to allocate up to 10 per cent of total salaries of those

supervised on merit pay.
- Decide on nature of immediate subordinates training to five days per year.
- Decide to initiate any legal action.
- Decide on tools and machinery in area of . . .
- Decide all purchasing policies.
- Decide if to accept tenders up to . . . for approved projects.
- Decide on all expenditures for . . . within approved budget.
- Decide on all effectiveness areas, measurement areas and authority for all unit members.
- Decide what per cent of the total marketing budget will be spent on market research.
- Decide organization structure.

Authority areas concerning personnel
Authority areas concerning personnel can become an endless list. As with other authority areas it is best to include only the more important ones. If you can dismiss personnel one need hardly add an authority area concerning discipline as well. In some organizations the personnel function has a high degree of power and in other organizations a very low degree. The degree of authority it has reflects directly in authority statements of managers generally. Output-oriented organizations tend to give little or no authority to such staff functions as personnel. However, they may have authority to know what is happening and the authority to report what is happening if they do not agree.

Authority areas relating to personnel matters often take this form:

- Decide to increase or decrease number of staff within specified limits.
- Decide on selection of new staff.
- Decide on promotions.
- Decide on transfers within departments.
- Decide salaries.
- Decide merit pay.
- Decide on dismissal.
- Decide on discipline.
- Decide on organization structure.
- Decide on outputs, measurement areas and authority.

How many authority areas?

Areas of authority could go on and on and on. But small is still beautiful. Those who might help you write authority areas are not, by and large, in a protection racket. Their job is not to cover you at every base, and surely nor is your own. Use the fewest areas possible that are clear to all of those involved. Anyone can easily write 100 authority areas. Certainly, any child could. Managers should learn to write fewer.

OTHER ISSUES CONCERNING AUTHORITY

You should now be reasonably familiar with the nature of authority as applied to your position. Here are a few other things that are worth thinking about.

"I have no authority"
A common complaint among middle managers is that they have no authority or do not have enough authority. Some even say they have no job. While not always true it is usual that these points of view are incorrect. In short, some managers think the job is much bigger than it is or the manager is simply not using the authority possessed. A general issue of 'I have no authority' is best settled with your co-workers and superiors.

Common problems with authority
There are several common problems with authority and these include:

● Not specified
● Not understood
● Not agreed
● Not sufficient
● Not utilized
● Not seen as a polite thing to talk about
● Not seen as worth the time to discuss or decide
● Not seen as independent of person and personality

You might think about all these and see whether any of these impinge on your thoughts about authority.

Obtaining more formal authority
If you want to obtain more formal authority you must go through formal channels. Your only formal channel is the person to whom you report.

Obtaining more informal authority

You obtain informal authority by virtue of your personal qualities. This is sometimes called leadership. Leadership does not mean Montgomery on the tank, necessarily. Leadership acts occur just as well on the shopfloor, in the union meeting and in the office. Never accept that things like team work, leadership and drive are somehow permanently appropriated to the more senior position. This is completely incorrect. If you want to find a leader, look at the voluntary organizations in your neighbourhood.

Authority is not and should not be a constant: When you have your authority do not assume that you should chisel it in granite. As with outputs for an output-oriented organization or an output-oriented manager, they will change over time. Authority may change over time as a function of these:

- As a function of learning and experience
- As a function of trust level
- As a function of acquiring more skills
- As a function of making greater role clarity
- As a function of trial and error over time

While changes in authority are very important the issue you may be faced with now is determining what your authority actually is and what it should be at this moment.

ACTION STEPS

1. Search for any written documentation that might relate to your authority. It may be that you have virtually no real statement of authority assigned to your position and that is not unusual.
2. Using the above information only, draft a statement of your authority areas in terms of the 'decide' format.
3. Now make a list, again using the 'decide' format, of what you think your authority actually is.
4. Now make a list of what your authority areas should be, based on the outputs you have formally or tacitly agreed with your unit top member.
5. Discuss the above with your unit as a whole including the top member and then the top member alone, in whatever is the most convenient sequence.

GLOSSARY

Accountability: The requirement to achieve outputs.

Authority (or, power):   The influence over the actions of others or the utilization of things by the exercise of both formal authority and informal authority.

Authority area: A short statement, prefixed with the word decide, identifying the authority associated with the position.

Command: Military term denoting the exercise of formal authority.

Formal authority: Influence over the actions of others or the utilization of things derived from the authority vested in the position one occupies.

Informal authority: Influence over the actions of others or the utilization of things derived from one's personal qualities.

Leader: Someone exercising a high degree of informal authority.

Leadership: The exercise of informal authority.

Manager: Someone exercising a high degree of formal authority.

Management: The exercise of formal authority.

Power: See *authority*

Responsibilities: Outputs.

Role clarification: A complete specification of effectiveness areas, measurement areas and authority.

Sapiential authority: Presumed authority based on knowledge.

The Application

Introduction

Part I dealt with the conceptual foundation of output-oriented management. That is, effectiveness areas, measurement areas and authority areas. These three led naturally to the creation of a Job Effectiveness Description. The central point of that Part was role clarification for the individual position.

Part II starts with the creation of the Job Effectiveness Description (JED). This provides a precise definition of the job which the manager has engaged. This document is produced from the principles behind output-oriented management of outputs, measurement and authority. This document needs to be inserted into the organization system and used productively. Part III explains how this is done.

After you have completed your own JED based on what you have learned from Part I, we move on to improving your JED and the JEDs of those with whom you work from the basis of thinking of the outputs of the team as a whole. You will want to discuss your JED with all members of the unit with which you work, which will include your superior and co-workers, then most probably with all of your subordinates as a group, and finally with your superior alone.

Also, while the JED is useful on its own for role clarification, it is a natural device to use for setting objectives. So this Part also deals with how to set objectives, how to match your objectives to your resources, and how to plan. The chapters covering these topics will lead you, naturally, to setting numerical objectives based on your JED and an agreement on them with all of those you work with.

Only after the JED is fully understood by all concerned should you move to objectives and then to planning. Too many approaches move to objectives first. By now, you know that it is better to get the role clarified first through the JED. Only then do you move to objectives and planning.

5 One-alone job effectiveness descriptions

> My advice to managers for years has been to burn their traditional job description. If they are timid, they could burn a photocopy, at least the symbol is there.
>
> W.J.R.

After reading this chapter create, formally, a JED for yourself. Show all three components as clearly as you can. You will need to balance brevity with clarity. The main error tends to be making lists too long. The most important point for you to observe in this exercise is that the three elements of outputs, measurement areas and authority areas fit with each other. Consider all three elements together, not singly. Later you will be doing this with others but it is best that you do it as thoroughly as possible.

JED CHARACTERISTICS

The characteristics of a good JED include:

- A complete specification of the effectiveness areas
- One or more clear measurement areas for each effectiveness area
- Statement of authority areas on which the effectiveness areas are based
- Agreed to by all those who occupy positions which relate to the JED position
- Seen as a flexible document as the situation changes
- As brief as possible
- As few copies as possible
- Used in a variety of ways
- Current

Job Effectiveness Description

Job
reference ——————————————

Draft
reference ——————————————

Effectiveness areas and measurement areas

Authority areas

Exhibit 5.1   The Job Effectiveness Description form is meant to be simple and clear

Components of the JED form

The JED form has very few components. It is simple and elegant and that is precisley what it is meant to be (see Exhibit 5.1).

The three obvious components of the effectiveness areas, measurement areas and authority areas form the two main sections. The two other items needed are job reference and draft reference. The job reference terminology may refer to a position by title or by number. The draft reference may refer to such things as draft number, draft date or whether it is individually proposed, team agreed or organization approved.

EXAMPLES OF THE JED

Here are some examples of JEDs which include:

- Production manager
- Bank manager
- Internal consultant
- CEO
- Office pool supervisor
- Training manager
- Area manager – consulting firm
- Cleaner, small office

These are intended to be illustrative only and, through the notes made on each, to illustrate that the JED must fit the situation and cannot arise from a book. The nature of the CEO's effectiveness area depends very much on the nature of the technology and how the CEO prefers to see the role. A bank may see a branch manager's job as being prudent and cost-conscious or may see the branch manager's job as being essentially that of a salesperson for the branch. An office pool supervisor may be able to decide on the relative priority of work that comes in or may have to ask another position concerning it. Job titles alone do not necessarily indicate what the effectiveness areas really are.

The JED can be worked out accurately for a particular position only when thinking of the organization as a whole and how it sees the role. The bank manager is a good example of this.

The notes that accompany each example will be useful to you in understanding the position and the JED for it. The notes contain such things as typical inputs for the position. It also contains a list of authority areas over which the manager in the position does not decide. Reading these will improve your understanding of the authority areas.

Job Effectiveness Description

Job reference   Production manager   Draft reference   Individually proposed

---

Effectiveness areas and measurement areas

1. Production level
   1.1 Number of units produced per week as per cent of target

2. Delivery times
   2.1 Per cent of delivery times met
   2.2 Amount of penalty payments per year

3. Cost levels
   3.1 Per cent of cost variance above or below budget

4. Quality levels
   4.1 Established quality control level within an average ± per cent each week

5. Raw material control
   5.1 Monthly raw material turnover
   5.2 Cost of production, or additional cost, in monetary units owing to inadequate raw materials during year

6. Machine utilization
   6.1 Average per cent of machine utilization over specified time period. Not less than ...

Authority areas

Decide overtime level up to 10 per cent of total wages budget
Decide organization and roles of staff
Decide specific allocation of overall agreed budget
Decide on 100 per cent of budget expenditures
Decide on daily optimum mix of product, machine and staff
Decide on production employee relations issues within company guidelines in document ...
Decide on all purchases relating to production

Exhibit 5.2   Job effectiveness description of a Production Manager

NOTES ON PRODUCTION MANAGER JED

Production, together with marketing, tends to be the easiest function for which to form effectiveness areas, and objectives and statements of them abound in the literature.

The most common effectiveness areas in production are:

- Production level
- Delivery times
- Cost levels
- Quality level
- Inventory control
- Machine utilization

The effectiveness areas can vary very much from position to position, however, depending on such things as whether or not:

- Continuous-flow process is used
- Plant has autonomy over policy, especially personnel
- Structure at the top is flat or tall
- Models change frequently

The 'daily' element in the authority of this JED suggests that this job has rather frequent changes in the production systems presumably because of filling to order. This job related to filling orders for inexpensive ballpoint pens with a variety of colours, shapes and sizes, with production up to a million per day. The production manager did not have to interact with others in the production process and bought supplies from outside. Aspects of the industrial relations issues in production might have been given to the personnel manager or the CEO in other circumstances. We are not certain of the extent of the authority of the production manager until we see the guidelines referred to in the authority areas statement. Sometimes production managers do not have control over raw material purchasing but this one did.

This production manager did not decide:

- on quality standards
- on products
- on amount to be produced
- on product modification
- on machine modifications

Inputs for this production manager included:

- walk the shop
- read reports
- make plans
- supervise immediate staff
- machine maintenance and repair
- monitor scrap and reject reports
- check raw material stock levels weekly
- visit suppliers
- conduct/attend meetings
- prepare budgets

They are listed here only to show how different they are from the outputs.

Job Effectiveness Description

Job reference	Bank manager	Draft reference	Individually proposed

Effectiveness areas and measurement areas

1. Bank loans
    1.1 Number of new loans made within established limits
         of ... to ... within time period
    1.2 Monetary value of loans outstanding within limits
         of ... to ... within time period
    1.3 Per cent of loan defaults to loans outstanding
         during time period
    1.4 Loan profitability as per cent of revenue to loans
         outstanding

2. New accounts opended
    2.1 Doctors   2.4 Dentists   2.6 Newsagents
    2.2 Solicitors   2.5 Estate Agents   2.7 Grocers
    2.3 Accountants

3. Bank charges
    3.1 Bank charges and commissions as per cent of total
         deposits
    3.2 Bank charge receipts in monetary units per cheque

Authority areas

Decide amount of time spent outside office in customer
   community
Decide how to spend specified advertising budget locally
Decide bank account charges
Decide overdrafts within specified limits
Decide loans up to specified limits

Exhibit 5.3   Job effectiveness description of a Bank Manager

NOTES ON BANK MANAGER JED

As indicated earlier the JED of a bank manager can vary a great deal from bank to bank and branch to branch and country to country depending on how the role is seen. In some banks the role is classically the 'country' banker who sits and waits for things to happen. In others the role is quite different. The thrust of this JED indicates the more active role for the manager. In this particular banking system the bank manager did have authority over charges to make to customers for such things as cheque clearances. A large number of banks now have this automated and automatically specified in advance but this one does not. This is reflected in the authority areas.

Measurement areas for new accounts opened could be refined in one or two ways. They could be either as an absolute amount of new accounts opened, the average balance in these accounts six months later or the per cent of each of the categories such as doctors and solicitors in the bank's market area actually obtained.

The measurement areas for bank loans might well be extended if seen as appropriate in terms of total monetary amount or the number of loans under a certain size and above a certain size but still within the loan limit. If appropriate, various of the measurement areas could be refined further in terms of personal loans and commercial loans.

This bank manager did not have the authority to decide the following:

- staff level
- interest rates
- size and nature of premises
- types of services available
- costs
- staff selection

The typical inputs might be:

- branch image
- customer relations
- meeting customers
- supervise staff
- time spent in office
- time spent out of office
- branch staff meeting
- reading HO instructions
- employee relations

Job Effectiveness Description

Job
reference __Internal consultant__   Draft
reference __Individually proposed__

Effectiveness areas and measurement areas

1. Consulted in competence area
    1.1 Number of times consulted by client A
    1.2 Number of times consulted by client B
    1.3 ... etc. ...

2. Advice accepted
    2.1 Per cent of times advice accepted by client A
    2.2 Per cent of times advice accepted by client B
    2.3 ... etc. ...

3. Advice accepted creates effectiveness
    3.1 Number of times advice accepted lead to more
         effectiveness by client A
    3.2 Number of times advice accepted lead to more
         effectiveness by client B
    3.3 ... etc. ...

Authority areas

Decide how to promote speciality
Decide if to recommend outside expertise within client's
   budget
Decide how to deal with requests for advice
Decide how to conduct assignments
Decide own travel and other expenditures within budget
Decide on days spent per project
Decide on emphasis and techniques for any project

Exhibit 5.4   Job effectiveness description of an Internal Consultant

NOTES ON INTERNAL CONSULTANT JED

The general line of thinking about the internal consultant as reflected in this JED was referred to on p. 24. This JED reflects a very well defined idea of the internal consultant's job. This idea is usually completely missed. This JED applies very widely to staff positions without power which might cover anything from industrial relations, pension funds to fire safety in buildings.

If JEDs can be created with valid decision statements for this kind of position then, as with the example of the cleaner, small office on p.110 surely there is little excuse for not using this idea for a variety of jobs.

It is important to note that this role does not give the internal consultant any authority to tell line managers what to do. Nor does it give the internal consultant any authority to go to a higher level in order to put pressure on the line managers who would not do what they were 'told'. It can be there if the organization decides it but it is not there in this case.

This consultant does not decide on who the clients might be, it might simply be all the plant managers and also does not decide on the area on which advice is given . . . it may only be fire safety. So this Internal Consultant did not have the authority to decide the following:

- client system
- general area in which to give advice

The typical inputs might be:

- Attend meetings
- Write reports
- Read
- Discuss projects
- Days spent on projects
- Personal competence
- Giving presentations
- Walk the shop
- Learn
- Be highly knowledgeable

Job Effectiveness Description

Job reference	CEO	
Draft reference	Individually proposed	

Effectiveness areas and measurement areas

1. Return on capital
    1.1 Annual per cent return on capital
    1.2 Annual trends in per cent return on capital against base of previous year
    1.3 Annual profitability in money units
    1.4 Annual profitability in money units per employee

2. Quality of decision-making
    2.1 Number of decisions made leading to more effectiveness in year
    2.2 Number of decisions made leading to less effectiveness in year

Authority areas

    Decide on annual divisional budgets
    Decide capital expenditures over ...
    Decide top team membership and remuneration
    Decide on employment of capital
    Decide on all aspects of company organization
    Decide to open new plant units
    Decide to close plant units
    Decide to cancel major product lines
    Decide to create new profit lines

Exhibit 5.5   Job effectiveness description of a CEO

NOTES ON CEO JED

The effectiveness areas of a CEO position are highly flexible. They differ from one organization to another and from one position to another, and they change over the length of time during which the top person grows into the job and comes to trust the subordinates more or builds the organization around a preferred style.

An extreme of authority can only be based on these five things.

- Decide own effectiveness areas
- Decide own measurement areas
- Decide own authority areas
- Decide own resources
- Decide own objectives

Those at the top of organizations are more likely to have one or more of these. If informal authority is high then more influence over these might occur. If you own the company and you are the CEO then you control all five. You can decide. If you do not own the company and you are still the CEO you may have to work things out with the shareholders' representatives you work with. The only point to be made is that these five are areas to be considered as an extreme case. For most managers none will apply at all as aspects of the system will decide most.

Trends in per cent of return on capital may well be stated in terms of five years. The objective might be stated in terms of regular growth quarter by quarter or might be, more realistically in some types of organization, not more than one decrease from a prior quarter per year.

The typical inputs might be:

- Meetings with directors, top team, major clients, community representatives
- Top team motivation
- Employee communication
- Walking the shop
- Community activities
- Read organization's reports
- Read financial publications

Job Effectiveness Description

Job
reference   Office pool
               supervisor   Draft
                                       reference   Individually proposed

---

Effectiveness areas and measurement areas

1. Production level
    1.1 Agreed production requests met each week

2. Delivery dates
    2.1 Agreed per cent of delivery dates met each week
    2.2 Number of user complaints about delivery timing
         each week

3. Costs
    3.1 Total staff costs per week
    3.2 Total overtime cost per week
    3.3 Per cent machine utilization per week
    3.4 Per cent of variable staff costs per week

4. Quality
    4.1 Number of complaints about quality each week

Authority areas

Decide priority of work and inform superior
Decide allocation of work to staff
Decide personnel matters within organization guidelines
Decide overtime up to 5 per cent of total salary cost
Decide all machine repairs up to ... money units
Decide machine replacement or new machines up to ...
  money units
Decide on staff replacements

Exhibit 5.6   Job effectiveness description of an Office Pool Supervisor

NOTES ON OFFICE POOL SUPERVISOR JED

The job of the office pool supervisor is seen by some as ranging from the 'dragon' to 'the queen bee'. How the office pool supervisor is seen is the function of the authority acquired or obtained and the level of resources related to the level of output required. Quite often the position does have the right to decide on work priorities and this tends to make those more junior somewhat upset. It is always a good idea to be absolutely clear about what the authority is in fact.

The office pool supervisor did not decide:

- stationery design
- machine typeface
- format of reports or letters

The typical inputs might be:

- Check on work quality
- Attend meetings
- Supervise staff
- Monitor future workload
- Advise stores supervisor on stationery and consumables usage

Job Effectiveness Description

| Job reference | Training manager | Draft reference | Individually proposed |

Effectiveness areas and measurement areas

1. Identify training needs
    1.1 Per cent of managers with training needs agreed
    1.2 Per cent of non-managers with training needs agreed

2. Meet training needs
    2.1 Per cent of managers with training needs met or scheduled to be met within six months
    2.2 Per cent of non-managers with training needs met or scheduled to be met within six months

3. Behaviour change
    3.1 Behaviour changes leading clearly to cost reductions per year as a per cent of relevant budget per year
    3.2 Behaviour changes relating to profit improvement per year as per cent of relevant annual budget per year
    3.3 Number of behaviour changes relating to service improvement per year

4. Conference facilities
    4.1 Conference facility utilization per cent by month

Authority areas

Decide frequency and method of conducting training needs analysis
Decide type, number and sequence of courses
Decide who attends courses
Decide on course design
Decide whether to design course or buy it in
Decide teaching method(s)
Decide if to involve outside trainers
Decide on which training staff to be used
Decide survey technique to be used to measure behaviour change

Exhibit 5.7 Job effectiveness description of a Training Manager

NOTES ON TRAINING MANAGER JED

This training manager had several trainers reporting directly and was responsible for a conference facility. Thus this training manager was not a training officer who would normally be measured by a seminar evaluation form but could take on more responsibility concerning behaviour change. For this some budget would be essential for the survey technique required to identify behaviour changes.

The typical inputs might be:

- Knowledge of course design
- Knowledge of training packages available
- Motivation of trainers
- Analyses, training needs surveys
- Attends heads of department meetings
- Conducts training staff meetings

Job Effectiveness Description

Job reference	Area manager – consulting firm	Draft reference	Individually proposed

Effectiveness areas and measurement areas

1. Profit
   1.1 Gross profit per month per consultant on staff
   1.2 Gross profit per month as a per cent of days sold

2. Sales
   2.1 Percentage sales increase over same month prior year
   2.2 Consultant invoiced days per month

3. Business mix
   3.1 Percentage of gross income from service A/B/C

4. Quality of service
   4.1 Per cent mix of quality, cost and time standards in client contract

5. Costs
   5.1 Percentage of average contract cost under plan per contract
   5.2 Percentage reduction for service A/B/C
   5.3 Consultant invoiced time per week average

6. Sales expansion
   6.1 Money volume of new contracts per three months
   6.2 Percentage of prior clients renewed per year
   6.3 Number of quality staff retained per year

Authority areas

Decide on staff selection
Decide on number of staff
Decide sales and promotion budget
Decide terms and conditions of all assignments other than those established as organization policy
Decide which assignments to select
Decide level of personal involvement with any assignment
Decide proposal cost, preparation and presentation
Decide which consultants to which assignments
Decide per cent of own time used for client prospection

Exhibit 5.8 Job effectiveness description of an Area Manager – Consulting Firm

NOTES ON AREA MANAGER – CONSULTING FIRM JED

Business consultants are usually knowledge workers who operate on a contract basis. A general set of effectiveness areas for a consultant is:

- Time utilization
- Meet contract terms
- Client effectiveness

While the manager of consultants might have these:

- Profit
- Sales
- Business mix
- Quality of service
- Costs
- Sales expansion
- Consultant quality

The position does not have the authority to decide all contract terms. Some are standard and in this position they included such terms as 'client will not employ the consultant for 12 months after the termination of the assignment', 'invoices should be sent weekly and paid monthly', and so on.

The manager might not decide:

- Geographic area of work
- Fee structure
- Consultant commission levels
- Consultant training pattern

The typical inputs might be:

- Visits to potential clients
- Meetings with other area managers
- Staying in contact with past clients

Job Effectiveness Description

Job reference: Cleaner – small office

Draft reference: Individually proposed

Effectiveness areas and measurement areas

1. Cleanliness
   1.1 Number of user complaints per week
   1.2 Per cent specifications met per week

2. Hygiene
   2.1 Number of user complaints per week
   2.2 Per cent specifications met per week

3. Level and frequency of waste disposal
   3.1 Number of user complaints per week
   3.2 Per cent specifications met per week

Authority areas

Decide within time agreed on own access to any part of office rooms
Decide equipment use
Decide route/sequence
Decide amount of dosage of cleaning materials to use
Decide start time/end time
Decide timing of own rest breaks
Decide when anything needs cleaning
Decide time spent on a particular thing to be cleaned

Exhibit 5.9   Job effectiveness description of a cleaner, small office

NOTES ON CLEANER, SMALL OFFICE JED

This JED is an elaboration of the notes made on the authority of a cleaner in a small office given in Chapter 4.

The single office cleaner working alone for a small office normally has all these authorities. A member of an office tower cleaning gang would have fewer but still indentifiable authorities.

Well, surely this point is worth repeating.

It is clear that office cleaners of small offices, at least, have identifiable authorities. It is not reasonable to expect that such authorities can be identified for all jobs?

The cleaner of a small office did not decide:

● When 'major clean' required
● On contract cleaning renewal (e.g. windows)
● When redecoration initiated

The typical inputs might be:

● Sweeping
● Polishing
● Emptying wastepaper bins
● Wash surfaces

This chapter gives you some examples of JEDs, covering quite a variety of positions. Notice the title of this chapter. It is meant to suggest that your first draft of your JED arises from thinking about your JED on your own with little input from those who occupy other positions that surround yours. As you will see from the next chapter, Unit Job Effectiveness Descriptions, there are some other things to think about than just simply your own position in isolation. However, it has been demonstrated quite conclusively that it is best to think about your position in detail first.

Up to this point you know what is meant by outputs, measurement areas and authority areas. That is exactly what the book has intended to achieve at this point. An entirely different topic is how these ideas can be used on a team basis. As simple examples, suppose two team members believe they are responsible for the same thing. Suppose in a team that there are some things for which no one believes they are responsible. Is the output of the unit top member identical to the output of the unit itself?

All these points will be settled but it is important for you now to create your own JED, as a learning step, before engaging the topics taken up in the next chapter. This prework before a unit meeting is essential.

ACTION STEPS

1. This chapter has asked you to create your own JED. Think about all three elements together rather than separately.
2. Check out your complete JED informally with someone else who has read this book.

6 Unit job effectiveness descriptions

When two do the same thing it is not the same thing.

Proverb

Perhaps the most important principle on which the economy of a manufacture depends, is the division of labour amongst the persons who perform the work.

Charles Babbage

Management must develop as broad a horizon as possible for every position, with guide posts along the way rather than rigid fences that hem the individual into a completely preplanned . . . existence.

Edward C. Schleh

The previous chapters have shown how to create a JED with a single position in mind. While this is very important as far as it goes, it does not go far enough. Individuals and individual positions are embedded in units, work teams, and one needs to look at unit JEDs as much as individual JEDs really to understand the individual JED. Too many books looking at managerial effectiveness and organization effectiveness overlook unit effectiveness, thus appearing to believe that organizations are run exclusively by individuals. They miss the interaction. This chapter deals with it.

ORGANIZATION OF UNITS

There are four types of unit organizations. While some units fit one type fairly squarely, some units may be a mixture of two or more. The four types of units are referred to as:

- Separated
- Related
- Dedicated
- Integrated

They differ primarily on the nature of the work interaction across the individual positions in achieving the unit output.

They can be defined as:

Separated:
   Characterized by a low level of work interaction across unit members except for top member inputs to unit members.

Related:
   Characterized by a low level of work interaction across all unit members.

Dedicated:
   Characterized by one unit member's outputs becoming another unit member's inputs with the top member inputs directed primarily to interfaces across immediate unit members.

Integrated:
   Characterized by a high level of work interaction across all unit members.

The separated unit

The separated unit is characterized by a low level of work interaction across unit members except for top member inputs to unit members. The regional manager and twenty bank branch managers would be an example of a separated unit. The individual bank managers really have little or no interaction with each other and do not add or detract very much from each other's effectiveness. It is much the same for some kinds of personnel unit which are organized along the lines of, wage and salary administration, training, safety and organization development. While all these are very important, the interaction across these positions is very low indeed, and thus, it is a separated unit. Managing what are essentially unrelated profit centres is another example, so-called 'teams' of encyclopaedia sales people or insurance sales people would be another.

   Types of unit that can be classified as separated include:

● A regional bank manager with bank managers as unit members
● Generally, any manager of a region supervising similar types of work in different locations
● A personnel unit
● A unit consisting of unrelated profit centres
● A chain of stores

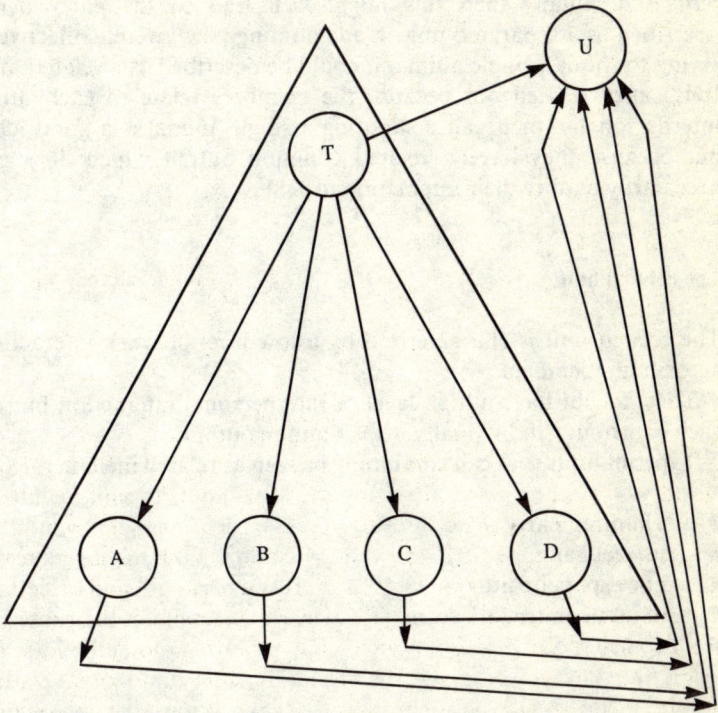

The separated unit organization is characterized by a low level of work interaction across unit members except for top member inputs to unit members.

Exhibit 6.1   The separated unit organization

- A sales 'team'
- A chef and assistant chefs
- A bank branch
- A typing pool
- A restaurant owner and key staff

These types of units do not necessarily always fit into the separated category. However, they often do. If the hunting party were shooting birds individually then this might well lead to the party being described as a separated unit. If the hunting party were, collectively, trying to shoot a single animal it could be described as a related unit. It is called related not because the members relate to each other interpersonally, or because shooting a single animal is a good idea, but because they have a related common output which does not necessarily require their interaction to achieve.

The related unit

The related unit is characterized by a low level of work interaction across unit members.

They do not have a high level of interpersonal interaction but do each contribute, individually, to a common output.

Types of units that can commonly be seen as related include:

- A hunting party
- A street gang
- A newspaper editor
- An immediate work team
- A lynch mob

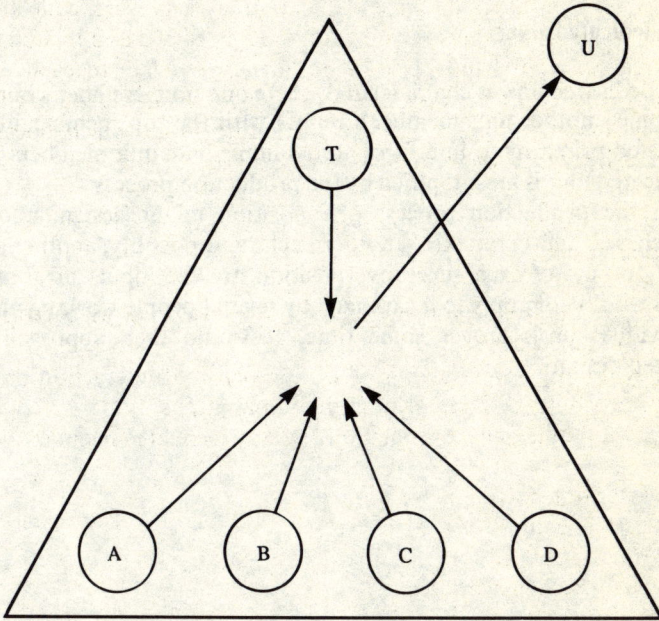

The related unit organization is characterized by a low level of work interaction across unit members.

Exhibit 6.2   The related unit organization.

The dedicated unit

The dedicated unit is characterized where one unit member's outputs become another unit member's inputs with the top member inputs directed primarily to interfaces across immediate unit members. The dedicated unit is most typified by the production process.

In the production process one position might design, another purchases, another makes, another packs and possibly, another sells. The outputs of each successive position are the inputs of another. This would not apply to a car made by several people working on the individual project over some time. It would then approach the related design.

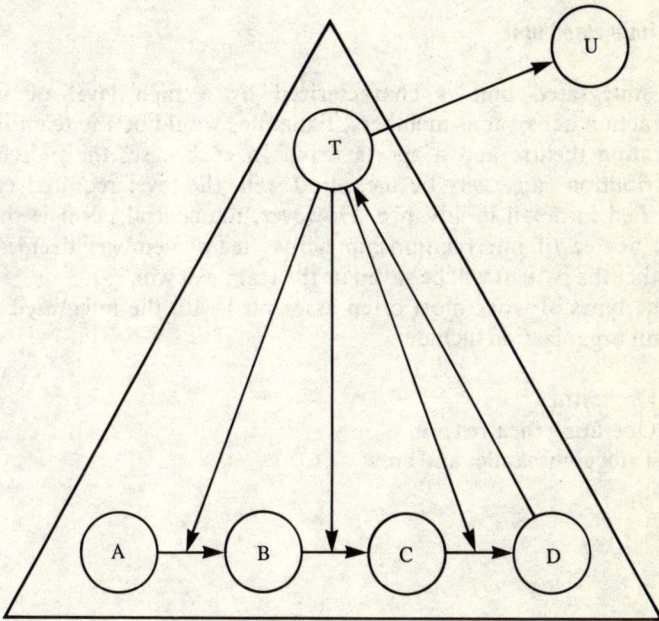

The dedicated unit organization is characterized by one unit member's outputs becoming another unit member's inputs with the top member inputs directed primarily to interfaces across immediate unit members.

Exhibit 6.3 The dedicated organization

The integrated unit

The integrated unit is characterized by a high level of work interaction across unit members. Examples would be the team in an operating theatre and a sports team. In each case, the individual contribution can easily be measured well, the level required easily specified in detail in advance. However, the central point is that a high degree of interrelationship across team members decides on whether the patient will be saved or the team will win.

The types of work most often associated with the integrated type of unit organization include:

- Orchestra
- Operating theatre team
- Tank commander and crew

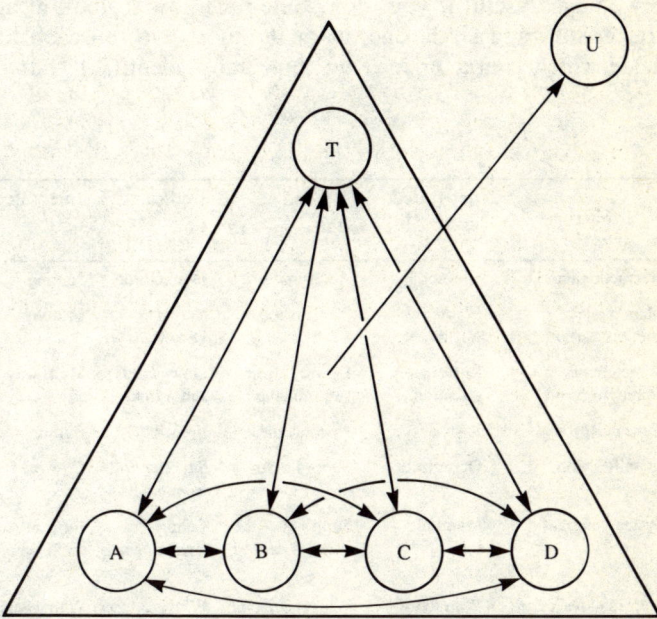

The integrated unit organization is characterized by a high level of work interaction across unit members.

Exhibit 6.4 The integrated organization

CHARACTERISTICS OF THE FOUR TYPES OF UNIT ORGANIZATIONS

Exhibit 6.5 gives identifiable characteristics of the four types of unit organization. It would be only seldom that a single, particular unit would fit all the characteristics for a particular type and none other. However, the list is very useful in helping you and your unit as a whole think about your team. It may well help identify some things you could seek to improve.

It would be useful if you took some time now to look at all the characteristics and circle one, or at the most two, on each line to indicate which characteristic you think most identified your team.

Factor	Separated unit	Related unit	Dedicated unit	Integrated unit
1. Interactional mode	Correcting	Accepting	Dominating	Joining
2. Main mode of communication	Written	Conversations	Verbal Directions	Meetings
3. Direction of communication	Little in any direction	Upwards from subordinates	Downwards to subordinates	Multi-way
4. Time perspective	Past	Unconcerned	Immediate	Future
5. Identifies with	Organization	Subordinates	Superior and technology	Co-workers
6. Systems emphasis	Maintains procedural system	Supports social system	Follows technological system	Integrates sociotechnical system
7. Subordinates judged on	Who follows the rules?	Who understands people?	Who produces?	Who wants to join the team?
8. Superiors judged on	Brains	Warmth	Power	Teamwork
9. Team mode	Clarifying, guiding and channelling	Supporting, harmonizing and coaching	Initiating, evaluating and directing	Setting standards, testing and motivating
10. Typical work situation	Administration, accounting	Managing professionals, training and coordination	Production and sales management	Interacting managers
11. Unlikely work situation	Non-routine	Low personal contact	Low-power	High routine
12. Employee orientation	Security	Cooperation	Performance	Commitment
13. Reaction to error	More controls	Pass over	Punish	Learn from
14. Reaction to conflict	Avoids	Smothers	Suppresses	Utilizes

Factor	Separated unit	Related unit	Dedicated unit	Integrated unit
15. Reaction to stress	Withdraws and quotes rules	Becomes dependent and depressed	Dominates and exploits	Avoids making decisions
16. Positive source of control	Logic	Praise	Rewards	Ideals
17. Negative source of control	Argument	Rejection	Punishments	Compromise
18. Characteristic problem of subordinates	Lack of recognition	Lack of direction	Lack of information	Lack of independence
19. Punishments used	Loss of authority	Loss of interest by manager	Loss of position	Loss of self-respect by subordinates
20. Undervalues	Need for innovation	Needs of organization and of technology	Subordinates expectations	Need for independent action
21. Main weaknesses	Slave to the rules	Sentimentality	Fights unnecessarily	Uses participation inappropriately
22. Fears in general	Emotionality softness and dependence	Rejection	Loss of power	Uninvolvement
23. Fears about others	System deviation irrationality	Conflict	Low production	Dissatisfaction

Exhibit 6.5   Characteristics of four types of unit organization

Then add up the four columns to get a very rough first impression. It would be helpful if you then did this with one or more other unit members and even more helpful if you did it with all unit members.

Building an organization

These four types of unit describe, reasonably well, the four typical molecular building-blocks of organizations. One has only to stand back from them to see how these four building-blocks can be used to help design and re-design organizations as well. While organization design issues are outside the scope of this book it is obvious that a top team would be well advised to start by asking what type of unit organization should be at the top. Then carry on the same question to the sub-units, and so on. Organizations can be seen as flows of outputs across systems. These four types can help you think about that with your unit and with your organization.

THE UNIT OUTPUTS DIAGRAM

The unit outputs diagram consists of four elements:

- Unit outputs
- Unit top member output
- Unit top member inputs
- Unit member outputs

Unit outputs

Unit outputs are the set of effectiveness areas for a unit which naturally include the outputs of the top member and all unit members summarized in some way. It is on these unit outputs that the unit top member objectives are set which are agreed with the top member's superior. In the prior chapter, when you considered your own outputs, you were probably thinking of unit outputs. You saw yourself as a top member and were naturally taking an overall view of your responsibilities. Unit outputs are sometimes simply an addition of each of the unit member outputs and the unit top member outputs. It is in the separated unit where this typically occurs. Unit members interact very little so the unit output becomes a list of the outputs of all of the individual positions. Sometimes unit outputs bear little resemblance to the outputs of unit members. A typical unit in a production setting is a good example. In this dedicated kind of unit, one unit member might buy, another unit member might make, another unit member might pack . . . and so on. None of these sets of outputs will appear on the unit outputs. The unit output may well be related to profitability. In short, the outputs of most team members, or all, are consumed within the unit.

Unit top member outputs

Unit top member outputs are the outputs of the unit top member having no overlap with unit top member inputs or with any unit member outputs. In short, it is the top member's unique contribution in output terms. It may well be that the unit top member has no unique outputs. The whole job may be in getting the unit to work so

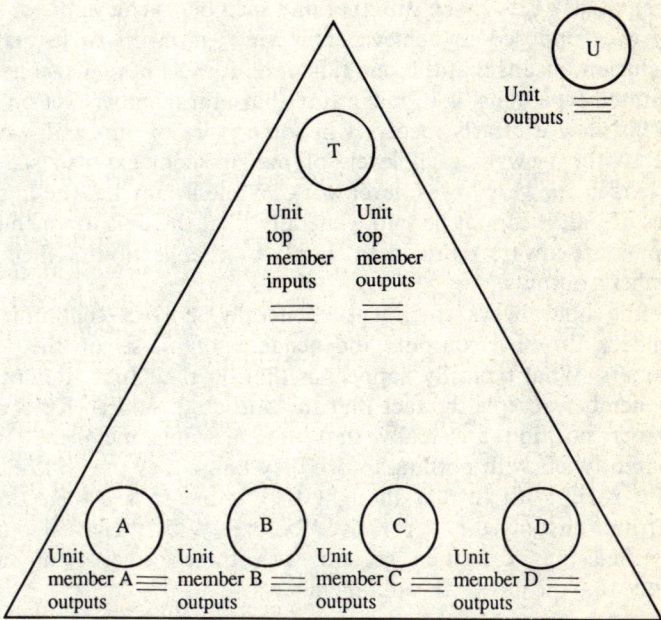

Unit outputs consist of the aggregate of the outputs of all the members of the unit, including the top members.

Exhibit 6.6   The unit outputs diagram

as to produce the best outputs possible in the unit as a whole. To take it to extremes, in the dedicated type of unit the main job of the unit top member is to optimize the working of the system and make sure that the interfaces between the unit member outputs work well. This may well lead to a lot of important inputs to the team but the main outputs are the team outputs. On the other hand, in a separated unit where most of the component parts run themselves, the top member may well have the opportunity to create a unique set of outputs. Later in the chapter examples of these are given.

Some managers of separated units incorrectly believe that their principal task is to make sure that unit members achieve the outputs they are supposed to achieve. This view, if taken to its natural conclusion, means that the sole function of levels of management, in separated-type units, is to make sure that unit members get on with it. This view is clearly incorrect in some types of unit and it could lead to the view that all levels of management exist to see that workers at the very lowest level work. While it may be true in some types of unit it cannot be said, generally, that the unit top member's outputs are always represented simply by a collection of their unit member's outputs.

While not always true, it is, generally, correct that unit top members do have outputs independent of those of their unit members. What typically happens is that, in their first attempt, the top member accepts the fact that the outputs proposed for the top member position are really those of the unit members. While apparently left with nothing to do, they know they are still filling a useful role. With further thought they come to see their unique contribution only dimly perceived before. With their real outputs identified they can then get on with these rather than simply monitoring the jobs of the unit members.

Unit top member inputs

Unit top member inputs are the activities of the top member to improve unit effectiveness. This may seem an unusual concept to introduce at this point in a book that is concerned with outputs. However, it has been found to be a very useful idea indeed in getting top members and a unit, as a whole, to think more clearly about the functioning of the unit. One of the important things that the identification of unit top member inputs accomplishes is to create much greater clarity about unit top member outputs and unit outputs.

Some of the responsibilities of the top member of any unit is to keep the unit functioning effectively. Some of the ways to do this are, naturally, inputs and come down to things like staffing, planning and budgeting. The top member knows that these are important, but also knows that these are clearly inputs in most situations. Many of the examples in Chapter 1 showing before and after sets of effectiveness areas reflect this dilemma. The first, and poor, set were usually very important inputs to the unit while the second set were, in fact, the true top member's, or unit's, outputs.

The typical inputs of the unit top member to the unit include such things as:

- Planning
- Staffing
- Allocating priorities
- Budgeting
- Goal-setting
- Management development

At high levels in the organization other such inputs as these may appear.

- Long-range planning
- Corporate strategy

These inputs may well be the outputs of a staff department. A long-range planning department's job is to create a long-range plan. The time-cycle and the measurement area must also be considered. It may well be that a CEO shows as an effectiveness area something along the lines of 'long-range objectives'. If this is to establish the objectives then it is clearly an input. If it is to achieve them in some future period then it is an output.

Are unit top member inputs needed?
Some managers, quite naturally, believe that a discussion of unit top member inputs is not really needed as the outputs are the thing. It has been found however that, without question, a discussion of them is a good idea. A discussion of them definitely helps the unit and the top member in particular to differentiate the important inputs the top member makes to help the unit become more effective from the unit outputs which, of course, are the top member's responsibility.

Unit member outputs

Unit member outputs are the effectiveness areas of a unit member.

They are the aggregate of the effectiveness areas of the unit which the unit member is actually the top member. Unit member outputs for unit members are exactly the same in concept as unit outputs for unit top members. They represent the aggregate of all for which the unit member is responsible.

EXAMPLES OF ERRORS

The following examples provide an understanding of how the concepts of the unit outputs diagram can lead to greater role clarification and effectiveness.
   Examples include:

- Confusing unit member outputs with unit outputs
- Confusing unit member outputs with top member outputs and unit outputs
- Omission of a key top member output
- Confusing objectives with outputs
- Failure to identify the top member outputs
- Some positions are clearly not needed
- One-over-one can work, or cannot work
- Overlap and underlap

Confusing unit member outputs with unit outputs

Here is an actual set of, so-called, key result areas for the CEO of a moderately large firm.

- To study the market for products and decide where to attack it
- To determine the specification of new products, and to sell them
- To design, make and distribute products
- To know where the revenue is to come from, where the expenditure is to go, and what the resultant profit should be
- To ensure the high morale of and secure employment for, employees
- To ensure the satisfaction of distributors and consumers
- To ensure that the company carries out its responsibilities to the community

What the CEO has done is to list each of the unit member outputs and has paid scant attention to unit outputs. On looking at this list it is fairly clear that this CEO heads a production operation. This kind of operation is run in a dedicated fashion. The unit member outputs are consumed within the unit and have no place on the unit output list. The CEO may well respond that this leaves only profit as the unit output. There is nothing wrong with that.

Confusing unit member outputs with top member outputs and unit outputs

During a unit outputs meeting the plant manager of a small detached plant prepared this as an initial set of outputs.

1. Operational costs
2. Product quality
3. Production targets
4. Product development
5. Technological change
6. Return on new investment
7. Fixed asset utilization
8. Management–union relations
9. Local government relations
10. Safety

He said he knew this list was too long. He was asked to separate those areas into top member outputs and unit member outputs and he produced these two lists.

Top Member Outputs
1. Operational costs
6. Return on new investment
7. Fixed asset utilization
8. Management–union relations
9. Local government relations

Unit Member Outputs
2. Product quality
3. Production targets
4. Product development
5. Technological change
10. Safety

He was then asked to separate top member outputs into top member inputs, top member outputs, and unit outputs and he produced this:

Top Member Inputs
8.   Management–union relations
9.   Local government relations

Top Member Outputs
1.   Overall operational costs

Unit Outputs
6.   Return on new investment
7.   Fixed asset utilization

   While very important in achieving outputs he saw that management-union relations and local government relations were, in fact, inputs. He saw that one of his own important outputs was to lower overall operational costs. None of the unit members could take overall control of this. Controlling overall operational costs could not be given to any unit member and must be his own. However, the unit outputs of return on your investment and fixed asset utilization were clearly a contribution of the entire unit.

Omission of a key top member output

A 1000-person subsidiary of a large electrical manufacturer made specially designed transformers. These were normally nine months in the production cycle and were so large that they were called elephants. The top unit design was conventional, with the CEO and the functions of design/engineering, purchasing, production and sales. In a unit outputs meeting where effectiveness areas of all unit members were to be studied and agreed it was obvious that no one was willing to accept the responsibility for meeting delivery dates. The CEO thought it was not a unit output nor a top member output. All of the other functions also wanted to pass the buck to each other. After discussion it became quite clear that the only person who could possibly take on that as an effectiveness area was the CEO. Attempts by the CEO to give the effectiveness area to an expeditor were quickly quashed because the expeditor did not have the authority to influence what was needed. In very much the same way, CEOs often do not really accept responsibility for profit and even go so far as to use such naive phrases as 'the buck stops here'. What we want is not a place where the buck stops but a position responsible for profit, or meeting delivery dates.

Top member and unit outputs that did not exist

An assistant CEO supervised four managers of profit centres as shown in Exhibit 6.7 and often wondered what the job really was as

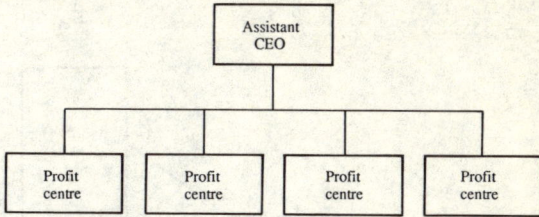

```
                    ┌───────────────┐
                    │  Assistant    │
                    │     CEO        │
                    └───────────────┘
        ┌──────────────┼──────────────┬──────────────┐
  ┌──────────┐  ┌──────────┐  ┌──────────┐  ┌──────────┐
  │  Profit  │  │  Profit  │  │  Profit  │  │  Profit  │
  │  centre  │  │  centre  │  │  centre  │  │  centre  │
  └──────────┘  └──────────┘  └──────────┘  └──────────┘
```

This unit looks very important but was not needed in this form.

Exhibit 6.7   The unit that wasn't needed

there was so little to do. The design of the four profit centres was such that there were no resources such as capital to allocate among them and they had no interaction. They were four quite independent businesses running very well on their own. It was a purely separated unit. At a unit outputs meeting all members of the unit, including the top member, decided to recommend that, as a unit, it be dissolved. The four profit centres became attached to other parts of the organization or became more independent and the assistant CEO assumed another role fully, rather than only nominally as in the past, in a different part of the organization. In this type of organization structure the main function of the unit top member would appear to be the ability to add.

Confusing objectives with outputs

A standard management text proposed Exhibit 6.8 as an example of an organization structure of four sales people, two sales managers and a marketing director. While it might be true as far as it goes, it does not go very far. It does show, in a crude way, the origin of the 10,000 units in sales but does not give any indication of what the top three positions do. It appears that, as with the prior example, their job is only to add. That might be an interesting top member input but it certainly is not a top member output. However, the sales levels would represent normal unit outputs in a sales organization.

This basic diagram drawn in terms of the outputs of the individuals involved, Exhibit 6.9, is much more revealing.

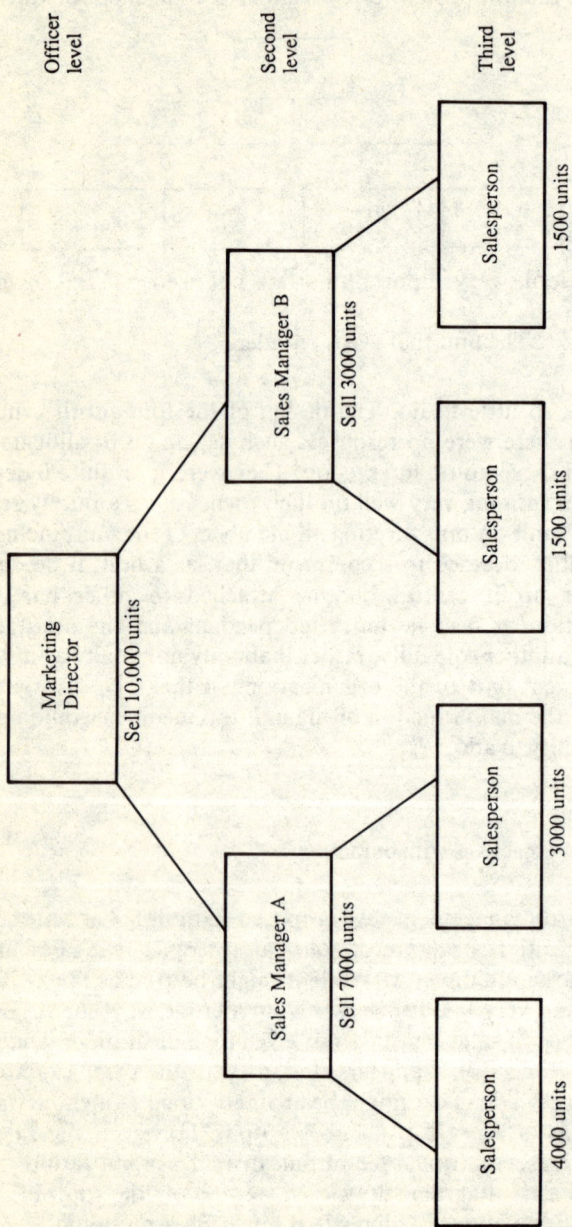

This over-simple approach leads to confusion in outputs implementation.

Exhibit 6.8   An incorrect view of vertical linking

132

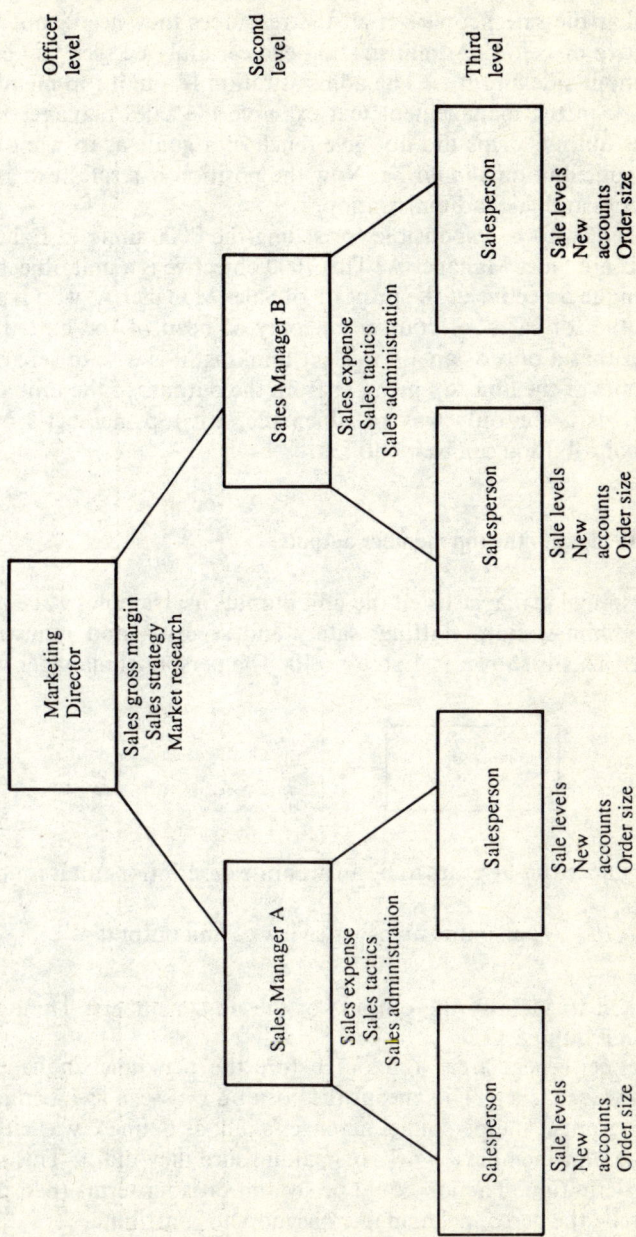

Here every position has its effectiveness areas and there is no overlap.

Exhibit 6.9 A correct view of vertical linking

133

The salespeople are responsible for sales levels. The two levels above are not. The sales manager is responsible for expense control (able to add or remove a salesperson), sales tactics (able to modify the direction of selling effort), sales administration (responsible for seeing that the salespeople get all the resources they need), not the level above or below. Administration can certainly be seen as being on the input side and it is. The administration is a unit top member input. So, in the management text example the sales manager had 'sales' as outputs. This did not give much of a guide as to what the unique contribution should be. Now the position has sales expense, sales tactics and sales administration.

But then, who is responsible for selling the 7000 units in Exhibit 6.8 if it is not Sales Manager A? This 7000 objective is a unit objective not a unique objective of the position of Sales Manager A, who is still responsible for sales, of course, but only as head of the unit. It is apparent that if only as an aid to clear thinking, it is wise to separate the outputs of the unit top member from the outputs of the unit as a whole. This is the only way in which the unit top member's own unique contribution can be identified.

Failure to identify the top member outputs

One personnel manager listed the unit outputs as: training, wage and salary administration, staffing, safety and security, and industrial relations. This is shown in Exhibit 6.10. The personnel manager was

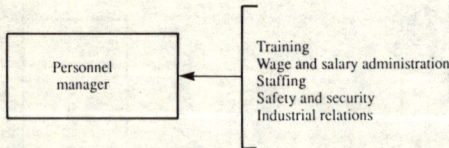

Personnel manager ←— Training / Wage and salary administration / Staffing / Safety and security / Industrial relations

At first glance this appears to be an accurate description but it is not.

Exhibit 6.10   A personnel manager's view of unit outputs

then asked to identify the outputs of the unit members. These are shown in Exhibit 6.11.

The effectiveness areas ran out before the personnel manager's position was reached. This meant the position was seen as having no unique outputs. The personnel manager's job, as defined, was either doing the unit members' work, or making sure they did it. This is a narrow definition. The job could be seen in broader terms than that and, surely, the personnel manager has more to contribute.

Personnel manager

Training officer	Wage and salary administrator	Employment manager	Safety and security manager	Industrial relations officer
Behaviour change	Wage equity	Recruitment quality	Thefts	Grievance administration
Performance improvement	Salary equity	Retention rate	Accidents	Contract terms
Facilities	Reward system	Career planning	Health	Negotiation
Advice		Organization		Union relationships

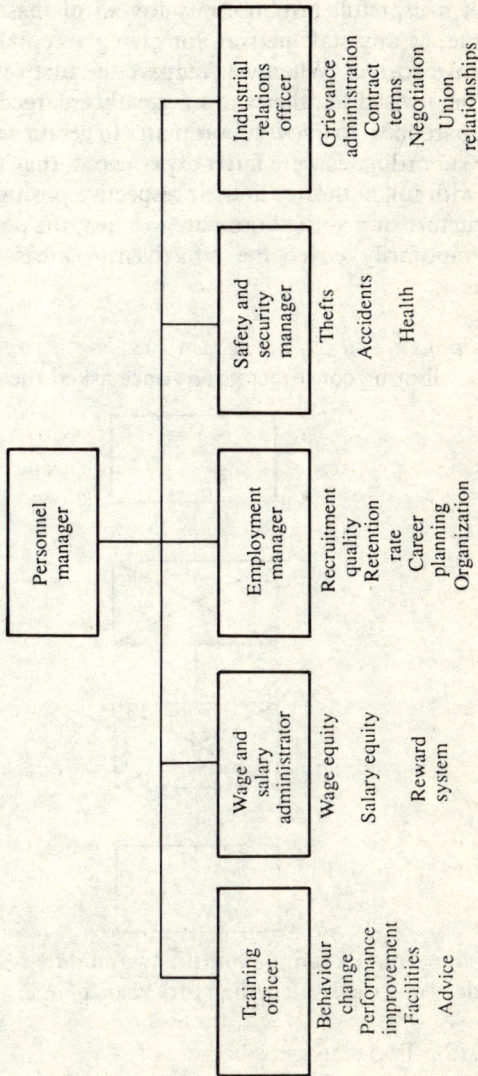

When your unit members share all of your outputs with you, what are you left with?

Exhibit 6.11 What are the outputs of the Personnel manager?

These questions were asked: What is your unique contribution? What is the biggest thing which could go wrong? What do you or could you do that the managers do not, because: (1) they do not have the ability or experience? (2) they do not have the time? or (3) they do not have the information? Why was your position created?

This personnel manager came to see that the unique contribution was in the areas of: personnel policy, working conditions, organization development and managerial effectiveness. The personnel manager could not accept full responsibility for all of these areas, but was responsible, as any staff person, for giving acceptable advice which would prove correct. When we compare the first set of effectiveness areas to the revised set, they show a greatly enlarged view of the job, and a preparedness to allow subordinates to get on with it.

As the subordinates were fairly experienced, they could be allowed to work with full authority in their respective positions. If a position in the structure or a key subordinate was lost, the personnel manager might temporarily cover the effectiveness areas of the position concerned.

Some positions are clearly not needed
A firm distributing consumer goods once asked the author to visit. I

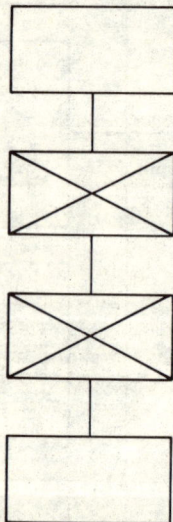

Perhaps an extreme example but the two middle managers did have heart attacks and died at less than fifty years of age.

Exhibit 6.12   Two managers died

asked to see the organization chart which consisted, in part, of the one-over-one-over-one-over-one relationship as shown in Exhibit 6.12. Then I expressed an interest in interviewing the four managers, but in particular the two in the middle. I was then told that things were not that way currently. The two managers in the middle had had heart attacks within a few months of each other and each had died at under fifty years of age.

It is risky to analyse this case without additional data, but an argument could be made that the deaths were hastened because the two managers tried too hard to make an impossible structure work. No job could possibly exist for the two in the middle. Had this group had an opportunity to conduct a unit outputs meeting and to try to make the unit outputs diagram fit to their situation they would have found it was absolutely impossible. They would have realized that their unit did not really exist. Some things cannot be solved by setting more precise objectives. The solution, in this situation, must come from changing an organization. For the outside observer it may be obvious, for those inside it is sometimes not. That is why a serious study of a unit in terms of a unit outputs diagram can be very important.

While not dealing directly with the human side of things, this example could be used to explain much strange human behaviour in an organization. An organization with clearer outputs is a quiet and pleasant place in which to work.

One-over-one can work, or cannot work

The importance of being clear on outputs at various levels can be illuminated further from the simple case of the one-over-one situation. The true nature of any one-over-one situation can be best studied by the analysis of the respective outputs. The one-over-one structure can be effective. It can occur, for instance, when the unit top member sees the work primarily as that of an outside representative and the unit member sees the work as that of an inside representative. If the top position is at the top of the firm, the unit top member may have effectiveness areas associated with government, community relations and strategy while the unit member has areas concerned with profitability. This is a common split between such roles as chairperson and managing director. Sometimes, however, a one-over-one position does not work because of overlap. Overlap occurs when two managers are responsible for the same thing, so one of them is not needed. One firm, on introducing output orientation, observed that it was common in the organization for senior managers at one level to have virtually direct overlap with their single senior manager at the next level, their so-called deputies. Either the senior manager or the deputy had no job. This point led to the removal of the deputy position. There is nothing wrong with having such deputies, of course, as long as they are recognized as being personal assistants, no more, no less, and are paid accordingly.

One such deputy tried to develop a set of effectiveness areas without overlap and actually produced these:

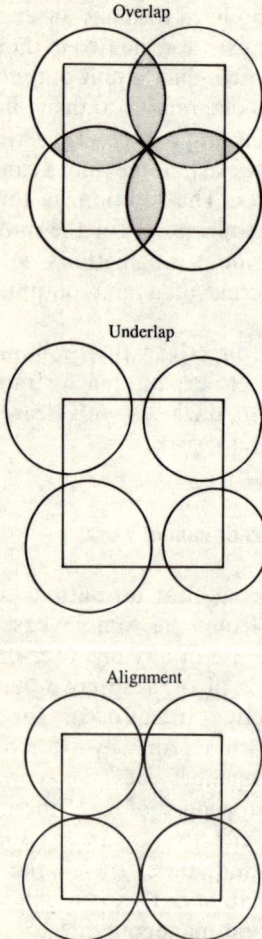

The shaded overlap is duplication, the white space underlap is assigned responsibility. Alignment is best.

Exhibit 6.13   Overlap–underlap–alignment

- Relieve director of detail
- Assist director on request
- Prepare for meetings
- Convey director's instructions

With these it became clear that the deputy did not have a managerial position. This was not the biggest part of the problem however which was that some others thought that there was a job.

These examples show full or 100 per cent overlap. It is a rare organization that does not have some instances of it. Overlap of less than 100 per cent is more common; the identification of effectiveness areas and a frank discussion of them on a unit basis is the best way to remove it.

Overlap and underlap

As indicated in the prior example overlap can be a serious organization design problem. So can underlap.

Overlap refers to the situation when two positions are responsible for the same thing and underlap when no position has been assigned a particular responsibility. Alignment is a condition of no overlap or underlap. These are illustrated in Exhibit 6.13.

Types of overlap

There are four types of overlap as illustrated in Exhibit 6.14.

- Duplicate overlap
- Full overlap
- Partial overlap
- Co-worker overlap

Duplicate overlap occurs when a superior and a manager have identical effectiveness areas. The situation of the director and the deputy is a good example. Full overlap occurs when a superior is responsible for all a manager does, plus some additional own effectiveness areas. This might occur with a brand manager reporting to a marketing director who makes all the decisions about brands thus reducing the brand manager to a clerk.

Partial overlap occurs when a superior-manager pair have not fully sorted out their effectiveness areas. In some parts of the job the locus of authority and responsibility is not established. The same kind of

Duplicate overlap

Superior

Manager

Full overlap

Superior

Manager

Partial overlap

Superior

Manager

Co-worker overlap

Co-worker A   Co-worker B

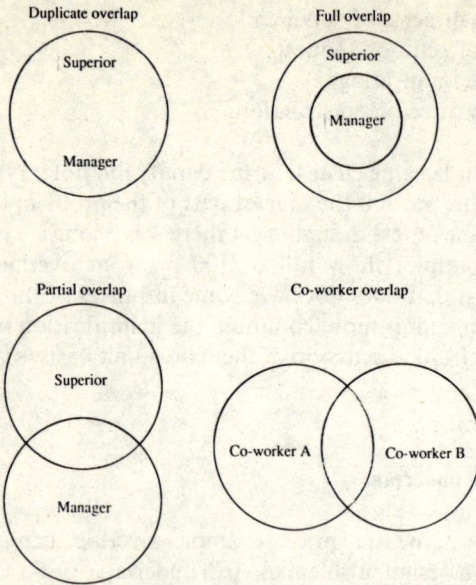

All are expensive and all can be avoided.

Exhibit 6.14   Types of overlap

thing can occur with co-workers, when it is called co-worker overlap.

While the idea of overlap seems so straightforward as to be almost trite, it nevertheless is still a principal cause of low managerial effectiveness and poor outputs implementation.

The unit effectiveness description helps to improve things. It is a written statement which specifies the effectiveness areas, measurement areas and authority of a unit, its superior and its managers. It separates and then brings together all the elements and so identifies overlap or underlap problems.

Alignment and output orientation

When one thinks in situational rather than managerial terms the importance of a proper alignment of effectiveness areas, measurement areas and objectives becomes obvious. Failure to align provides an important explanation of many unsuccessful attempts to implement output orientation. The present position is something like this:

(Alignment of the effectiveness areas and measurement areas between levels)

> Can be difficult to do and is usually done poorly. If done well the problems that arise from having a layer of too many managers would be brought out.

(Alignment of the objectives between levels)

> Usually easy to do when an overall plan exists.

(Alignment of the effectiveness areas and measurement areas among co-workers at the same level)

> Can be done easily if clear functional area distinctions exist. 'Who has the authority?' must often get resolved first.

(Alignment of the objectives among co-workers at the same level)

> Usually fairly easy to do but conflicts arise if roles, authority distribution and organization structure are right but misunderstood or are wrong.

This suggests that effectiveness areas and measurement areas are most difficult to align vertically, though when an overall plan exists it is not so difficult to align objectives. Also, effectiveness areas and measurement areas can be aligned horizontally, but questions of authority distribution must often be settled first. The horizontal alignment of objectives may be easy but this too must involve agreement on such things as roles, authority and organization structure.

FOUR TYPES OF MEETINGS

In addition to the Managerial Effectiveness Seminar described in Chapter 10, the Reddin organization has found it useful to use four quite different types of meetings.

These are:

● The unit outputs meeting
● The unit objectives meeting
● The unit review meeting
● The one-on-one meeting

All of these meetings are effectiveness-oriented and all are highly involving. The Managerial Effectiveness Seminar should precede any. To avoid this usually means one does not understand the need for overcoming resistance to change and how applied behavioural science can make things much, much easier.

The biggest gap in attempts to improve managerial effectiveness is the lack of use of the work unit or team to facilitate the change. Most implementations are based on a one-to-one design, where a superior speaks to each of the subordinates in turn. Virtually no managerial effectiveness improvement method even tries to get the full team together, superior and all subordinates, to work out effectiveness areas, objectives, and improvement plans as a group.

One reason why these meetings are avoided is the fear of disagreement. Another is that early attempts using such meetings were predictable as to outcome. What was needed was a device to train a team as a unit which was always safe and usually effective. In response to this need, the unit outputs meeting was developed. It has been under continuous test and revision as the Team Role Laboratory for twenty years. It is now widely used.

Teamwork in industry is clearly acceptable. This is Drucker's view:

> In business, teams are used a good deal more than the literature indicates. They are regularly employed for short-term assignments in every large company. They are common in research work. Team organisation, rather than the hierarchy of rank shown on the organisation chart, is the reality in the well-run manufacturing plant, especially in respect to the relationship between the plant manager and the heads of the technical functions reporting to him. Many tasks in process manufacturing or in mass production new style can only be done if organised on a team basis.

He clarifies the view that teamwork depends on clear objectives and responsibilities:

> It is therefore of genuine importance that management understand what team organisation is, when to use it, and how. Above all, it is important that management realise that in any real team each member has a clearly assigned and clearly defined role. A team is not just chaos made into a virtue. Teamwork requires actually more internal organisation, more co-operation, and greater definiteness of individual assignments then work organised in individual jobs.

It is hardly reasonable not to share his view today.

Teamwork is not a group activity where everyone does their own thing and responsibility is blurred. Members of a football team or a mountaineering team all have clear roles, clear effectiveness areas and a clear leader. We still call them 'teams' or units, and appropriately so.

The unit outputs meeting

The unit outputs meeting, usually lasting for two to three days, consists of the unit top member and all unit members. The main outputs of the meeting are to establish the unit outputs diagram and to make changes as necessary in unit organization structure, policies and procedures.

In the three-day unit outputs meeting, a manager and all immediate subordinate managers discuss their outputs and decide how best to improve the way they work together. The unit outputs meeting has been described as situational management for a team and also as a work-study conference for a team. Each of these descriptions does reflect the essence of the design. The emphasis is not on personality or subordinates' rating of their superior, but on individual and unit effectiveness areas. The unit outputs meeting is usually conducted by company or external trainers.

After about twenty hours of prework has been completed by each unit member, the meeting is held. The meeting requires each unit member, including the top member, to state own effectiveness areas, describing what programmes are needed to meet them and then specifying what each unit member could do that would enable the top member to improve managerial effectiveness. Another key activity is the design of an optimal organization chart for the unit. This single activity can lead to a structural change which is often long overdue and definitely needed before effectiveness can increase.

The unit outputs meeting leads directly to a clear definition of the unit's role in the organization. With this established, unit effectiveness areas and unit outputs may be prepared. Often the preparation requires some type of unit reorganization, which the unit designs and implements. Flexible job trading usually occurs and leads to the talents of individual managers being better utilized through job enrichment. Needless to say, the enthusiasm and commitment generated by this activity leads to the solution of many problems.

The unit outputs meeting takes place only after all unit members have participated in the Managerial Effectiveness Seminar. The seminar induces a readiness to change, for which the unit outputs meeting provides the vehicle.

The central outputs of the unit output meeting include:

- *Role clarity*: Each unit member has a much greater understanding of the correct role to suit the overall unit situation
- *Changes in effectiveness area, measurement areas and authority*: Changes should occur in all of effectiveness areas, measurement areas and authority. If no, or very few, changes have occurred the meeting has probably resulted in polite discourse rather than a meeting to introduce change
- *Moving effectiveness areas round the unit*: In many units, but not all, some reasonably obvious issues will arise which can be solved by moving effectiveness areas around the unit.

The overall outputs of the unit outputs meeting are:

- Far greater unit and managerial effectiveness
- The unit role is better defined
- Unit effectiveness areas are established
- Unit outputs are established
- Unit is reorganized if it needs it
- Unit member effectiveness areas are established
- Unit decision-making is improved
- Talents of individuals are better used
- Individual jobs are enriched
- Motivation increases sharply

The unit objectives meeting

The unit objectives meeting, usually lasting 1–1½ days, consists of the unit top member and all unit members. The main outputs of the meeting are to establish, for an agreed period, the objectives of the unit, the unit top member and the unit members.

In many organizations this kind of meeting is somewhat unusual. In so many organizations objectives are usually set on a one-on-one basis rather than a unit basis. The theme running through this book is that outputs can generally better be achieved by working on a unit basis and this meeting is designed to help this process. In the prior unit outputs meeting, the outputs of the unit and all unit members will have been decided and after that, JEDs agreed. This meeting then, brings the unit together again to make sure that their objectives align. The meeting is also highly motivational in encouraging managers to set higher, but yet realistic, objectives with their peers and to expect as much from their peers.

The unit review meeting

The unit review meeting, usually lasting one day, consists of the unit top member and all unit members. The main outputs of the meeting are to review the achievement of objectives of the unit as a whole, of the unit top member and all unit members.

There is little question that a manager's co-workers or peers are in an excellent position to evaluate effectiveness. This is not true in every situation in every organization, but there is no question that it is better than not doing it at all and, usually, better than simply asking the top member to make the appraisal. The issue is to create conditions where all unit members will deal with this issue openly and well, and be in the role of coach rather than judge. As with many of these meetings it is advisable for an outsider to be present for at least the first meeting as the true purpose and methods of the meeting can be misunderstood.

The one-on-one meeting

The one-on-one meeting, usually lasting from four to eight hours, consists of the unit top member and each unit member in turn. The main outputs of the meeting are to review the unit member's JED, to agree unit member's objectives for a future period, to identify any blockages to achieving objectives that might exist and to identify help from the top member that will be made available.

One-on-one meetings are usually badly designed and poorly handled. Just one of the unrecognized reasons for this is there has not been agreement at the start on the JED. The meeting may be dispensed with altogether if the unit review meeting is used. Or both can be used. Traditional management practice is to use only one of these four types of meeting and that is the one-on-one. The method described here has many obvious advantages over that.

The sequence of the four meetings
The meetings should be conducted in the order given here. If one or more meetings are omitted this will not change the advisability of the basic sequence proposed.

Are all the meetings always needed?
The simple truth of the matter is that most organizations operate using only the one-on-one meeting. Another simple truth is that many organizations have shown enormously high profit improvement by using two or more of the meetings. Those in a position to decide

should seriously consider using all four meetings as a trial in at least some parts of the organization. The effects are easy to measure.

The Managerial Effectiveness Seminar first

There is no doubt among those who have used it that a highly desirable step before the unit engages in a unit output meeting is that all members should attend the Managerial Effectiveness Seminar (Chapter 10).

ACTION STEPS

1. Agree with your unit if investigation of the Managerial Effectiveness Seminar for your unit would be a good idea.
2. Agree with your unit to hold a Unit Outputs Meeting.
3. Agree with your unit to hold a Unit Objectives Meeting.
4. Agree with your unit to hold a Unit Review Meeting.
5. Identify your inputs to the unit for which you are the top member.
6. Identify the unit outputs of the unit for which you are the top member.
7. Review the four types of unit, separated, related, dedicated and integrated. Reviewing the characteristics given in Exhibit 6.5 make a rough estimate of the degree to which your unit is one or more of these four. A good way to do this is privately to circle one, or at the most two items on each line and then to do this with others, preferably all members of the unit.
8. Agree with your top member to hold a one-on-one meeting.
9. Agree with each of your subordinate unit members to hold a meeting with you as top member.
10. Identify your outputs of the unit for which you are the top member.

GLOSSARY

Areas alignment: When effectiveness areas for a set of related positions have no overlap or underlap.

Dedicated unit organization: A unit characterized by one unit member's outputs becoming another unit member's inputs with the top member's inputs directed primarily to interfaces across immediate unit members.

Horizontal alignment: When effectiveness areas for two or more related positions at the same level have no overlap or underlap.

Integrated unit organization: A unit characterized by a high level of work interaction across unit members

Member: See *Unit Member*.

One-on-one meeting: The one-on-one meeting, usually lasting from four to eight hours, consists of the unit top member and each unit member in turn. The main outputs of the meeting are to review the unit member's JED, to agree unit member's objectives for a future period, to identify any blockages to achieving objectives that might exist and to identify help from the top member that will be made available.

Overlap: When two positions are responsible for the same effectiveness area.

Related unit organization: A unit characterized by a low level of work interaction across unit members.

Separated unit organization: A unit characterized by a low level of work interaction across unit members except for top member inputs to unit members.

Top member: See *Unit Top Member*.

Underlap: When no position has been assigned an effectiveness area which is needed.

Unit: A set of related positions including a unit top member and one or more unit members.

Unit effectiveness description: A written statement specifying the effectiveness areas, measurement areas and authority of a unit taken as a whole.

Unit member: A member, other than the top member of a unit, normally referred to as subordinate.

Unit member outputs: The effectiveness areas of a unit member.

Unit objectives meeting: A meeting usually lasting 1–1½ days, consists of the unit top member and all unit members. The main outputs of the meeting are to establish, for an agreed period, the objectives of the unit, the unit top member and the unit members.

Unit outputs: The set of effectiveness areas for a unit which naturally include the outputs of the top member and all unit members summarized in some way.

Unit outputs diagram: A diagram containing the four elements of all unit member outputs, unit top member outputs, unit outputs and unit top member inputs.

Unit outputs meeting: A meeting usually lasting two–three days, consists of the unit top member and all unit members. The main outputs of the meeting are to establish the unit outputs diagram and to make changes as necessary in unit organization structure, policies and procedures.

Unit review meeting: A meeting usually lasting one day, consists of the unit top member and all unit members. The main outputs of the meeting are to review the achievement of objectives of the unit as a whole, of the unit top member and all unit members.

Unit top member: The head of a unit often called the superior.

Unit top member inputs: The activities of the top member to improve unit effectiveness.

Unit top member outputs: The outputs of the unit top member having no overlap with unit top member inputs or with any unit member outputs.

Vertical alignment: When effectiveness areas for two or more related positions at different levels have no overlap or underlap.

7 How to set objectives

Watch out when a man's work becomes more important than its objectives, when he disappears into his duties.

Alan Harrington

The output-oriented manager thrives on demanding yet realistic objectives.

Soon after agreeing effectiveness areas, measurement areas and authority with all of those concerned you will want to establish the objectives for your position based upon each measurement area. It is pointless to do any of this until those who must relate to your objectives have also agreed on your JED. When you have made a draft of your objectives you will meet with one or more others to agree them. This may be with your superior or your whole co-worker team with superior present.

You now know the link between effectiveness areas, measurement areas and outputs. Here are three straightforward examples showing the direct link.

Effectiveness area	Measurement area	Objective
Sales	Unit sales territory 'A'.	Unit sales of 680 in territory 'A' during 199–.
Accidents	Accident per cent decrease.	Decrease accidents by 12 per cent during 199–.
Accounting information	Introduction of new code of accounts in branches.	Have new code of accounts operating in 16 branches for at least 6 months by the end of 199– with an error rate of less than 0.3 per cent.

SOUND OBJECTIVES ARE MEASURABLE

An objective is useful only if its attainment is measurable. It if is not measurable it is impossible to determine whether the objective has been achieved. 'To increase profits' is an unsatisfactory statement of an objective as it does not say by how much or when. A better statement would be 'To increase profits to 200,000 units during 199–'. Two essential and measurable elements of an objective are:

● Time (how soon)
● Quantity (how many)

Two other measurable elements which are sometimes included in objectives are:

● Quality (how well)
● Cost (how much)

These last two items are often omitted from the statement of the objective, as they are inferred from the wording, or the facts of the situation.

Unsatisfactory objectives
It is an easy matter to detect unsatisfactory objectives. Without training, managers sometimes propose such objectives as:

● Satisfy my superior
● Keep my subordinates happy
● Keep in-basket clear
● Maintain sound communication
● Continue cost-saving investigation

One manager proposed the following as a complete set of objectives for the position:

● When authority and accountability for executive are defined
● When effective control is available to measure action
● When motivating forces in department are positive
● When effectiveness communication is maintained with others from the top down

While all these may be desirable conditions, they are unsatisfactory as objectives, or even as statements on which measurable objectives could be based.

Specifying time in objectives

Time is one of the easiest elements to include in an objective. It should never be omitted. There are four basic forms which are used in this book.

End form	EO (end of) JUL (by the end of July)
	EO 199– (by 31st December 199–)
Beginning form	BO (beginning of) JUL (by 1st July)
	BO 199– (By 1st January 199–)
During form	DUR (during) JUL-NOV (From 1st July to 30th November)
	DUR 199– (From 1st January 199– to 31st December 199–)
Specific form	On 16th DEC (On 16th December)
	By 16th DEC (On or before 16th December)

If the year is not stated it means the current year. The end form is most widely used as objectives are usually in terms of achieving something by a specific date. It is better to express a date in terms of a month end rather than in terms of the beginning of the next month. 31st August seems a long way from 1st September. The earlier date tends to avoid procrastination. The specific form tends to be used when a manager's objectives interlock tightly with those of others.

'By 16th JUL have recommendation and sample survey results prepared on which package design should be used for product "Y".'

Length of time of objectives
Objectives are most often set for yearly or quarterly time-periods. But the battle does not win the war nor the sale win the customer forever. Managerial effectiveness is not concerned solely with the present or short run but with the long run as well. Objectives, while set for quarterly or one year time-periods, must still reflect an understanding of the future. A failure to do this can lead to a variety of problems. A marketing manager who decides to introduce a new brand without looking at brand strategy several years ahead is obviously in error. Also in error is a plan to reduce maintenance expenditure without considering long-term machinery capability.

Any public servant knows that it is unwise to start in new directions shortly before an election. The larger the unit the longer-term the objectives usually tend to be. As a very rough guide objectives are most often set for the following time periods:

Corporate	1 to 5 years
Divisional	1 to 3 years
Departmental	1 year
Managerial	3 months to 1 year

If an objective is set for too short a time-period, it may be nothing more than a prediction. In the short term nothing much could be done to change things anyway. If an objective is set for too long a time-period, it may be simply a hope, as too many non-controllable events could occur in the interim.

Specifying quantity in objectives

All objectives must be quantified in some way or their achievement cannot be measured. If you cannot measure it forget it. The units most often used are monetary or physical but others are also used:

Monetary units:	'60,000 sales by EO DEC 199–'
Non-monetary units:	'Total of 60 new accounts by EO 199–'
	'Reduction in model change time from 28 days to 25 days by EO 199'–
Proportion:	'Average of 28 per cent share of national market during 199–'

It is not satisfactory for objectives to use such words as the following without specific quantification:

● Increase
● Decrease
● Maximize
● Minimize
● Satisfy
● Optimize

These words at most indicate direction only and not how much.

Quantifying measurement areas and so converting to objectives
In the left-hand column below are measurement areas taken from Chapter 3. On the right-hand side a quantity and time has been placed on each, thus showing the conversion of a measurement areas to an objective. This is the only way it should be done. Objectives should be seen as measurement areas, and measurement areas should be seen as effectiveness areas with far greater

specificity and therefore clarification. If the effectiveness areas are wrong then everything is wrong. That is why a programme of output-oriented management starts with role clarification and not with setting higher objectives.

Per cent above 199–	Increase volume of product 'X' by 5 per cent for each of next four quarters above quarterly averages of 199–
Profit of territory	Within ± 10 per cent by end of 199–, achieve same profit levels across all territories.
Unit sales by product	Increase unit sales of product 'A' to 50 per cent above totals for products 'B' and 'C' by end of 199–
Inventory level	Reduce the inventory level at dockside warehouse to one fifth of the annual average for the months JAN–MAR.
Reject ratio	Lower the 'reject to good product' ratio from 1 to 10 to 1 to 12 within this calendar year.
Tons moved	Double the tons moved by haulage division 'A' in second half of year over the first half.

The problem of the level of the objective

One of the central problems in setting objectives is deciding on the level of the objective. Should the market share be increased 2.4 per cent or 3.6 per cent? Should waste reduction be 4.2 per cent or 5.3 per cent? Even with a perfect job effectiveness description it still comes down to a matter of judgement. In some continuous-flow production operations which have changed very little over the years, setting the objective is fairly easy. In other situations where the environment is volatile and unpredictable, perhaps caused by competitive actions, setting the correct level of the objective can be quite difficult.

An objective should be attainable with a manager's level of motivation, competence, authority and resources. The objective must be commensurate with the manager's and subordinates' level of experience, training, skill, capability and motivation. It must also be compatible with the level of resources that the manager can obtain. Objectives may well reflect a more ambitious level of performance than previously. This is expected to result not from working harder but from working smarter and with better vertical and horizontal alignment.

The quantitative element of an objective may reflect these levels:

- As they have been in the past
- As they are now
- As they could be now
- As they could be in the future

The selection the manager makes will depend on a number of factors. It is one of the most important decisions that will be made. The manager must decide what the appropriate level of effectiveness is for the situation.

The decision requires a manager to consider the previous level of attainment. Was it too low? Is there anything that can be done about it? To be avoided is the predictive objective which sets the level at what could probably be attained without any effort.

Sophisticated output implementations lead to a variety of objectives being tied to different budget levels. A marketing manager will say, 'I can obtain 32 per cent of the market if I am given a market budget of 800,000, but with 900,000 I can obtain 35 per cent.' One CEO says:

> Our budgets are not an objective, but are the results of objectives. Each year we operate with a minimum budget level which represents the amount of money we believe it is going to cost to do a job which satisfies our minimum objectives and in which we have a high confidence level. We also operate with a quota level, which represents substantially increased performance. Financial plans are made for both levels of operation and are determined to be possible and practical. Budgets indicate what we expect to spend to get the job done. Within the budget we indicate the most important factors. And these are the standards which represent the percentage of the sales in money units we are willing to spend to get various parts of the job performed. Obviously, the standards are more important than the budgeted amounts, since we are willing to spend more money than we have budgeted if we can get the increased business on standard costs.

The factors to consider when deciding on the level of an objective are:

- Level necessary to achieve 1–5 year plans
- Objectives of associated positions
- Budget available
- Possible additional budget available
- Skill of manpower resource
- Motivation level of manpower resource
- Past performance experience

Some managers like the concept of the 'ratchet principle' sometimes called 'stretch'. Both of these refer to obtaining a higher performance than previously with a similar resource level.

Bands of objectives
Because the most appropriate level of an objective is sometimes hard to determine with any precision, the idea of bands of objectives becomes very useful. Using this method three objectives are set. One is the planning figure such as might be used if only one objective was set, another is the low band figure which is believed to be the lowest performance possible and acceptable. The other is the high band figure which will represent an extreme condition on the high side. Sophisticated managers setting objectives use methods of this kind. Setting a single objective does not make it more accurate. It just looks more accurate to the naive observer. For many positions the bands will be very narrow, representing a degree of predictability. In new positions and in market situations the bands may be fairly wide.

Out of control limits
In production systems, in particular, out-of-control limits are sometimes set. These are a higher and lower objective limit and a deviation outside of this range is seen as a cause for some investigation and correction. This general approach was derived from quality control methods. In some situations, particularly in production, these limits may be checked on a continuous basis so there is a second-by-second, minute-by-minute, or hour-by-hour check. For middle and senior management levels, if they are set at all, the measurement may be more like a month or three months.

Priority of objectives

The importance of each objective should be indicated by assigning it a priority of 1, 2 or 3. Number 1 is assigned to the objective of the highest priority, and so on. Several objectives will have the same priority. Such assignment of priorities helps to keep a perspective, especially when there are many objectives for one position.

With only a few objectives, it is a relatively simple matter to assign priorities. When there are many objectives assigning relative weight is more difficult. An aid to doing this is the method of paired comparisons. The procedure is as follows:

1.   Each objective is assigned a number.
2.   The basis for assigning priority is established. This would

presumably be 'its importance to the position' or 'its importance to the company plan'.
3. Each objective is compared with each other objective, and one of them is assigned a higher priority.
4. The number of choices each objective receives is tallied, and from this the objectives are arranged in the order of priority.
5. The rank orders are converted to priorities of 1, 2, and 3.

Errors to avoid in objectives

In drawing up their objectives managers should be wary of these errors which frequently occur:

● Objectives too high (overload)
● Objectives too low (underload)
● Objectives not measurable
● Cost of measurement too high
● Too many objectives
● Too complex objectives
● Too long time-period
● Too short time-period
● Unbalanced emphasis

Most of these are self-explanatory and have been discussed earlier.

Managerial effectiveness can seldom be obtained by achieving a single objective, no matter how broadly it is written. Effectiveness is multidimensional. Profit, for instance, may be obtained at the risk of losing customers or by sacrificing human resources. Sales may be obtained by unduly increasing credit risks. Any manager who sees effectiveness in simple black-and-white terms may perform well in the short term but not in the long term. On the other hand, a large number of objectives usually indicates only that the essence of the job has not been understood.

While opinions differ, more than ten or so objectives probably indicate a fragmentation of the job rather than seeing it as a whole. Complex objectives tend to be produced as hedges against unsatisfactory performance. Hidden in them are 'ifs' and 'buts'. Except for the top team, objectives need not usually cover more than a year, while less than a three-month time-period is usually considered too short. Unbalanced emphasis would occur if there were five objectives covering 20 per cent of the effectiveness areas of the position and one objective for the other 80 per cent.

Managers should expect that they and their subordinates will make all these errors at least once or twice in the introductory stages of installing an output orientation system.

Your objective must be commensurate with the authority
As explained in Chapter 4 the objective needs to match your authority and remain within your authority. You cannot take responsibility for something over which you have no authority. This idea is expressed well in your specification of effectiveness areas and measurement areas but it is worth thinking about it again in setting your objectives. It may be for instance that you have a very small range of authority over your objectives. In some situations they may be handed to you. In some situations they may be a direct function of an objective set in other parts of the organization.

Think about your resources
Resources may be relatively fixed or relatively flexible. If flexible it is critical for you to think in terms of different levels of objectives with different levels of resources. It is not so much that you can reduce cost by such an amount but rather how much more could you reduce cost successfully if you were given more resources to do it. It is normal for the brand manager interested in high output to have a running conversation with the marketing manager along the lines of 'if you give me X amount more I can increase market share by Y amount more. But if you give me X plus then I can produce Y plus.'

However, most managerial jobs do not have the flexibility of resources implied by these examples and your objectives will be set on what you reasonably expect to have for the time period under consideration.

Tests of sound objectives

Sound objectives can be easily distinguished from unsound ones by being tested against this list.

Test of Objectives

Sound	*Probably unsound*
Measurable (quantitative)	Non-measurable (qualitative)
Specific	General
Results (output) – centred	Activity (input) – centred
Realistic and attainable	Minimum or unattainable
Time-bounded	Time-extended

Many factors in this list overlap somewhat, but, taken together as well as separately, they serve to identify clearly the characteristics of sound objectives that managers would want to establish for their positions. A good objective must be measurable, for without this its achievement cannot be established. It should be specific rather than general, so that what is being measured is unambiguous. 'Most product lines', is not as good a statement as 'product line, A, C and S'. It should focus on results or output rather than activities or input, that is, on what a manager achieves rather than on what is done. 'Implement budget control' is not as good as 'Have budget control system in full operation'. It should be seen as a realistic and attainable objective to both the superior and the subordinate rather than as a minimum or unattainable objective. It should be time-bounded with clear time limits for completion rather than being time extended.

Who agrees objectives?

There are four widely used methods of agreeing objectives, these are:

1. The manager initially
2. The superior initially
3. The manager and superior together
4. The manager and unit together

This first method where the manager drafts the objectives initially has certain dangers as it requires the manager to determine how the department fits into the company as a whole, size up its strong and weak points, determine its total capability and perhaps without guidance from the superior or co-workers to reach certain conclusions in isolation.

The second method where the superior drafts the objectives initially, does perhaps, at first sight, seem the natural way to do things and is still used by some. The problem with this is that it is not much more than giving a more specific order than usual. It certainly does not contain all the elements of planning, involvement and commitment applied by outputs orientation. A serious weakness of this method is that it does not tap the ideas or develop the manager and it certainly does not get the manager involved.

The third method which is the most common in the output concept overcomes many of the platitudes concerning whether objectives should come from the superior or the subordinate. The question is asked the wrong way. Objectives flow from corporate strategy and both superior and subordinate should contribute as much as they can at the appropriate time. Participation should always be used if subordinate can contribute to making a decision better. It should also be used if their commitment to the objective is important and if this commitment can be increased by participation.

With this method both sides can contribute fairly evenly to the objectives and both will then have a thorough understanding of what the drafted objectives mean and imply. Because of inexperience on both sides the initial objectives may not be perfect. Far more important however will be the joint commitment to a start. This method also gives the fullest opportunity to arrange and agree the resources and authority necessary for the achievement of these jointly agreed objectives.

The fourth method is in some ways an extension of the third method in so much as once again there is an opportunity for full discussion and above all alignment of each unit member's objectives, the recognition of the necessary authority to achieve these objectives and the allocation of resources which in some cases may mean sharing when resources are in short supply.

Review of attainment of objectives

The function of the checkpoint meeting is to review the degree of attainment of objectives. As a minimum it is attended by a manager and the superior but it is better if the superior is there with all the manager's .co-workers as well. Then the objectives of all are considered at the same meeting. This makes for better integration across functions.

The checkpoint meeting

It takes one to two hours per person and is normally held quarterly or half-yearly but can be held whenever needed. The checkpoint meeting makes output-oriented management come to life in an organization. It makes the whole process real and facilitates an integration of outputs into other organization systems such as budgeting.

The objectives are reviewed and for each objective at or past its completion date these questions are asked:

● Was the objective met?
● Why was there variance from it, if any?
● Is the measurement area adequate?

And for each other objective:

- Is progress satisfactory?
- Is corrective action needed?
- Is amendment to the objective needed?

And for new objectives:

- Clear statements are made

The focus of the checkpoint meeting is, naturally, the extent to which the objectives have been met and the reasons for under achievement, if any. Several objectives will have been easily met; some will be seen in retrospect as having been impossible to meet.

When objectives are not met

During the early stages of output introduction, objectives will frequently not have been met. The rules to follow are complete openness about the degree of attainment, a focus on causes in terms of what was or what was not done, a discussion of any corrections that can be applied immediately, and a decision on how to avoid failure in the future.

In summary, when objectives are not met, consider:

- What was done
- What was not done
- How to correct now
- How to avoid in future

If the objective was not met, the cause should be identified. It may be one of the following:

- Objective too high
- Insufficient resources requested
- Insufficient resources supplied
- Poor planning
- Failure to follow plan established
- Unanticipated events (changed conditions)
- Insufficient motivation
- Managers do not work effectively with staff advisers
- High staff turnover in unit – no trained replacements
- Insufficient coaching of subordinates

If the objective was significantly exceeded, an inquiry should also be made. While usually desirable, its achievement could have caused problems to others. The following questions are important:

● Was the objective too low initially?
● Why did over-achievement occur?
● Can it be repeated?

Checkpoint meeting errors
The checkpoint meetings are designed to eliminate most of the horrors of appraisal schemes and interviews. Many such schemes in industry still are little more than paperwork and are known to have little effect. More and more firms, recognizing their lack of effectiveness in changing behaviour, have discontinued the formal appraisal scheme. Fortunately, such ideas as outputs allow such firms to have another start, this time on the right foot.

The climate in the checkpoint meeting is that of rational people making a review. When the review finds underachievement, the causes for it are identified so as to reduce the possibility of recurrence. The climate is not one of criticism or even of praise. Studies have demonstrated that, as a general rule, neither criticism nor praise improves performance. In fact, criticism reduces performance.

The most common errors at CPMs are:

● Traits or personality discussion
● Emphasis on incidents – nagging
● Hiding own views
● Focus on activities, not results
● Focus on 'no-control' items
● Being too participative
● Being too rigid
● Implied emphasis on 'pleasing me'
● Discussion of salary

A discussion of a manager's personality will not help change it or improve the performance. It is of no value to tell managers they 'push too hard' or are 'too easy-going'. These things will not change them and they will resent it. They were engaged to perform, not to conform. Discuss performance not personality inputs. The true title of some appraisal interviews is 'How to be more like me'. Some appraisers, in an attempt to drive a point home, keep harping on it. 'If you had not . . .' or 'If only you had . . .'. This doesn't usually work with the children or spouse, why should it work with managers? A checkpoint meeting is an opportunity to be candid. The superior should show candour from the outset. Hiding one's own views will only lead to a defeat of the implied contract – a meeting to improve performance.

It is not helpful, though it is comforting, to dwell on 'no control' items. These are things which inhibit performance but which cannot be changed: 'If only we could get another pair of hands.' 'If only the government regulation had not changed.'

A balance is required on the part of the superior between being participative and being rigid. If too participative, the importance of formal review of performance will be lost. If too rigid, the commitment of higher performance, which may be generated, is lost instead.

Some superiors, with the best of intentions, give the impression that the major reward for high performance is that they will be pleased. It is no part of a subordinate's job to make a superior happy. The job is to obtain output, not praise.

Salary discussion is usually avoided at the checkpoint meeting.

ACTION STEPS

1. Set objectives for all of your measurement areas. Review these objectives with all the others whom they might impact.
2. Test your objectives against the tests of sound objectives.
3. Consider for which objectives you might need to set a high and a low band and set them.
4. Ask your subordinates to set objectives.

GLOSSARY

Checkpoint meeting (CPM):   A superior-manager meeting, usually held quarterly, at which the manager's progress towards objectives is reviewed.

Objectives: Effectiveness areas which are as specific, as time-bounded, and as measurable as possible. Specific output requirements of a management position.

8 How to plan

Make a model before building.

A.N. Whitehead

A journey of a thousand leagues begins with a single step.

Lao-Tzu 540 B.C.

Don't be afraid to take a big step if one is indicated. You can't cross a chasm in two small jumps.

David Lloyd George

The output-oriented manager knows that objectives without plans are dreams and therefore spends all the time needed on planning. The output-oriented manager creates a detailed plan for every measurement area linking to an objective.

This chapter shows how to convert an objective into a plan, a plan into a schedule, and a set of schedules into an activity schedule which every output-oriented manager needs. Some will be struck by the simplicity with which the topic is treated. It is simple because what is needed is simple not complex. Sound and lengthy books have been written about planning. The average manager, however, needs only the guides given here – and a decision to start.

In output-oriented organizations a special emphasis is given to manager planning. This refers to the production of a step-by-step plan which will lead to the attainment of an objective. Corporate planning is important of course, but it is manager planning which is missing. Managers normally resist the discipline involved in planning to achieve their own objectives. But when they have gone through one or two cycles they see what an important tool it is.

Planning is not an addition to a manager's job. It is a way of managing. Managers who say they have 'no time for planning' are those who have no time to get properly organized. Output-oriented management properly applied must have an emphasis on planning.

This chapter will show how to bring together on a single sheet of paper what has been covered so far. The Objective Planning Form is a simple form on which to record an effectiveness area, its measurement area, the associated objective, the priority of the objective and the plan of activities. This form is very similar to other forms used to record objectives. Its main difference is the space given to record the complete programme of activities necessary to achieve the objective.

For any objective there must be a plan and a timed schedule. Plans are a statement, prepared in advance, of what is to be done. A schedule is a plan with timings. Without plans managers muddle through to their objectives, which if achieved, were almost certainly too low to begin with. A plan identifies what is seen as the best route towards achieving an objective. Planning is a purely intellectual process, and to plan well managers need to sit and think.

Sound advance planning has many benefits: it increases a manager's thinking time and decreases the doing time. In this way brains are substituted for effort. Crisis management is less likely to occur, as most eventualities have been thought out in advance. In-basket material will always be drastically reduced, as key activities have been decided and agreed in advance and managers do not need to be continually reminded of them.

Plans may consist of a few sequential steps or they may be considerably more complex. While determining and approving objectives is the joint responsibility of the superior and each manager concerned, plans are the sole responsibility of the managers themselves. It is their responsibility alone that their plans lead to the achievement of their objectives.

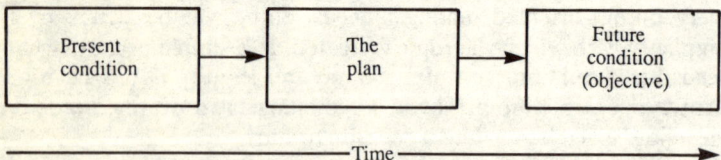

Objectives without plans are dreams; plans convert objectives to reality.

Exhibit 8.1   Plans lead to objectives being achieved

A plan is the means by which it is proposed to convert a present condition to some future condition. The future condition is the objective, as shown in Exhibit 8.1.

If the objective could have been achieved without the plan, it was not an objective but a prediction. Managers are not paid to allow predicted futures to occur: management is not needed for that. Management is paid to cast up alternative futures, select one of them, which is the objective, and work to achieve it by a plan.

PLANS CONSIST OF A SERIES OF LINKED ACTIVITIES

In this first section of the chapter, activities are discussed, in the second section plans are the topic, and in the third section detail is given on the objective planning form which shows how to link effectiveness areas, measurement areas, objectives and plans together.

In this section on activities the following will be covered:

- What is an activity?
- Qualities of a good activity
- Some frequently occurring activities
- Things to consider when identifying and linking activities

What is an activity?

An activity is something a manager does. The key word in the activity should be chosen so that completion of the activity is unambiguous. Such words as administer, manage, arrange, observe and others shown in the list below are usually unsuitable prefixes for activities, as all are vague and each could mean many different things. Better words are indicated in brackets.

Poor activity indicators
(and better substitutes)

Administer (approve)	Examine (decide)
Analyse (decide)	Expedite (attain)
Arrange (implement)	Facilitate (provide)
Assist (advise)	Follow-up (review)
Assure (notify)	Investigate (decide)
Collaborate (achieve)	Manage (obtain)
Consult (ask)	Observe (appraise)
Cooperate (achieve/inform)	Participate (decide/inform)
Coordinate (decide)	Search (find)
Develop (prepare)	Study (appraise)
Discuss (inform/prepare)	

The words we use can show we do not mean anything. Better but not always appropriate substitutes are in parentheses. Better prefixes include change, close, complete, decide, deliver, purchase and train, and others shown in this list.

Better activity indicators

Adopt	Approve	Authorize
Advise	Assemble	Calculate
Announce	Assign	Cancel
Appraise	Attach	Change

Circulate	Implement	Release
Classify	Inform	Represent
Collect	Initiate	Request
Compile	Inspect	Require
Complete	Install	Requisition
Conduct	Instruct	Review
Control	Interview	Revise
Construct	Issue	Schedule
Correct	Locate	Scrutinize
Decide	Maintain	Secure
Delegate	Make	Select
Deliver	Notify	Sell
Design	Obtain	Separate
Determine	Organize	Start
Discover	Originate	Submit
Distribute	Outline	Summarize
Divide	Plan	Supply
Draft	Prepare	Tabulate
Establish	Programme	Teach
Find	Provide	Tell
Formulate	Purchase	Trace
Give	Recommend	Train
Hire	Record	Verify .

Most of these words mean that something will get done.

While some words such as these can have ambiguity, they are less ambiguous than the previous examples given. The purpose of the two lists is not to initiate a debate on exceptions to the words in them, but to make one point clear: the wording of the activity should be such that all involved would know when it is completed. When applicable, finish is better than start.

Qualities of a good activity

The qualities of a good activity are:

- The activity is separate from other activities
- It is stated briefly
- It is understandable
- It avoids detail which arises naturally from other activities
- Its completion is easily measured

Some frequently occurring activities

In drafting plans for your objectives you may want to think of some of these steps to include in one or more of the plans, as they do frequently occur and are sometimes overlooked. These are phrased rather generally here to give the basic idea. The particular wording here may not be appropriate for you.

- Objective approved by/with
- Plan approved by/with
- Budget approved by/with
- Obtain all necessary information concerning the objective
- Checkpoint meeting to review progress toward objective
- Date objective to be achieved

Things to consider when identifying and linking activities

In selecting the best activities, and their sequence, the following questions should be asked:

- How broad or detailed should the activities be?
- Is it best to work backwards from the objective or forwards to it?
- Which activities must precede which?
- Which activities may be concurrent?
- For which activities does a time constraint exist?
- Which activities must be completed by a certain time?
- Which activities must be done by the same person?
- Which activities cost more or less if done at different times?
- Which activities are similar enough that they may be grouped?

Except for those managers, usually engineers, who are involved in complex construction projects, this is all that the average manager really needs to know about arrow diagrams and networks. Managers are best employed in making plans with what they already know rather than in learning more about planning that they will not use. The only real difficulty in simple planning is that managers do not do it.

ACTIVITIES LINKED TO PLANS AND SCHEDULES

A set of activities creates a plan, putting dates on a plan creates the schedule. The following topics are in this section:

- Putting dates on activities
- Activity networks

- The activity schedule
- Simple plans
- Standing plans
- Qualities of a good plan
- Planning problems

Putting dates on activities

A schedule is a plan with timings. So to create a schedule, you put a
date on your activities. There are some obvious factors which effect
the construction of a schedule and some not too obvious. In deciding
what dates to put on a plan these factors are most important:

- The earliest start point
- The latest finish point
- Key date ties with other schedules
- Staffing required and available for each activity
- Equipment required and available for each activity
- Uncontrollable timed inputs from others

Here is an example of a simple schedule which shows the objective
and a plan with timings. (EO is an abbreviation for end of.)

Objective:
Have plant in single shift operation at 70 per cent capacity by EO
Aug 199–

Plan:

1.	Complete design by	EO Mar 199–
2.	Complete construction by	EO Dec 199–
3.	Install all equipment by	EO Feb 199–
4.	Hire and train staff by	EO May 199–
5.	Start-up by	EO June 199–
6.	Operation at 70 per cent capacity	EO Aug 199–

Activity Networks

When the number of activities in a plan goes much over ten, it is
often useful to make an activity network. The basic idea is very
simple. It involves linking numbers which represent activities with
arrows which show the sequential relationship of the activities. A
diagram of a particular combination of activities and arrows is called

Exhibit 8.2 A simple network

an 'arrow diagram' or 'activity network'. The simple network in Exhibit 8.2 shows two activities and by the use of the arrow indicates that activity 1 must be completed before activity 2 is started.

A more restricted network in Exhibit 8.3 shows that activities 1 and 2 must be completed prior to activity 3, and activity 3 prior to activity 4.

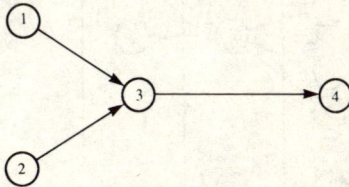

Activities 1 and 2 can and should proceed simultaneously and must be completed before starting activity 3 – it is simple but is also important.

Exhibit 8.3 A restricted network

This planning concept is of enormous usefulness to managers, and using it can shorten considerably the time taken to achieve objectives. Time is always money. Most managers who do not plan, unwittingly assume that all their activities concerning an objective are sequential. Thus they wait until one activity is completed prior to starting the next. They might instead have initiated work on several activities simultaneously.

The reason they do not do this is that they believe their work may become too complex. They think this because they do not have a plan. Plans simplify and shorten the time to achieve objectives.

Exhibit 8.4 shows four examples of networks with five activities having various sequential relationships. Network 1 shows that each activity must be completed in turn before proceeding to the next. In all, five time-periods are needed. Network 2 shows that activities 1, 2 and 3 may be worked on at the same time but all must be completed prior to activity 4, and that activity 4 must be completed before activity 5 is started. Network 3 shows that while activities 1 and 2 may be worked on simultaneously, each respectively must be completed prior to activities 3 and 4 being initiated, and both 3 and 4 must be completed prior to 5 being initiated. Network 4 shows a common type of network for managers. Activity 1 has to be completed and perhaps a plan made, after which several activities may be initiated and completed (activities 2, 3 and 4), usually by a manager's subordinates, and after that a decision or evaluation is made by the manager (activity 5).

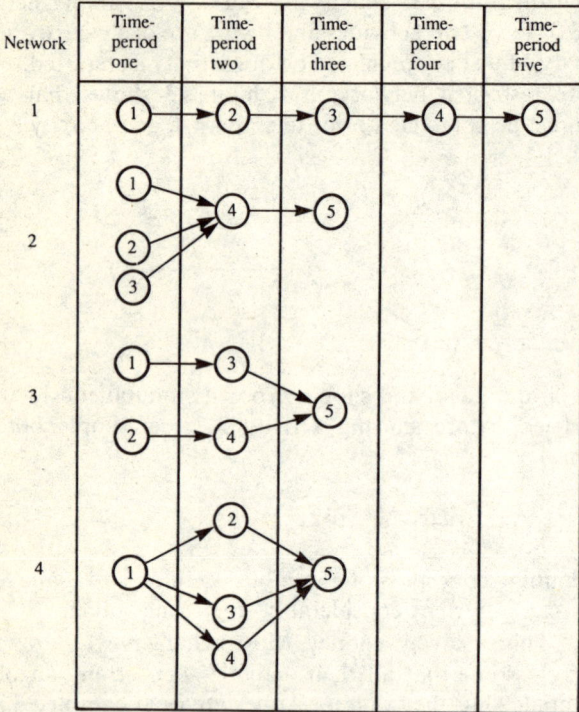

This kind of analysis leads to things being done faster and on time.

Exhibit 8.4   Networks of five activities

The activity schedule

If it is assumed that for each of the four networks just considered, each activity or set of simultaneous activities took a month to complete, starting 1 January, the timing of each would look like the schedules in the accompanying table.

Plan One		Plan Two	
1.	EO Jan	1.	EO Jan
2.	EO Feb	2.	EO Jan
3.	EO Mar	3.	EO Jan
4.	EO Apr	4.	EO Feb
5.	EO May	5.	EO Mar

Plan Three	*Plan Four*
1. EO Jan	1. EO Jan
2. EO Jan	2. EO Feb
3. EO Feb	3. EO Feb
4. EO Feb	4. EO Feb
5. EO Mar	5. EO Mar

These timings can be presented conveniently on an Activity Schedule shown in Exhibit 8.5. This schedule shows, for instance, that the manager's plan is to complete seven activities by the end of January, another seven by the end of February, and so on. A trained secretary can assist a manager by giving a list of activities to be completed for each month in the third week of the prior month, or a wall board may be used. Without having such a schedule a manager is less likely to achieve 'high outputs'. With a schedule it will become very clear whether the manager is taking on too big a job or too small; if the job is too big, such a schedule will show what type of assistance is needed, and when.

Network	Activities				
	Jan.	Feb.	Mar.	Apr.	May
1	1	2	3	4	5
2	1 2 3	4	5		
3	1 2	3 4	5		
4	1	2 3 4	5		

A planning board like this helps a manager keep on target.

Exhibit 8.5 An activity schedule

Simple plans

Here are examples of two simple plans, without dates, showing the use of appropriate key words.

Objective:
  Increase service sales on Product A from 2.6 per cent to at least
  2.9 per cent of market during 199–.

Plan (activities):
  1. Discover by analysis of sales records of the past four years
     what are the weak and strong markets and what is the
     marketing mix in fact.
  2. Discover competitors' product and marketing mix over the
     past four years.
  3. Conduct a two-day marketing strategy meeting to develop
     new marketing strategy.
  4. Implement the proposed strategy.
  5. Discover by survey why existing users do not use the service
     more.
  6. Discover by survey why some do not use the service at all.
  7. Prepare a draft of my analysis of problem and our proposals
     on how to increase utilization and distribute to users and non
     users.
  8. Conduct a one-day meeting to discuss my draft and obtain
     agreement on improvement methods.
  9. Implement the meeting proposals.

Standing plans

Very often the same kind of objective may occur year after year, even
for many different managers in a single firm. A firm with several
brand managers, for instance, will have many similar objectives
concerning brand launch or market penetration. A firm with several
plants will have many objectives relating to quality control and other
typical production type objectives. It is then often useful to prepare
sets of simple, carefully worked-out master standing plans which can
be used, at their discretion, by managers who have common
objectives.

Qualities of a good plan

The tests of a good plan are:

- Has a clear objective
- Has clear activity steps
- Activities are properly arranged in sequence
- Has suitable progress checkpoints identified

- As necessary takes into account other plans by the manager
- As necessary takes into account plans of other managers

As managers gain experience with planning, they will grow into their skill to satisfy all these tests with each plan they make.

Planning problems

If a manager's plan does not lead to the attainment of the objective, the plan or its implementation was faulty. At the end of the year review of the attainment of objectives it is most useful to review the plan of activities itself. Plans fail for one of three reasons: something was left out, something was put in, or the activities of others were not anticipated. As managers gain experience in planning, partly through some of their plans failing, they will learn how to think more clearly about these three things which arise from poor planning and which lead to failure.

The most common errors in planning are:

- Not doing it
- Planning only two to four activities when many more are needed
- Not recognizing that for many objectives several activities may proceed simultaneously
- Becoming so fascinated by the plan that its associated objective is seen as secondary
- Failure to review a plan when the objective is not met
- Omission of key activities
- Failure to allow for activities of others that might hinder one's own plan
- No review of progress
- Stating activities vaguely so that their completion is uncertain

Resistance to planning
There is much resistance to planning simply because some managers do not want to do it. These objectives take many forms and their nature depends upon the creativity of the manager involved in resisting change and the nature of the manager's particular emotional defences. We have all heard things like:

'It takes too much time.'
'It is only for big firms.'
'I don't want to get involved in long-range planning because we

174   *The Output-Oriented Manager*

don't even know whether we'll exist next year.'
'I prefer to think only about the bottom line.'
'Planning takes too much time.'
'I keep my plans in my head – it has worked for years.'
'Planning creates too much paperwork.'
'I am over my cost budget and that's all I can think about right now.'
'I am well under my cost budget so I must be doing something right without planning.'
'My job is too simple for planning.'
'My job is too complex for planning.'

The real reasons that some managers do not plan include

- Planning takes time away from other work
- The effects of planning are not always visible in the short term
- Past failures of planning due to unpredictable and uncontrollable events
- Failure in past planning owing to poor planning
- The misperception that planning somehow ties one down
- Lack of intellectual capacity
- Lack of logical reasoning ability
- Pending environmental uncontrollability
- The organization's failure to provide a one- or two-day course on planning to help those who need it
- A current crisis – or recurring crises
- Difficulty learning how to plan well

THE OBJECTIVE PLANNING FORM

The Objective Planning Form (OPF) is for use by individual managers. One is completed for each objective and all the important facts impinging on that objective are included on the form. This form has been used by tens of thousands of managers. When output-oriented management is introduced in particular companies, managers are asked what changes they would like to see in the form. Virtually all want no changes.

In this section we shall review the form itself, Exhibit 8.6, and the particular use to be made of each section of the form, and then, Exhibits 8.7 to 8.10 give examples of completed forms.

Objective Planning Form

Manger _____

Draft date and
draft number _____ ____

Serials

Effectiveness Area	
Measurement Area	
Objective	Priority

Plan	Person	Completion date	Status

Actual Performance

Exhibit 8.6   The objective planning form

Objective planning form

This one-page form is used by all managers, one per objective, based on a single measurement area. In some situations only one copy is made, that is for the manager. It is more usual for two copies to be made, with the second copy for the superior. It is very seldom a good idea to distribute this form to other parts of the organization as this tends to give the impression that authority and responsibility are diffused. No matter how many copies are sent round, the authority is sited on the manager whose objective it is. It is not usually desirable to discuss the planning steps on the form with others with whom the managers interact. There is just too much detail and the action plan is the manager's responsibility not the unit members' responsibility. Unit members want to know effectiveness areas, measurement areas and the objectives, not the detail of the plan.

The objective planning form consists of these headings. The use of each will be explained in turn:

- Manager
- Draft date
- Draft number
- Serials
- Effectiveness area
- Measurement area
- Objective
- Priority
- Plan
- Person
- Completion date
- Status
- Actual performance

Manager

Insert here the name or the initials of the manager whose objective it is.

Draft date

Insert the date that this current objective planning form was created by the manager.

Draft number

Insert here the draft number. If the draft is the first then insert '1', and so on. It is quite common, particularly in the early stages of setting clear objectives, for the objective planning form to go through several drafts. Instead of numbers, standard in-company terms might be used such as preliminary, intermediate and final.

Serials

A number is assigned to each objective and each activity. If the objective is the third a manager has established for the position then '3' is inserted. The activities for this objective are numbered sequentially 3.1, 3.2, 3.3 and so on.

Effectiveness area

Each Effectiveness Area is identified. Several planning forms may have the same Effectiveness Area. There is one OPF per measurement area.

Measurement Area

The measurement area associated with the objective is identified.

Objective

Under this heading is inserted a statement of what the manager plans to accomplish, stated as clearly and specifically as possible. There may be more than one objective for a particular effectiveness area, in which case additional objective planning forms are used. There is only one objective per measurement area.

Priority

Insert 1 or 2 or 3. 1 indicates highest priority. 3 is the lowest.

Plan

The specific activities the manager will undertake as steps toward achieving the objective. These are essentially inputs, and care must be taken that they are not seen as substitutes for, or supplementary to, the objectives. This list is designed solely to assist with planning. It is the manager's, not the superior's, responsibility that the programme of activities proposed lead to the attainment of the objectives. Indicate also the best checkpoint date at which the progress towards the objective is to be formally reviewed. List the checkpoint as a separate activity.

Person

Insert here the initials of a person responsible for completing the particular activity of the plan.

Completion date

Insert here the date by which the activity is planned to be completed. (It is convenient to use such abbreviations as EO for end of or BO for beginning of, or DUR for during.)

Status

Insert here the word 'done' (or something similar) to indicate the activity has been completed. Alternatively, indicate the date when it was completed.

Actual performance

A record of the extent to which the objective, not the programme of activities, was actually achieved, as measured by the measurement area established, in the time-period set. This is worded in similar fashion to the objective so that comparisons may be made. In addition, it includes a statement of whether the objective was over achieved, just achieved, or under achieved. If under achieved a note on why this occurred should be given.

EXAMPLES OF COMPLETED OBJECTIVE PLANNING FORMS

Here are four completed examples of actual pages of objective

Objective Planning Form

Manger A CEO

Draft date and
Drat number JAN 199–   TWO

Serials

Effectiveness Area Paper Products Ltd.

Measurement Area Existence of company, its catalogue, its inventory and its administrator.

Objective
By EO 199- have Paper Products Ltd. ready to go into full operation with catalogue printed, inventory in stock with forty paper product lines and administrator appointed.

Priority 1

Serial: 3

	Plan	Person	Completion date	Status
3.1	Initiate name search in three countries	CEO	EO FEB	DONE
3.2	Establish product line	CEO	EO MAR	
3.3	Plan budget	CEO	EO MAR	DONE
3.4	Appoint administrator and agree effectiveness areas	CEO	EO APR	
3.5	Contract all test designs and production responsibility	CEO	EO APR	
3.6	Incorporate	ACC	EO ARP	
3.7	Checkpoint	CEO	DUR MAY	
3.8	Survey competitors and customers	CEO	EO JUN	
3.9 '	Approve all product designs	CEO	EO SEP	
3.10	Decide staffing and location	CEO	EO OCT	
3.11	Design catalogue and pricing	CEO	EO OCT	
3.12	Mail preliminary promotion piece	MKM	EO NOV	
3.13	Catalogue mailing ready	ACM	EO DEC	
3.14	Inventory ready	PRM	EO DEC	

Actual Performance

From nothing to something in fourteen steps.

Exhibit 8.7   Paper Products Ltd.

planning forms, they include:

- Putting a new Company into operation
- New code of accounts
- Consumer market research
- Subordinate's effectiveness in meeting objectives

Putting a new company into operation

Exhibit 8.7 shows one of the Objective Planning Forms of a CEO of a pulp and paper producer. One of the effectiveness areas concerned a new company, Paper Products Ltd, that the CEO was responsible for bringing into full operation. The objectives might have been improved by adding a quality measure in terms of sales potential or a favourable comparison between the products of Paper Products Ltd and those of competitors. The measurement area is clearly stated again except for the quality measure, though it is still quite satisfactory.

The fourteen-step plan could easily be contracted or expanded, but this is not important. Some managers prefer to work with a few and some with many steps. This CEO has used the EO (End Of) date form, except for 3.7, the checkpoint.

New code of accounts

The measurement area of Exhibit 8.8 has a clear quality control measure. The programme provides for planning, a trial run, a checkpoint, and then full implementation.

Note the wording of the actual performance section, which parallels that of the objective and states deviance. No explanation was given, but might have been, of why the objective was not fully achieved.

Consumer market research

Exhibit 8.9 is that of a market research project leader. The effectiveness area is one of several for this position, including industrial surveys and internal company surveys. The objective is quite well worded, as is the measurement area.

Objective Planning Form

Manger A. N. ACCOUNT

Serials

Draft date and draft number FEB 199–   ONE

Effectiveness Area Accounting Information				
Measurement Area All branch accounts coded using new systems with less than 3 errors in 1,000 discovered by monthly audit team.				

4	**Objective** Introduce new code of accounts fully into all branches by EO JUL 199–			**Priority** 2

Serials	Plan	Person	Completion date	Status
4.1	Obtain approval to introduce	ANA	EO MAY	APR
4.2	Design implementation plan	ANA	EO JUL	JUN
4.3	Visit all branches to explain implementation plan	ANA	EO AUG	SEP
4.4	Conduct minimum 3 days training for all account clerks	TRM	EO SEP	SEP
4.5	Introduce in West Branch	ANA	EO NOV	NOV
4.6	Conduct 1 day seminar on West Branch introduction problem	TRM	EO JAN	JAN
4.7	Checkpoint	ANA	DUR FEB	FEB
4.8	Introduce into all branches	ANA	EO MAR	APR

Actual Performance Introduced new codes of accounts fully into 5 of 6 branches by EO July 199–. Each branch alone exceeded allowable 3/1000 error rate with 15/1000 error rate in August inspection. No problems anticipated in reducing this to desired level. Objective was substantially achieved.

A simple plan but important for those who must adjust to it.

Exhibit 8.8   Accounting information

Objective Planning Form

Manger A MARKETEER

Serials

Draft date and draft number   MAR 199-   ONE

Serials					
	Effectiveness Area Consumer Surveys				
	Measurement Area Availability of twenty copies of report to management and their acceptance of its quality.				
6	**Objective** Have full report of national consumer survey available to management EO JAN next year showing profiles of our ten major products and the profiles of the main competitors for each.			**Priority** 2	
	Plan	**Person**	**Completion date**	**Status**	
6.1	Make final revisions objective	AMM	EO MAY		
6.2	Decide question and answer sheet formats	AMM	EO MAY		
6.3	Select sample	AMM	EO MAY		
6.4	Proof and print questionnaire	AMM	EO JUL		
6.5	Mail sample	PRM	EO JUL		
6.6	Contract for computer and programmer time	AMM	EO JUL		
6.7	Design analysis procedure	AMM	EO JUL		
6.8	Complete analysis	AMM	EO OCT		
6.9	Draft final report of research design and findings	AMM	EO NOV		
6.10	Write final report and submit	AMM	EO DEC		
6.11	Reproduce final report	TPS	EO DEC		
	Actual Performance				

It may be staff but it is output.

Exhibit 8.9   Consumer surveys

Objective Planning Form

Manger A. BOSS

Draft date and
draft number DEC 199-   TWO

Serials

	Effectiveness Area Subordinate effectiveness
	Measurement Area Agreement by myself and, each subordinate that each objective was fully achieved using the measurement **area** decided.

Serials	Objective			Priority
2	All subordinates achieve their objectives for this coming year.			1

	Plan	Person	Completion date	Status
2.1	Hold monthly meetings with AJM and TST to coach on method of achieving their objectives.	ABO	DUR YEAR	DONE
2.2	Hold meetings on 12 Feb., 26 May,	ABO	ON FEB 16	DONE
	4 Jul., and 3 Sep., with team	ABO	ON MAY 26	DONE
	to discuss best method of	ABO	ON JUL 4	-
	facilitating the achievement	ABO	ON SEP 3	DONE
	of the objectives for the year.			
2.3	Obtain 25% increase in clerical assistance available to unit during year.	ABO	EO JAN	DONE
2.4	Be available to any subordinate for a 30 minute meeting with no more than a four day delay.	ABO	DUR YEAR	DONE
2.5	Meet twice, in Jan. and May, with all the superiors of all those managers with whose objectives my subordinates'	ABO	DUR JAN	DONE
	objectives must align.	ABO	DUR MAY	DONE

Actual Performance Not fully achieved. Four subordinates substantially achieved **their** objectives **but** two did not.Reasons: Subordinate JKR was not coached sufficiently in planning, subordinate RTI possible difficulties with production division were not sorted out early in the year and got worse.

The difficult one with many possible different plans.

Exhibit 8.10   Achievement of subordinate objectives

Subordinates meeting objectives

A second objective associated with the subordinates' effectiveness area is that concerning meeting objectives set. Exhibit 8.10 shows such a plan. This plan involves, in essence, a high degree of coaching assistance, especially for two subordinates. Such a plan as this commits a manager's time and enables everyone concerned to mark diary dates.

SUMMARY – PLANNING AND THE OUTPUT-ORIENTED MANAGER

- Planning is not an addition to managerial work.
- The only problem with planning is how to get managers to do it.
- An objective without a plan is a dream.
- Planning, at least, simulates the future and can often help to create it.
- Planning costs nothing except management time.
- The most successful firms in the world insist managers spend at least a month a year on planning – it is called the budgeting process.
- Planning substitutes dreams for reality.
- Planning helps a manager control the environment rather than the environment controlling the manager.
- Planning is a superb way to ensure linkage of one part of the organization with another.
- An agreed plan sharply reduces conflict and unnecessary memos and meetings.
- Planning does not control the manager, it enables the manager to respond quickly to a changed situation.

ACTION STEPS

1. Create a plan for one of your objectives and check it with some others who might help you improve it.
2. Create a plan for all of your objectives and check them with others who might help you improve them.

GLOSSARY

Activity: A particular thing a manager actually does or intends to do.

Activity network::   A diagram of a particular combination of activities connected by arrows to show their sequential relationships.

Activity schedule: A visual arrangement of activities over a time period.

BO: Beginning of (usually a month but could be a year).

EO: End of (usually a month but could be a year).

DUR: During (during a particular period).

Objective planning form (OPF):   A form used to record a single objective of one measurement area together with priority, activities and plan.

OPF: See *Objective planning form*

Plan: A sequence of activities.

Schedule: A plan with timings.

PART III
The Benefits

Introduction

Output-oriented management can benefit you in many ways. As a bare minimum it helps you with job security. It also helps you with whistling on your way to work rather than whistling on your way home. In short, motivation to do well.

Some naturally and easily jump into output-oriented management. For many, however, it is the hard road. The road is often made more difficult by the environment such as the ageing firm which needs new ideas. Chapter 10 discusses training managers for output-oriented management.

As you really are serious about the idea of outputs you will be interested in Chapter 11 which shows how many systems in the firm can be built around the ideas of outputs and effectiveness.

To become an output-oriented manager you must do some things differently. If you do not, then you will stay at precisely your current level of effectiveness, unless the environment changes in some way. Chapter 12 gives you ideas on what you might do to become an output-oriented manager.

9 Output-oriented management benefits you

> If a man has a talent and cannot use it, he has failed. If he has a talent and uses one half of it, he has partly failed. If he has a talent and learns somehow to use the whole of it, he has gloriously succeeded and won a satisfaction and triumph few men will know.
>
> Thomas Wolfe

> No one has a greater asset for his business than a man's pride in his works.
>
> Mary Parker Follett

Being a output-oriented manager can benefit you in many ways. These benefits include:

Benefits relating to your personal effectiveness:
Obtaining greater rewards
Improved family security and happiness
Preferred career route
Enjoying work as much as play
Higher job satisfaction
Lower job stress

Benefits relating to your self-development:
Acquiring a transferable skill
Working smarter not harder
Advancing your own management development
Improved situational sensitivity

Benefits relating to your effectiveness:
Improving your effectiveness
Getting your authority clarified
Improving your performance measurement
Better planning
Developing a sound basis for setting objectives
Becoming more objective about your situation
Flexible job trading

BENEFITS RELATING TO YOUR PERSONAL EFFECTIVENESS

As you know, personal effectiveness refers more to what you want to get from the organization than what you may give it. One of the most important results in being an output-oriented manager is to improve your personal effectiveness, that is, meeting your objectives in terms of what you personally want. While the situation varies from manager to manager you will find some of your personal needs here:

- Obtaining greater rewards
- Improved family security and happiness
- Preferred career route
- Enjoying work as much as play
- Higher job satisfaction
- Lower job stress

Obtaining greater rewards

This book cannot guarantee that if you learn to achieve higher outputs you will obtain greater rewards. There is little doubt, however, that in the long run it is the more effective manager who gets ahead and gets rewarded for it.

A well-designed organization usually ensures that managerial effectiveness, and only managerial effectiveness, leads to personal rewards. While organizations do vary in the extent, speed and accuracy of rewards for effectiveness, there can be little doubt that, in the long run, the effective manager is the rewarded one. The rewards are usually concrete in terms of salary, level of position and advancement rate. Other rewards more important to some are fulfilled ambitions, assured security, self-actualization, personal satisfaction or happiness in the form of job enrichment, or plain job survival when there is a decline in business. This book is designed to show managers how they can be more effective and thus obtain the rewards that being so, brings.

Improved family security and happiness

There is no question that the output-oriented manager has improved family security and happiness. In the long run, the effective manager is the one who is rewarded most. It does not always happen in the short run and it does not happen in every organization all the time, but there really is no question, the race does go to the swift. You may be seeking job security, job mobility or a higher salary or all three. Higher outputs can only help you with them.

Preferred career route

It is highly probable that you do not want security of tenure in your present position, or want to move to another organization. What you are interested in is your preferred career route in your *current* organization. A preferred career route is a common organization reward for managers who are more effective. In some organizations, it is true that a major move may occur only once every ten years. In other organizations that are growing rapidly such moves might occur every two years or even less. The point is that if you want to move in the organization a good way to accomplish it is to become more effective.

Enjoying work as much as play

Most of us enjoy work as well as play. What we do not enjoy is being hindered when doing either. What makes organized games fun is that effectiveness areas, measurement areas, objectives, roles, authority and responsibility are clearly defined. They are learned as a child and readily understood by all concerned. Those who do not want organizations to be structured should consider the degree of structure in games and the enjoyment we have when playing them. Most dissatisfaction in organizations stems from a lack of clarity concerning such things as authority and from vague performance standards, not from the existence or absence of them. Output orientation can help sort things out and make work more enjoyable.

Quite apart from monetary rewards, most of us find intrinsic enjoyment in a job well done. If we did not, we would not spend so much time building and sailing our boats, growing our roses, or processing our films. An important reward that we seek in these and other activities is the knowledge that we have performed well. This is true also in most kinds of managerial work, and this intrinsic reward must be recognized and understood when motivation to work is being considered. However, concrete rewards are also usually enjoyed by all of us. These may relate to promotion, to still more interesting work, increased responsibility, or more pay.

Well-designed organizations are quiet places in which to work. Poorly-designed organizations are death-traps since role conflict can and does kill. We all can draw on our experiences in our own companies of a clumsy change followed by a heart attack, or the hard-working person in a non-job getting an ulcer, or a lifetime of organizational stress leading to a breakdown. If two people, for example, are responsible for the same thing one of them is not needed; out of respect to both, the issue should be resolved.

Worklife can be a great game, but to play it effectively, we must know all the groundrules, respect our co-workers, agree to the objectives, and know the score. People are rational animals capable of both good and evil and motivated most when they both understand, and can perform in the position in which they find themselves. Work is not intrinsically evil. What is evil is poorly-designed work. People want to work and they want to play – there is no difference – the manager's job is to create situations where they can.

Higher job satisfaction

It is obvious that with the knowledge of how to do your job and the authority to do it that your job satisfaction will increase. As it happens, it will also increase if you become more effective. Several studies have been made linking job satisfaction with more effectiveness and the results show very clearly that the more effective managers are the more satisfied ones. Job satisfaction was shown, in an investigation of ageing, as the strongest predictor of longevity. So, if you are happy at your work you live longer. Job satisfaction and general life satisfaction were far better predictors of living longer than such things as physical examination, smoking, or even of genetic structure. It is a truism that most people, if not all, are pleased when they do a good job. That is the link between managerial effectiveness and job satisfaction.

If properly introduced by those above you and if properly understood by you the methods described in this book can lead to much greater job motivation for yourself. This motivation, of course, arises from knowing what your job is, having the authority to do it, and agreeing on these with your superior and co-workers. Consequently, motivation is what you are allowed to do to yourself not what others do to you. The same applies to your subordinates, of course. What this book does is to put you much more in control of your situation. If you really want to engage it and perform well in it, you have a much better chance of doing so after working through this book.

Lower job stress

Hundreds of scientific studies have been conducted into the causes of
stress at work. There are many causes and most are obvious. The
causes include such things as the general level of job dissatisfaction,
poor relationships with superior or others, belief that the job is of
little value, not understanding the job, not having the resources to do
the job well, lack of recognition and undue time pressure. Some of
these occur in some jobs for all of us sometimes. They can be greatly
decreased, however, with the many ideas in this book pertaining to
clarity about roles and candid discussion about how best work might
be done. The problem is not just work stress but what work stress can
lead to. High work stress has been related to a variety of physical
ailments, particularly heart disease, arthritis and peptic ulcers.

BENEFITS RELATING TO YOUR SELF-DEVELOPMENT

You have a major responsibility for your self-development. This is
shared by others in your organization including your superior and
specialized departments. However, most self-development is what
you will do yourself, for yourself. The mere fact that you have come
this far in the book means that you have a high interest in your self-
development and that of others. Through being an output-oriented
manager, your self-development is fostered by:

- Acquiring a transferable skill
- Working smarter not harder
- Advancing your own management development
- Improved situational sensitivity

Acquiring a transferable skill

The ideas in this book do not apply to your job alone. They will
apply equally well and equally effectively to any other job you may
have, in any kind of work. The time you spend on clarifying your
current outputs will help you enormously in any job to which you
may move. You will find that when you meet potential future
superiors you will be asking, 'What outputs will I be responsible for?'
They may well show you the old-fashioned job description showing
your actions, they may show you a job specification suggesting what
you should be like. None of this will hurt you. You will show them
your understanding of how business organizations should operate by

asking what the outputs are. You will push in terms of how you will be measured and precisely what your authority is and whether your authority is commensurate with your responsibility. There is no need at all to be pushy about all this but it is very important in any future job to which you might move to know exactly what the job is.

You may well discover that the person suggesting that you enter the new job does not in fact understand it and this may lead you to think twice about whether you are interested in the position.

The concept of outputs as applied to individual jobs has been tested and used in over twenty countries. Should your organization work internationally and should other countries use these ideas you will find that the common language this book provides gives an immediate starting point for such things as project teams, design of other types of temporary organization structures.

Working smarter, not harder

Working harder does not necessarily mean becoming more effective. This book may well lead you to think, reflect and plan more rather than putting more hours in or slavishly 'doing' when you should be thinking about being smart.

> A less effective manager of a purchasing function worked very hard. He worried a lot, he always took home work at night and sometimes put in work at the weekends. He was told by his team members – and this was supported by a consultant working with the team – that he 'worked too hard'. He was highly offended by this and took it as a personal insult.

This manager could not see the wood for the trees and did not want to, because that would mean that his behaviour would have to change. He would have to sit and think about the job and have to delegate more. It was change he was frightened of and he hid it by saying he had to work hard. A popular defence for less effective managers is that 'my job demands that I put in long hours'. In some particular situations that may be true in the short term. Most jobs, however, are designed to be done in normal working hours not excessive hours.

A manager's true worth to the company may sometimes be measured by the amount of time the manager could remain dead in the office without anyone noticing it. The longer the time, the more likely it is that the manager makes long-run policy decisions rather than short-run administrative decisions. The key decisions in a company are long-run and may refer to market entry, new product introduction, new plant location, or key appointments. The person making these should not get involved, as can happen, with short-run issues. If that happens, then the manager has not decided on the output measures of the job or does not have the skill or opportunity to create conditions where only policy issues reach that level. Work smarter not harder.

Advancing your own management development

In various ways this book provides you with a comprehensive management development programme. One part of it is the learning you will do as a result of working through the book and developing your own job effectiveness description. Quite another, is the further learning you will do in looking at your unit as a whole in output terms and working with your unit members to develop a higher candour level about each others' outputs and how effectiveness should be measured.

Improved situational sensitivity

It is very common for managers to mistake symptoms for causes. So-called personality conflicts, for instance, are very often caused by a role conflict based on a poor distribution of authority, leading to a clash of objectives. As the managers involved might normally have a drink together and perhaps even been known to play a game of golf, it is unlikely that it is their personalities that clash but rather that their work roles clash. In similar vein, a very poor diagnosis is that of poor communications. If you take that diagnosis at face value it suggests that one should send people on communication courses. Any intelligent manager would know this is the last thing that is needed. Poor communication means that parts of the organization are not fitting together properly. There is lack of alignment. This is an organizational problem, not a personal problem. Would anyone seriously consider improving communication by running courses on how to write letters, how to write clearer memos, how to run a better meeting or even how to listen? These may have their use in very particular circumstances but they really do not help at all in improving communication generally. The reason is that poor communication arises from other than the individual differences that these courses are designed to change. It is certain that with a set of job effectiveness descriptions communication vastly improves.

Initial drafts of effectiveness areas by the managers themselves can form an excellent basis for diagnosis of the fundamental problems in the organization such as:

● Power concentration
● Power diffusion
● Decisions made too high up
● Decisions made too low down
● Low trust level
● Poor information system
● Lack of corporate strategy
● Lack of planning
● Control from outside the organization
● Emphasis on maintenance, not change
● Incompetence

Look at this list from a new perspective. Your perspective now emphasizes role alignment, clarity about authority, effectiveness areas that fit with those of others, and clear measurement. Many of the problems listed above in your organizations can be traced directly to these . . . not personality conflicts.

BENEFITS RELATING TO YOUR EFFECTIVENESS

The whole thrust of the approach outlined in this book is on improving your effectiveness. It does this in a variety of ways. All of these are the benefits you will obtain from being an output-oriented manager:

● Improving your effectiveness
● Getting your authority clarified
● Improving your performance measurement
● Better planning
● Developing a sound basis for setting objectives
● Becoming more objective about your situation
● Flexible job trading

Improving your effectiveness

Your effectiveness is bound to increase if some of the following are improved.

- Your understanding of the outputs of your work unit. This applies to unit outputs, your unit top member's outputs, your outputs and the outputs of the other unit members.
- Your understanding of your subordinates' outputs.
- The establishment of clear measurement areas for all outputs.
- An open meeting with your unit top member and other unit members as a whole on unit outputs, measurement areas and authority.
- An open meeting with your unit top member on your outputs, measurement areas and authority.
- Concrete periodic feedback through measurement areas.
- Better all-round communication, candour and feedback.

Working more effectively with unit top member co-workers and subordinates

The methods described in this book can lead naturally to your working more effectively with those in your situation. You can share a common language, a common interest in effectiveness and some practical tools like the JED to help the effectiveness of each other.

Getting your authority clarified

Working through this book will definitely help you to agree your authority. It makes no promise about your getting more authority, and you may get less. You may find you have very little. Some 'deputies' at various levels in organizations have very little authority but they think that they have.

If your effectiveness areas and measurement areas are the same as your unit top member's then one of you is not needed. This general point is still an extreme case. It is used to make the point that this book leads to clarification of authority not necessarily obtaining more or less. One consultant who had used the ideas in this book in a variety of organizations reported:

> There is nothing in 'output' theory which proposes that managers should delegate more or that decision levels should go downward or that participation is a good thing. However, I have almost consistently observed that in organizations using the 'output' ideas it uniformly happens. Since the theory does not propose it I have of course been interested in why this might arise. My conclusion is that it is almost a general case that larger organizations, in particular, tend to keep authority higher up and push down responsibility. Of course, when writing job effectiveness des-

criptions the authority and responsibility must match. Senior managers come to the decision of either accepting all the effectiveness areas of those lower down, as they have the authority higher up, or pushing down the authority. They soon understand that they are trying to run the organization on a 'we keep the authority, you take the responsibility basis'.

Improving your performance measurement

As we saw in Chapter 3 improved knowledge of performance improves performance. If you know how you are doing you will probably improve should you wish to. You want to know exactly where you stand in terms of managerial performance and you want to know how others stand too. Accurate measurement is the only way to do this and the method described in this book can supply you with a high level of accuracy.

Better planning

Better planning can provide you with a road map. It gets you to think of where you are starting, where you want to go, how you are going to get there, what you need to get there, and who will get you there. All of this can only help you sleep more peacefully. Plans do not constrain you, or they need not. The existence of a plan makes it much easier for you to change direction or to put more emphasis on a particular direction. With no plans you cannot easily do either. Your plans, when integrated with those of others, can make your organization a quiet place in which to work. While they take time to create they will undoubtedly improve your job satisfaction as well as your effectiveness.

Developing a sound basis for setting objectives

There are many unsound bases for setting objectives and you may have had experience with one or more of them. They lead to confusion, unnecessary work and conflicts ... quite apart from lower effectiveness than necessary.

Once you have developed your JED, which as you know consists of effectiveness areas, the associated measurement areas and your authority, it is a very easy step to move to setting objectives if you wish. Essentially this next step is to put numbers on the measurement areas. If you have as a measurement area 'scrap rate per cent decrease' then the next step is to put a number as to how much per cent. In similar fashion, the university director of physical education may have swimming pool load factor as one of his measurement areas for the effectiveness area 'plant utilization'. By putting a number on the measurement area it becomes an objective. The important point about this method is you do not start with objectives you start with outputs and effectiveness areas and measurement areas. The start has to be with outputs otherwise one would put numbers on inputs, and there are many examples in this book of what a big trap this is.

Becoming more objective about your situation

Your situation exists as a reality. But you may not be seeing it. People seldom want to change and the best way to avoid changing is to distort your view of the situation you are in. Distortions vary with personalities. For some the distortion is simply to deny that certain aspects of the situation exist. For others it might be rationalization – 'I didn't want that job really'? For still others it might be projection, 'That person is resisting' when it is really the person saying it. Developing JEDs, particularly on a team basis, helps eliminate distortions. One can describe one's perception of the situation through effectiveness areas. If all of the listeners disagree with your perception it might be you who is wrong. It is quite possible that your vision is now 100 per cent, it is probable that it is somewhat lower than that. This method can help you improve your objectivity about your situation. If you distort the situation you must become less effective.

Flexible job trading

Flexible job trading means exchanges of parts of jobs, as described by effectiveness areas or measurement areas, with others. Especially in smaller organizations, it is common for the unit to sit down and discuss effectiveness areas and for unit members to realize that parts of jobs should be offered to other unit members. As organizations grow or change the need for this is heightened. So, one has the opportunity to respond very quickly to changes that are needed on a unit-by-unit basis. This is virtually impossible to do if one is faced with the traditional job description, or the traditional job specification. It is simplicity itself to do if each unit member has on a newsprint chart the effectiveness areas for the position occupied. All of these are put up for the unit, the superior and all unit members, the unit as a whole looks at this and thinks how to improve the design. Yes, it actually happens and it may well happen with your unit. It cannot possibly happen unless you all understand your outputs first and these are expressed in a shortlist of six to eight four-word statements with everyone understanding what they mean. You have not got a hope of doing this if you sit down with your job description in front of you and talk about it with others.

ACTION STEPS

1. Review these seventeen possible benefits from being an output-oriented manager.
   Benefits relating to your personal effectiveness:
   Obtaining greater rewards
   Improved family security and happiness
   Preferred career route
   Enjoying work as much as play
   Higher job satisfaction
   Lower job stress

   Benefits relating to your self-development:
   Acquiring a transferable skill
   Working smarter not harder
   Advancing your own management development
   Improved situational sensitivity

   Benefits relating to your effectiveness:
   Improving your effectiveness
   Getting your authority clarified
   Improving your performance measurement
   Better planning
   Developing a sound basis for setting objectives
   Becoming more objective about your situation
   Flexible job trading
2. Indicate for each the ones which have a high (H) average (A) or low (L) priority for you.
3. Consider the ones you rated high only and consider how the ideas in this book can help you achieve them. Make an action plan to achieve them.

10 Training for output-oriented management

Education does not mean teaching people to know what they did not know, it means helping them to learn to behave as they did not behave.

Ruskin

Untaught we cannot look in the right direction.

Plato

Some mangers and some smaller firms can start applying the ideas of this book immediately. However some managers, and larger firms in general, can usually benefit from some form of training in outputs. The ideas concerning outputs are good but usually some reinforcement and practice in application is needed. For this reason the Managerial Effectiveness Seminar (MES) has been designed. It is the primary method used by the Reddin Organization for over twenty years to introduce or to improve output orientation within an organization.

This chapter describes the objectives, design and effects of the MES on the manager and on the organization. It should be particularly useful for those who see that a successful implementation will have to involve overcoming resistance in individuals and in the organization as a whole. This is how the MES has been used most successfully to introduce output orientation. Consistent reports are received to the effect that without the MES being used as a first step the introduction of output orientation would have been far less effective. Training managers, in particular, will find this chapter very useful as it will give them some training design ideas for improving effectiveness. Managers not in training roles will also find the chapter useful in that it gives yet another framework to thinking about improving one's own effectiveness and that of others.

SEMINAR OBJECTIVE

The objective of the MES is the clarification of the manager's effectiveness areas, measurement areas, authority and objectives. In addition to its emphasis on these four separate points, leading to the construction of the JED, it also teaches several techniques of output orientation and shows how a manager may work with these techniques to obtain greater effectiveness.

At the end of the seminar, managers are highly conscious of themselves as key figures in situations where effectiveness could be increased. They are more open to change. They see themselves rather than others, as keys to greater effectiveness. They are capable of applying an increased number of sound output principles and techniques to achieve effectiveness.

The theme running through the seminar is that managerial effectiveness is the central issue in management. It is the manager's job to be effective. It is the only job. In fact, the seminar carries the issue further to point out that it is any manager's true social responsibility to be effective. The pens used on the seminar have 'Any manager's true responsibility' printed on them.

THE SEMINAR IN OUTLINE

A language for outputs

Organizations introducing output orientation need a specific, tightly defined language which everyone uses. Managers who talk and work together need a common set of concepts which they share and agree on. Without such a set, objectives are often hard to arrive at and are not well connected as they are based on different ideas. Disraeli spoke for many when he said, 'If you want to converse with me, define your terms.' The theory on which this book is based has a reasonably elaborate language concerning outputs. As an example, three kinds of effectiveness are distinguished: managerial, personal and apparent. Some managers learn a great deal from having this pointed out to them. They never saw effectiveness as having three sides before. Such concepts provide a language to make discussions and analysis more precise.

Questions raised

The seminar makes salient these questions for the individual manager.

- What are my effectiveness areas now?
- Should I try to change my effectiveness areas?
- What are my measurement areas?
- What is my athority?
- How should I plan?
- What are my objectives?
- How can I improve my superior's effectiveness?
- How can I improve my co-workers' effectiveness?
- How can I improve my subordinates' effectiveness?
- Should I be doing this?
- How can I manage time better?
- How can I make decisions better?
- What can I do now?

Direct application

Participants create a number of documents to help them apply effectiveness concepts to their actual work situations. These include:

- A draft Job Effectiveness Description which serves as a basis for clarifying the manager's role in the organization.
- A rating of the manager's effectiveness by the seminar team as well as by seminar instruments.
- An Effectiveness Improvement Plan with month by month progress checks.
- A Management Style Profile, which provides an assessment of style strengths and weaknesses as well as a guide to desirable future behaviour.
- A Situational Analysis of the manager's actual work situation.
- A Team Skill Diagnosis, which provides an assessment of team skills as well as a guide to sound team operation.

DESIGN OF SEMINAR

The MES is a six-day, residential, instrumented laboratory. The seminar starts at 5.30 p.m. on the first day, and ends at 12.30 p.m. on the sixth day. This time span normally covers Sunday evening to Friday noon. Hours are long. Each morning starts promptly at 8.00 a.m. in the main room. Teams frequently work from then until past midnight. About 80 per cent of the seminar takes place in team rooms with four to eight managers, which approximates the usual span of control. Participants with close working relationships, such as superior to subordinate or co-worker to co-worker, may attend the same seminar, but are not placed together on the same team.

The MES confronts the teams with a wide variety of problems to solve, generally related to methods of achieving managerial effectiveness through the recognition of the reality of a situation and the best approach to it. Teams solve problems in their team rooms, then meet with other teams in the main room to report on their decisions and to compare their effectiveness in making them and in reaching them. As an example of the emphasis on effectiveness, one full day of the seminar is spent solely in each team reaching agreement on the effectiveness areas for each team member. Most managers on this day discover that there is more potential for contributions in their job than they had considered. They experience a new and rewarding understanding of how to be effective. They develop an increased awareness for assessing job demands. They learn to apply what they have learned at the seminar to their actual work situations. They enjoy their work more. They understand better. They are more effective.

Some of the many reasons why the MES is effective for introducing output orientation include:

* The basis of the seminar is managerial effectiveness.
* The seminar in its various activities stresses measurement.
* Team work and team objectives are given very high priority on the seminar.
* The seminar puts teams into a team appraisal mode at least once a day and sometimes this internal team critique will last for several hours.
* Non-evaluative feedback is formally taught and much practice is given.
* Each participant receives a thorough grounding in what is meant by outputs and effectiveness areas.
* The seminar stresses change as an absolutely necessary part of the manager's job.
* The seminar recognizes both the needs of the organization and the needs of the individual.
* The seminar, without question, provides a substantial 'unfreezing' effect on the manager which is a powerful conditioning for accepting any new system such as outputs.
* The seminar, while recognizing the rationality and logic of output orientation, also recognizes the inherent level of irrationality of many managers. It deals with this by demonstrating conclusively that some managers have a very high distortion level about themselves or their situation. This bridge must be crossed before talking rationally about output orientation.

THE SEMINAR AS UNFREEZING

There is that well-known model of Kurt Lewin who suggests that an analogy can be made between physical systems and human systems in terms of change. If you want to change a block of ice first you unfreeze it, then you change it, then you refreeze it in the new shape. With managers and with organizations unfreezing is needed first. This can be accomplished by the MES, then change is introduced. There is little doubt that the MES alone has a profound impact by unfreezing the organization. When a large number of managers from a single organization have participated, the seminar has a deep effect on the organization and considerably increases the readiness for change.

Unlearning must sometimes precede learning

Much light can be thrown on the nature of resistance by referring to carefully controlled experiments. What follows may be seen by some as an extreme or unusual example. It is neither. It mirrors precisely what happens concerning resistance in organizations large and small. The experiment involves a fish tank almost filled with water with a glass partition in the centre, a big fish on one side and small fishes on the other side.

Exhibit 10.1   Unfreezing needed here

In this experiment, then, the big fish is separated from its natural prey, the small fish, by a glass partition. It can see them but cannot get at them. What happens, quite routinely, is that the big fish attempts to get closer to the small fish but continually bumps into the glass partition. After doing this a few hundred times the big fish learns it will only hurt itself and stops. So far what has happened is fairly obvious. What happens next is not. The glass partition is removed, the small fish surround the big fish and the big fish makes no attempt to eat them. The big fish, in fact, dies of starvation in what is a sea of plenty. It has learned only too well that the small fish are unavailable and that if it tries to reach them pain will result. It has difficulty in unlearning what it has already learned so well. The fish has been conditioned into not being able to learn or respond to a new situation. This experiment reflects precisely what is observed routinely in planned change programmes. Management thinks it is a good idea to 'remove the glass'. This may be their wish to introduce a new climate or new methods in the organization. Other managers in the organization, most having been around for a long time with a different system, have learned only too well to 'not go after the smaller fish'. Top management may initiate training courses, wave flags or give speeches all concerning the fact that they have removed the glass but the middle managers simply do not believe it and do not respond. Their problem is that they have some unlearning to do because the prior learning was so effective. Not learning but *un*learning. In short, they need unfreezing. They need to see what is really in their current changed situation rather than what used to be there. That is the problem of middle managers; they have an unlearning problem. Top management decides it wants to introduce a new scheme, such as output orientation, for example. The attitude of middle managers is often that they do not like change or change will not work or that change is not necessary, and so they resist it. They have to unlearn that and learn the new situation. Managerial effectiveness results from a match of style to situation. Then the three key skills of an effective manager may be logically described as situational sensitivity, style flexibility and situational management skill. A manager needs situational sensitivity to diagnose a situation and either style flexibility to match the style to it or situational management skill to change the situation itself.

The situationist's prayer	*3-D Theory*
Give me the serenity to accept what cannot be changed,	Style flexibility
the courage to change what should be changed,	Situational management skill
and the wisdom to distinguish one from the other	Situational sensitivity
St Francis	

It is these three qualities, style flexibility, situational management skill and situational sensitivity, that a manager acquires through working life, usually referred to as experience, that lead to increased managerial effectiveness.

Self-awareness

A key step in improving effectiveness is in facing one's own behaviour. If a manager believes that the style being used is relationship-oriented when it is really task-oriented, this distortion can only lead to lower effectiveness. The increased awareness needed is about one's own behaviour, one's own situation and one's own effectiveness. The seminar accomplishes this by many techniques. An obvious and fairly straightforward one is to provide a variety of tests so that it is a fairly easy matter to compare the manager's own perception of style with that of others on the seminar and with the reasonably accurate test itself. Another technique is to review case studies, to decide on the styles being used and then to compare these judgements with others on the seminar. The self-awareness techniques are based very much on tested case studies and questionnaires and team discussion and agreement on results. In short, we think the best way to lower distortion level is to encourage feedback from others on the reality of the situation as presented. Obviously, this is precisely what we want to be used back home.

QUESTIONS TYPICALLY ASKED ABOUT THE SEMINAR

Managers who are interested in this seminar naturally have several questions. Here are some common ones together with their answers.

- What do I do each day?
- Is the seminar right for me?
- Will the seminar apply to me?
- What about the MES and the organization?

What do I do each day?

The seminar can be seen as having five stages in learning.

Prework

You will receive a pre-work kit. This consists of three texts, wall charts and a seminar workbook. The basic text is based on the ideas in this book. The general seminar workbook contains questionnaires, effectiveness inventories, seminar tasks, case studies, team diagnosis instruments and other learning aids. Depending on your prior knowledge, capacity and dedication, seminar pre-work generally takes from 50 to 100 hours to complete.

Days 1 and 2

You will work in teams to increase your understanding of the basic concepts relating to effectiveness. By the end of day two – Monday evening – you will have a thorough understanding of the pre-work and have a common language concerning outputs with which to approach the more complex aspects covered during the rest of the seminar.

Day 3

The effectiveness concepts are applied to a case study so their practical application is demonstrated and learned. Team-building skills are also practised and reviewed. At the end of the third day team members evaluate the performance of their teams. Teams usually engage in open and candid discussion on their performance. The skills to identify ineffective performance and to discuss it openly are rapidly built.

Day 4

This day is spent on effectiveness. You are provided with a sharp and objective view of your individual role. You also receive the practical skills needed to define your own job and those of other managers in output terms. You will also get the confidence and practical skills needed to define effectiveness areas in an open team setting.

Day 5

The fifth day is spent on managerial behaviour. The objectives of this day are:

- To provide you with useful feedback on your own effectiveness.
- To improve your skill in appraising the effectiveness of others.
- To improve your skill in giving useful feedback on effectiveness.
- To improve your skill in receiving feedback on effectiveness.

Day 6

The last day concentrates on situation management. You will be provided with an opportunity to consider what personal changes you could make which would improve your managerial effectiveness in your on-the-job situation. You will also learn to give important practical guidance in a team setting. If the seminar is an in-company one then a senior manager will attend to receive feedback from seminar participants.

Post-seminar

This is on-the-job application: After the MES, you will use the conceptual and printed tools the 3-D MES has provided. You may use them to redefine your position in output terms, to work with subordinates, co-workers and your superior on objectives and also to change your less effective behaviour, or you may decide to change your work situation.

It has been determined conclusively that the seminar effects are magnified when the actual work team meets in the months after the seminar to apply the seminar ideas to the work team itself. The whole point in management training is what is called transfer of training and the transfer is greatly facilitated when a superior and all immediate subordinates sit down to discuss their effectiveness areas and other things that impinge on their managerial effectiveness.

Is the seminar right for me?

Some managers are concerned about whether the seminar is right for them. Some managers are concerned that their education is limited, they have not read a book in years and simply wonder whether they can handle the concepts. In some countries the seminar is regularly used with those with only four years' education. These participants are rather apprehensive but they find that by the second or third day they are well into the swing of things. Help can be provided by prior participants or others before the seminar so that they can work through the book with someone with more knowledge. This person does not give the answers but rather explains the concepts. The truth of the matter is that those who feel they may not be up to it learn something important from the seminar, that they are up to it and could expect much more of themselves. Eighty per cent of the seminar time is spent in team rooms. And, the important thing, if someone does not understand a concept or a term or an idea being developed, they can always ask someone else on the team. The seminar is not an examination, it is a developmental helpful experience. Some managers are concerned about their style and their effectiveness and are worried about it being exposed to others. All personal material of this kind is the property of the team and never leaves the team room. Often teams bring out team results on various things but none of this is ever identified with specific individuals. Your team members will know your effectiveness well because they have worked with you for a week. Also, they will tell you what they think of your effectiveness as you will tell them about theirs. But this is the limit of it. There is never ever any feedback to management or to other teams. Never. Again, development not assessment. In any case, the theme of the seminar is that team members help each other to improve.

Teams are normally of from four to eight members. On a public seminar team membership is assigned randomly. On an in-company basis the key rule is that no one on the team has a working relationship with others on the team on a day-to-day basis. The whole idea of the seminar is to give a chance to a trial for developing team skills, natural feedback, consensus testing, complete resolution and many other things. This is best done with a stranger rather than with someone who you are working with every day.

Will the seminar apply to me?

There is much evidence that the seminar has wide applicability. This evidence relates to levels, functions, ages, types of organization and countries.

The use of the MES across levels
The seminar has a demonstrated effectiveness at all managerial and supervisory levels. General Motors, for instance, uses the seminar from plant manager level down to general foreman level. When the seminar is used as part of an organization development programme it is obvious that all levels of management and sometimes supervision attend the same seminar. In any organization the identical seminar can be attended by the CEO and the lowest-level supervisor. The absolutely identical seminar is used for CEOs, generals, admirals, high and low-level civil servants, line crew supervisors, bottling line supervisors in a brewery, supervisors of cowhands on a ranch, PhDs and those with only a few years of any education. One series of seminars was attended by the middle and top management of the largest weapon system designer in the world, about 3000 employees and half had their PhDs. In some companies it is common for different levels to be attending the same seminar. The reason that all this is seen to work is that the seminar teaches basic truths about management effectiveness which, simply, are applicable to all managerial positions. Nothing more than that. The concepts apply broadly.

The use of the MES across functions
The seminar has obvious application across all management functions. Some organizations send their top 250 managers and in one case more than their top 1700 managers, through the full six-day residential seminar. Most types of functions naturally need to attend. No adverse effects, by functions, have been reported. Sometimes the

seminar is used to train a particular function only. Examples include production, sales, and in one case the administrative function of the head office.

The use of the MES across ages

Age, young or old, is no deterrent to the effectiveness of the managerial effectiveness seminar. Managers of 21 and up to the age of 75 have participated. In one seminar in a family company the parents, aged 72 and 75, attended the seminar along with their children of about 40. An older manager of 64 came to a seminar staff member at the end of one seminar and said: 'I only wish I'd taken this many years ago.' He was not saying it was not effective for him rather he was saying it could have been even more effective earlier. Age does not limit learning about managerial effectiveness. One's perceptions of one's age and what it means might. So, you only have two more years on the job. They could be a very important two years in leaving your best mark and in training your successor in the best way. The managerial effectiveness seminar can help. There is no room for the argument 'These managers will retire in about 18 months, why try and develop them'? One can do a lot, either way, in 18 months.

The use of the MES across types of organization

Broadly, the seminar has been used to improve the effectiveness in organizations as diverse as production organizations, marketing organizations, military organizations, government organizations and virtually any other type you can think of.

The MES has been used successfully by groups as diverse as Imperial Chemical Industry directors, General Motors plant managers, 35 employees of a 100 employee bakery, 20 employees of a 125-strong brewery and the top 200–400 supervisors and managers in many firms and government departments in the United States, Canada, United Kingdom and many other countries.

Many organizations have used the full one-week residential MES to introduce management by objectives to as many as 250 managers. Others have used it for higher numbers, and one bank used it to introduce management by objectives programme to over 1700 managers.

The use of the MES across countries

The MES has been conducted in these countries: Argentina, Australia, Belgium, Brazil, Canada, Eire, Ethiopia, Finland, Germany, Guyana, Hong Kong, Jamaica, Kenya, Mexico, Netherlands, Norway, Singapore, South Africa, Spain, Sweden, Trinidad and Tobago, United Kingdom, United States of America, Venezuela and Zimbabwe.

As an example of transnational application one of our staff members recently conducted two MESs back to back in Ethiopia. They wanted two, and back to back, because of the overwhelming response to prior ones there. The seminar was attended, in the main, by the most senior government and military officials of this Marxist country. About a month later the absolutely identical seminar was conducted by the same staff member for the CEO and supervisors of one of the largest cattle ranches in the USA. Both seminars were very well received as suiting the specific needs of participants.

Seminar availability
The seminar is available on an in-company basis in any country at any time. The only limiting factor is language. The seminar is now translated into these languages: Dutch, Finnish, German, Norwegian, Portuguese, Spanish and Swedish. When the seminar is introduced into a new language area and is not yet translated, more time is then taken on pre-work and some of it is done through lectures by those who speak the local language and the main room talks are subject to immediate translation. Naturally, in team rooms, the local language may be used. Public seminars are conducted in several countries and, while it is better to start with in-company seminars, some may wish to attend public seminars instead.

What about the MES and the organization?

The MES is used either as management development where the focus of change is the individual manager or for organization development where the focus of change is the organization as a whole. Whether used for management development or organization development the MES is best used on an in-company basis. That is, all participants are members of the same company, the top person of the unit or the CEO attends the last day of the seminar and the seminars are normally conducted by in-company trainers. All this can help very much in transferring the things learned on the seminar into the organization itself.

When large companies use the seminar simply as management development, they do not link it to any later team building or make any particular attempt to transfer the things learned back to the job. Their general assumption is that the climate of the firm can produce the necessary follow-up needed and what the seminar really has to do is to get managers unfrozen enough to engage their work situation on their own. However, the seminar was originally designed as a first step in a two (or more) stage organization development programme.

A very common use is to see the seminar as the unfreezing stage and then other activities leading to a change stage and then to a flexibility maintenance stage. The most common next stage is the team meeting of Chapter 6 which takes the actual work team of superior and all immediate subordinates for several days to look at their situation in an open, candid way and to agree to change it, by consensus. The team meeting is designed to capture the spirit and ideas of the MES and transfer them to the actual work setting.

A typical in-company MES

The typical in-company MES starts on Sunday at 5.30 p.m. and ends on Friday at 12.30. It is normally held at a rural hotel which most or all participants would not know. The seminar size depends upon the organization design but often is six teams of about seven people each. At the first in-company MES some of the top team will be there. The CEO may well be on the first seminar as a participant but if not would attend, in any case, Friday at 10.30 and give a problem concerning the organization for teams to present ideas about. The usual problem concerns improving productivity but it might be introducing change or how best to introduce a systemic change such as organization redesign or management by objectives. All the comments of all the managerial teams at the seminar are distributed to all the managers of the organization. This feedback produced by the CEO's session at each seminar is used as raw data for diagnosing the ills and opportunities for increasing effectiveness of the organization. The CEO always finds that the experience is enjoyable and realizes that it must be done much more in a variety of other ways.

Internal staff

Most MESs are run by company staff members. Sometimes these staff members are drawn from the personnel and training departments and sometimes from the line or other staff functions. As a general rule we find that our post-seminar reaction forms show higher results when the seminars are conducted by internal staff even though they were never trainers.

One bank trained fifteen staff members to conduct seminars and all of these staff members had been branch bank managers at one time in their career. They all started as cashiers. They were excellent trainers.

Low seminar costs

Seminar costs are low compared to most management seminars of similar length for a variety of reasons.

- The optimum, not maximum, number on the seminar is 42 and the maximum is 72. The reason that this high number can be maintained is that 80 per cent of the seminar takes place in team rooms. Lecturing is nominal. Teams teach themselves.
- For even the largest seminar, a maximum of only two staff members are needed.
- The seminar is highly structured and this makes it easy for client staff to conduct the seminars after only one as participant and co-training on three.
- Some organizations purchase the seminar design outright for use within their organization and this clearly leads to a lowering of average unit cost.
- Some companies prefer to print the seminar material and pay a royalty and we allow this.

A typical in-company start-up

Typically a company will start by conducting a trial of two MES back-to-back as a pilot study, using consultant staff. Two or more of the senior management team should be among them. These managers then meet as a committee to make an evaluation and report on the relevance of the programme to the company. If the report is favourable, the MES is continued incompany for other managers.

In the interests of increasing output orientation you owe it to yourself and your organization to look further into the availability and suitability of the MES.

ACTION STEPS

Your position may be such as to not allow you to gauge all these action steps but it is worthwhile to consider them.

1. Should I attend an MES?
2. Should the company use the MES as an initial training and unfreezing step?
3. Should we attempt to design our own MES?
4. Is it essential that our senior managers participate?
5. Should all or most of our middle managers participate?
6. Should we arrange an incompany trial?
7. Should we find out how to access it?

11 Organization-wide use of the JED

If everyone else would agree to move, we would be the first to change.

Unknown

The form of organisation should be such as to allow or induce the continuous coordination of the experience of men. Legitimate authority flows from coordination; not coordination from authority.

Mary Parker Follett

Large and small organizations, but particularly larger ones, tend to be riddled with what might be called competing systems or competing bases of systems. The accountants decide the budgeting systems, the mainframe people design the management information system, the personnel department designs the job evaluation method, and so on. They all too often start from completely different philosophies about how the organization is to be run. The concept of outputs gives them a common philosophy on which all such systems should be based. In short, if you truly want to create an output oriented organization, work very hard on linking the main systems around the concept of outputs. This linking is accomplished through the job effectiveness description.

WHAT SYSTEMS CAN BE LINKED TO THE JED?

Systems that be linked to the JED include:

- Basic corporate philosophy
- Management information system
- Objectives
- Appraisal
- Budgets
- Job specification

- Selection
- Job evaluation
- Organization design
- Teamwork
- Rewards

The JED and basic corporate philosophy

The JED contains the key elements needed to focus an organization as a whole on outputs. Thus the JED can form the basis of basic corporate philosophy. The organization decides to put outputs at the centre of the organization and to build other systems around it.

The JED and the management information system

The JED contains one or more measurement areas for each effectiveness area. These measurement areas, then, are the most important ways in which a manager should actually be measured. It should be obvious that the management information system (MIS) must be designed around the measurements that managers want. Very often the MIS is designed somewhat independently of what managers want and rather what those in control of the mainframe think they should have. This sets up two competing measurement systems where only one is needed. It is obvious which one is needed. In those organizations with too many so-called knowledge workers one finds that senior management sometimes actually believes these knowledge workers should design the MIS to suit what they would like to know about the managers and their performance. If what they want to know is not what the manager needs to know, and not what the team has reached agreement on, something must be wrong somewhere. So, if you want to improve your MIS, use your JED as the start and end point.

The JED and objectives

The JED contains measurement areas on which 100 per cent of objectives in an organization should be set. No other method is needed or should be used. While not clearly enough understood, it is obvious that objectives for managerial positions arise by one method only. This method consists of putting agreed numbers on measurement areas. Suppose a manager has an output of 'swimming pool utilization' and the measurement area is the load factor on the pool expressed in terms of the number of hours when at least twenty people are in it. The objective is obviously derived by agreeing a number of hours of load. In short, objectives are derived by putting numbers on measurement areas. This can be the only possible way. In the early, very crude attempts at management by objectives people thought that it was an independent new system with independent and different ideas. This is not the case. If one wants to have objectives for managers or to design any kind of management by objectives scheme, one must clearly start with outputs.

The JED and appraisal

Through a review of the objectives based upon its measurement areas, the JED provides the soundest possible basis for appraisal. With an agreed JED created, based firmly on outputs, no organization needs a separate set of criteria for an appraisal form. Managers should be appraised on only one factor: that is, the extent to which they achieve the output requirements of their position. These output requirements are expressed very clearly by the objectives based on measurement areas which in turn are based on effectiveness areas. No one needs to know whether a manager excels in initiative. The organization needs to know whether or not the manager achieved the output requirements of the position.

The JED and budgets

Budgets are related to the objectives based on the measurement areas that the JED contains. This is the only possible basis. Budgets can be based on an input orientation or an output orientation. Those budgets based on input orientation take the general view that the main point of budgeting is to keep the organization ticking over in a predetermined way. Those based on output orientation deal very clearly with the issue of 'how much is needed to achieve that objective stated in output terms?' The change of budgets to output orientation can be a long and difficult task. It is not essential that budgets be 100 per cent output oriented still to have an output organization, however, it is obviously very desirable to have them as output-oriented as possible. When budgets remain input-oriented what managers tend to do is to ignore them more and more and see budgeting as an independent system to suit other parties, not themselves.

The JED and job specification

The term job specification is somewhat loosely defined but it is normally taken to mean what the job is and what it involves. The very last thing an organization needs is any job specification other than the JED itself. The JED contains all the elements needed for a complete job specification. If necessary, an appendix might be added which lists the personal qualities most likely to lead to the attainment of the outputs specified in the JED. This could only be done when there is factual knowledge about what these qualities might be. In most organizations there is little such factual knowledge except where specialized technical expertise is required.

The JED and selection

The JED contains the essential elements needed to write an advertisement for a position or to aid in selection for a position. Sometimes job specifications are created for advertisements. They are not needed. The JED, perhaps slightly rewritten, is quite sufficient. Would you not have liked it when you were hired for your most recent job to have had a very clear JED in front of you describing your outputs with precision, how you will be measured and your authority specified? Obviously, many organizations are already doing this, but too many are not. Managers are attracted to output-based advertisements. Several have reported that it was the clarity of the advertisement that most attracted them to the job. Others have said that the explicitness of the advertisement made them realise that it is not the kind of job they wanted at all . . . so, everyone saved time and money.

The JED and job evaluation

The JED contains all the information necessary for job evaluation. There is no need for yet another job description to be written by consultants based upon different principles than outputs. There are many proprietary and non-proprietary job evaluation schemes. In all, about eight are reasonably well recognized by experts in the area. The majority use a set of criteria which might include level of responsibility, unsocial hours, number supervised and many, many others. Points are assigned to these to indicate relative weight and then each job is evaluated on a point basis and from this the salary band for the job is derived. One very interesting research study compared most of the well-known methods across a wide variety of jobs and this showed that no matter what the proposed criteria, the rank order of ratings of the jobs turned out to be very similar. What this means is that the rating methods, while appearing different, are really not very different.

There is one very simple method of job evaluation based on outputs. This is known as the Reddin Outputs Method. The method involves as many people as possible in looking at successive pairs of JEDs and based on what those descriptions contain, asks the simple question, 'Which of these two jobs has greater value to the organization?' This leads to a natural rank order of jobs from which the appropriate salary level is derived. While this method is important in itself, the key point about it is, again, that the basic philosophy of the method is outputs and this integrates with everything the firm does. This method is to be described in Reddin, W.J., *Pay for Outputs* (Gower, forthcoming).

The JED and organization design

The creation of JEDS can lead directly to ideas concerning re-organization. When one has a one-over-one situation it sometimes occurs that the top position has the authority and the deputy position has essentially none. The problem is not only that the deputy is there at all but also that though this job barely exists it is often valued quite highly in monetary terms when it perhaps should be devalued to the level of a senior secretary. A good rule in thinking about JEDs and organization design is: If two people are responsible for the same thing, one of them is not needed. Whenever JEDs are constructed on a team basis and the contributions of each team member to the team's output is carefully considered, it sometimes becomes obvious that a position should be eliminated or moved and sometimes that a position should be added. All of these can be seen as organization design issues which the JED can help highlight.

The JED and teamwork

While team work is not a system in the normal sense it can be seen as one and there is little doubt that the JED helps enormously in developing it. Sports teams and jazz bands have very clear outputs, measurement areas and authority. Those involved enjoy being part of the organization and, at most times, do it simply for fun. Why not use these ideas to design our work teams as well? A superb weekend for a team, after they understand what outputs really are, is to derive and agree upon the JED for the top member and all team members and the team as a whole. The more obvious objective of such an event is to increase role clarification and finish with JEDs being agreed. However, the latent and far more important objective is to build a team around the concept of outputs.

The JED and rewards

Rewards, or merit pay, can be seen as that extra payment, usually given annually, for superior performance. Superior performance can only be judged in the light of objectives being exceeded as a function of the manager's own efforts. Needless to say, the objectives are based on the JED. The JED cannot be used to decide the total amount of money to be used for rewards, such as 10 per cent of total salary base, or how much an individual manager should receive, but it does give a basis for deciding, relatively, which manager should be rewarded over others.

USING JEDS

Chapter 13 shows how a large organization used the JED to integrate many of its systems. In doing so it had to overcome many of the problems that commonly arise when a serious attempt is made to integrate systems around the concept of outputs. These problems are easily recognizable and acknowledging them openly is one method to help overcome them. They include:

● Some systems based on inputs
● Some systems entrenched
● Some systems independently controlled
● Some systems competing with each other
● Some systems inconsistent with each other
● Resistance in those who control the systems

There is little doubt that a superb way to overcome resistance and to spread the idea of the common philosophy of outputs is through the

Job Effectiveness Description

Job
reference _____

Draft date and
draft number _____

Effectiveness areas and measurement areas

1.   Effectiveness area

   1.1 Measurement area

      1.1.1 Objective

2.   Effectiveness area

   2.1 Measurement area

      2.1.1 Objective

   2.2 Measurement area

      2.2.1 Objective

   2.3 Measurement area

      2.3.1 Objective

3.   Effectiveness area

4.   Effectiveness area

Authority areas

1.   Decide . . .

2.   Decide . . .

3.   Decide . . .

4.   Decide . . .

Exhibit 11.1   Uses of the JED

Five systems based
on particular elements
of the JED

Six systems based
on the JED as a
whole

**Management
Information
System**

Based solely on
the measurement
area

Corporate Philosophy

The JED as a whole
expresses the entire
output philosophy of
the organization

Job Evaluation

The JED as a whole is
used for paired com-
parisons to evaluate
the outputs of one job
against the other for
basic pay structure

Objectives

Created solely by
putting numbers
on measurement
areas

Job Specification

The JED as a whole is
the whole job speci-
fication needed

Budgets

Created only with
objectives based
on outputs in
mind

Selection

The JED as a whole
should be used for
selection by placing
it, in possible abbre-
viated form, as the
advertisement

Appraisal

Based only by the
extent to which
objectives are
achieved

Rewards

These should be
based only upon
objectives which
are achieved well
above normal

Teamwork

The JED as a whole
is created by the
team and this builds
teamwork

Organization Design

The JED as a whole
helps you to identify
overlaps and underlaps
in the organization
and linkages needed

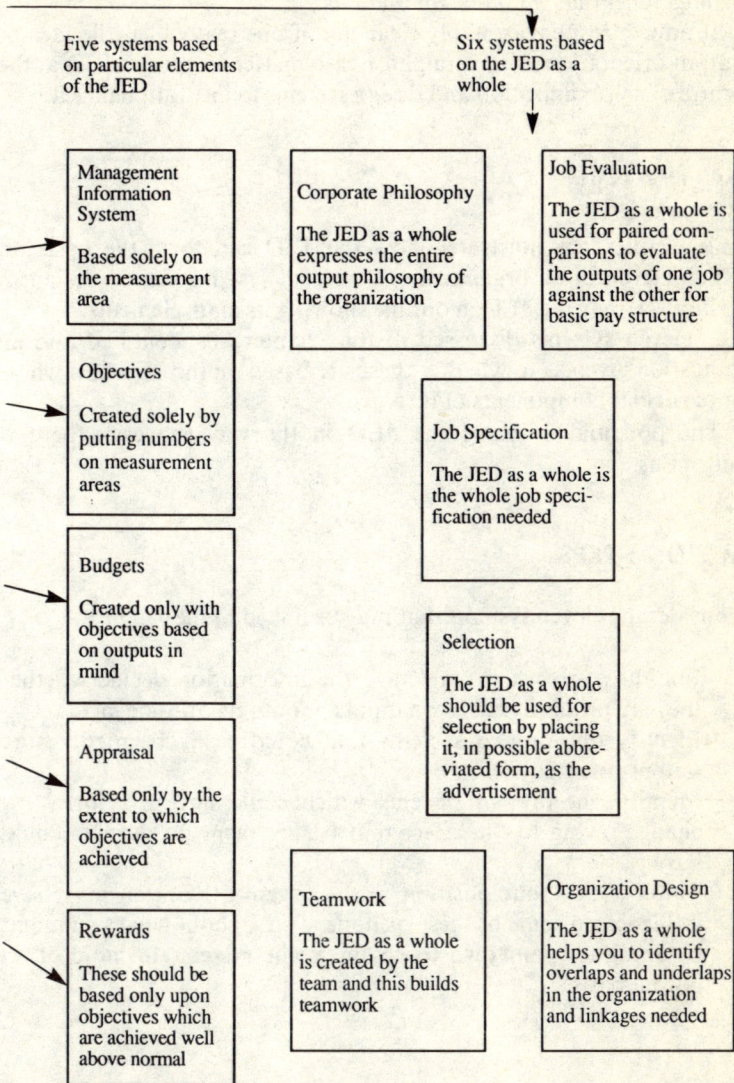

These are the eleven systems which may be linked directly to the
JED.

Exhibit 11.1   Uses of the JED (concluded)

managerial effectiveness seminar described in Chapter 10.

Imagine that this single document, the JED, could be used as the conceptual basis for most important internal management systems. What a relief that would be for all of us.

It now must be reasonably clear that if one really likes the idea of output orientation it is a straighforward matter to put the JED at the centre of an organization and design systems to institutionalize it.

IN SUMMARY

This chapter has illustrated how the JED can form the basis on which eleven of an organization's internal systems can be designed. Exhibit 11.1 gives a JED in outline showing its main elements.
The eleven systems discussed in this chapter are identified and an indication given as to whether these are based on the JED as a whole or particular components of it.

The potential of using the JED in the way suggested here is enormous.

ACTION STEPS

Consider the eleven systems that may be linked to the JED.

1. For those on which you have the information decide whether they are primarily based on inputs or outputs or some mix.
2. Identify one or two systems that could easily be made more output-oriented.
3. Identify one or two systems which could have a priority for change owing to the effect that basing them on outputs could have.
4. Think about your position in the organization; you may have influence on some of these or none. Think about what you might be doing on your own to change some systems to more of an output basis.

12 Plan to become an output-oriented manager

The secret of success in life is for a man to be ready for his opportunity when it comes.

Benjamin Disraeli

I will pay more for the ability to deal with people than any other ability under the sun.

John D. Rockefeller

This chapter contains 47 specific recommendations on which you might act. All the recommendations are raised with only one thing in mind and that is how to help you achieve an even higher output orientation. As a start, you might like to read over each of the headings to get a general idea of the suggestions made. You may not be able to take action on most of them in the short term but you can check some now that you think you should and want to accomplish soon. Many of these recommendations arise directly from earlier chapters. For these a reference is given. Other recommendations such as those concerning time management and reading are not discussed elsewhere in the book.

At the end of the chapter is an Action Checklist. You will find this a handy method of making decisions concerning these recommendations.

THE RECOMMENDATIONS

The 47 recommendations fall into these ten sections:

1 Basic recommendations
2 Meetings with others about effectiveness
3 Improving your decision-making
4 Giving work away
5 Recommendations for changes in your behaviour
6 Reading

7 Time management
8 Training and development
9 Fundamental questions
10 Other changes for you to decide

Most of the recommendations are directed to the middle or senior manager, and may not relate to your position. If so, you may revise some of them to suit your situation. If you are the CEO or on the top team of a reasonably autonomous unit, there will be many additional things you will want to do to help introduce high output management throughout your organization. Similarly, if you are in personnel or training or an internal or external consultant, other ideas will come to mind about how you might improve your effectiveness and that of others.

BASIC RECOMMENDATIONS

The five basics for the output-oriented manager are effectiveness areas, measurement areas, authority, resources and objectives. In working to use these five basics to improve your output orientation you are invited to consider these recommendations:

1 Decide your effectiveness areas
2 Decide your measurement areas
3 Determine your authority areas
4 Create your job effectiveness description
5 Burn your existing job description
6 Decide your objectives
7 Establish your resources
8 Create your first objective planning form
9 Create an objective planning form for all of your measurement areas

Decide your effectiveness areas

You will want to decide your effectiveness areas as soon as possible. Perhaps you have a very good idea of them now or perhaps you think you do, but really do not. It is important to you in achieving higher output if you have a clear understanding of what your outputs really are. (See Chapters 1 and 2).

Decide your measurement areas

Your will most probably want to improve your measurement areas so that you can come to grips with your outputs and effectiveness areas. Improving your measurement areas may be as straightforward as having someone count what is already in your files. You may have to buy your own mini-computer if your company has not supplied one. There is no need to wait for those promises of mainframe support which always take longer to come than is planned and which, so often, do not provide the information you want. In short, you should take action yourself soon on deciding your measurement areas. (See Chapter 3).

Determine your authority areas

You will want to determine your authority. It may take longer than you think. It will not, suddenly, all become clear from a single meeting, it is usually done over time. Also, in determining your authority you may well be changing it by acquiring some or giving some to others. All this also takes time. After working on your outputs, your measurement areas and your authority you are in a position at least to make a first draft of your job effectiveness description. (See Chapter 4).

Create your job effectiveness description

After deciding your effectiveness areas and measurement areas and determining your authority you are in a position to create your job effectiveness description. (See Chapter 5).

Burn your existing job description

It is recommended that you burn your existing job description. As you well know, it is no use to you at all and you never refer to it. For too many managers it possesses an almost magical power. They think that by having it that they have something. Actually, they have nothing. As you know, it was probably created as part of a job evaluation scheme and has little to do with your outputs. If you are reluctant to burn your job description you might consider why. If you really think it does mean something, attach it as Appendix 'A' to your JED and never refer to it.

Decide your objectives

Make (at least) a first draft of your objectives for some future time-period. You may have well developed objectives already but they may be rather more on the input side than they should be. If this is your first time at setting objectives you may find you are too ambitious. Those who want to become output-oriented managers, quite naturally, set more ambitious objectives for themselves. This should be true in your case. The issue remains, however, that the best objectives are the realistic ones, though still high enough to recognize your attempt to do better than expected. If your environment is highly volatile or you are new to setting objectives you may want to use the bands of objective ideas. That is, use three numbers instead of one; one representing a very high attainment, one a planned attainment and one a low attainment. (See Chapter 7).

Establish your resources

As part of setting your objectives you will want to make sure you have the resources needed to achieve them. There will be something of an interplay between the resources you have, or might get, and the objectives you have set or might change. Where resources are relatively flexible an opportunity exists for having an array of objectives to suit an array of resource levels.

Create your first objective planning form

The objective planning form is simple to use and highly practical. It is reasonably certain that once you start to use it you will wonder how you did without it before. The form has been very well tested exactly as it is in many different types of organization and it should suit you very well. Learning to use it well is an important skill on your way to achieving higher output orientation. (See Chapter 9).

Create an objective planning form for all of your measurement areas

It is usual to create an objective planning form for each measurement area. If you want to measure an effectiveness area in two or more different ways you will have two or more different sets of action steps to reach your objective and this would create the need for two or more objective planning forms. (See Chapter 9).

MEETINGS WITH OTHERS ABOUT EFFECTIVENESS

We have all been to meetings which were useless. Properly designed, however, meetings with a shared set of concepts and a common language and an intent to improve effectiveness can only be useful. This book has provided you with a clear common language to use with others in your search for greater effectiveness. The meetings referred to here are all work-oriented and highly focused on improving effectiveness. Here are the recommendations:

10   Meet with your co-workers and superior together on effectiveness areas
11   Meet with superior alone on effectiveness areas
12   Meet with all of your subordinates together on effectiveness areas
13   Meet with your co-workers and superior together on JEDs
14   Meet with your superior alone on your JED
15   Meet with all of your subordinates together on JEDs
16   Hold a one-to-one with each of your subordinates
17   Hold a one-to-one with each of your co-workers

These meetings may be combined in various ways. It is a very good idea to stay with the sequence given, however. (See Chapter 6).

Meet with your co-workers and superior together on effectiveness areas

It is relatively rare for a superior and all subordinates to sit down for a day – and sometimes longer – to discuss how their system is designed in terms of outputs. It can be highly productive. It helps everyone become more objective and to have a common understanding of the game they are playing, the team composition and the rules. It is not a discussion of performance, it is a discussion of how are we actually designed now and what are we trying to do.

Only after you have met with your co-workers and superior together on effectiveness areas is it a good idea to have a one-to-one with your superior on them. If you do this in reverse order the effectiveness areas brought to the team meeting will tend to be considered as 'given' and the superior put in the role of the expert judge to sort things out rather than the team being seen as the natural vehicle for this task. You may well combine this meeting on effectiveness areas with a discussion of measurement areas and authority and, even possibly, objectives but it is a good idea to keep these things separate as, if you get the outputs wrong, everything else is wrong. (See Chapter 6).

Meet with your superior alone on effectiveness areas

After the team of which you are a member has met on the effectiveness areas of the unit, the top member, yourself and your co-workers, you would want to move naturally to meeting individually with your superior alone on your effectiveness areas. (See Chapter 6).

Meet with all of your subordinates together on effectiveness areas

Establishing clear effectiveness areas is best done top-down. It is impossible, in fact, to do it bottom-up. So, as suggested in previous points, meet first with the unit of which you are a member and then with your superior, and only after that, have a meeting with all of your immediate subordinates together on effectiveness areas. At this meeting you are, of course, in the role of superior just as your superior was in the meeting you previously attended. (See Chapter 6).

Meet with your co-workers and superior together on JEDs

By now you will be becoming an expert on outputs and it is the time to meet with the unit of which you are a member to work on the fine detail of measurement areas and authority. (See Chapter 6).

Meet with your superior alone on your JED

By now you will be quite an expert on outputs and JEDs and it is time to clarify your own with your superior. (See Chapter 6).

Meet with all of your subordinates together on JEDs

In the same way that you met as a unit member with the other unit members and the top member on all the JEDs, it is important that you hold an identical type of meeting with the unit of which you are the top member. The one-to-one with each of your subordinates will then be designed by you and the particular subordinates involved depending upon the emerging needs. (See Chapter 6).

Hold a one-to-one with each of your subordinates

You have held some one-to-ones with each of your subordinates but probably not too many, if any, on outputs, effectiveness, JEDs and what support you can give them to help them become a high output manager. The meeting might be based on help needed from you to achieve the subordinates' outputs, it might be further detailed clarification of some aspect of the JED. (See Chapter 6).

Hold a one-to-one with each of your co-workers

Good organizations work well from the top down and the bottom up. Even better organizations also work well laterally. It could almost be a general rule that not enough time is spent by managers on meeting with co-workers to settle problems before they even start. A key question when working with co-workers is 'How can I improve your effectiveness without lowering my own?'. (See Chapter 6).

IMPROVING YOUR DECISION-MAKING

You can learn a great deal from thinking about the decisions you have made and the ones you should make. Effectiveness can never be achieved unless the right decisions are made. Decisions are a manager's stock-in-trade. A lack of decision-making can lead to prolonged low effectiveness. Moreover, managers, in reviewing their decisions, often find that most could have been made months or years before. Timing is obviously as important as accuracy. At any one point in time a manager usually has several important decisions that should be made. On some, action is postponed for good reasons; on others, it is postponed for perhaps no reason at all. There is no value in making decisions hastily or too far in advance. But there is often no point in postponing them too long either. Managers might well prepare a list of all the decisions facing them. This is not the usual list of things to do – it is a decision-list of decisions. The list should have the most pressing decision, which is not necessarily the most important, at the top. This list can be used as a guide to action. There is, however, a great temptation to make the list and then ignore it, or make it and then start with the easiest decision rather than the most pressing one. You are invited to consider these recommendations:

18 Make a list of your decisions outstanding
19 Make one or more decisions now that you have been postponing
20 Analyse your past decisions
21 Make a decision list with timings

Make a list of your decisions outstanding

A list of your decisions outstanding might surprise you. For some managers it runs to several pages and it is something of a shock. The realization arises that a lower-than-appropriate output occurs not because bad decisions were made but because few decisions were made. Sometimes doing nothing can cause the problem to disappear but that is not the general case. If your list is very long, you will have to start asking yourself some obvious questions.

Make one or more decisions now that you have been postponing

As you make the list suggested in the prior suggestion it will almost certainly become clear to you that some decision that you have been postponing could and should be made immediately.

Analyse your past decisions

It is well worth your time analysing your past decisions. A key question relates to timing. Were some or most decisions made too late or even made too early? Do you have a built-in tendency to avoid making decisions which can be revealed by analysing your past ones? Also analyse which decisions were correct in the light of later events and which ones were clearly incorrect. Analyse the incorrect ones in more detail to attempt to discover what flaws you had in your decision-making. For instance, do you characteristically think you have all the facts when, in truth, you do not?

Make a decision list with timings

For as many decisions as possible make a list of when you think each should be made and do what you can to stick to the list. (See Chapter 4).

GIVING WORK AWAY

One method of becoming an output-oriented manager is to give some of your work away thus leaving you with more time to concentrate on all those important things you want to do but cannot find time to complete. The recommendations made here include:

22 Stop doing some things
23 Give some parts of your work away
24 Give your in-basket to your secretary
25 Remove your desk from your office

Stop doing some things

Make a list of the jobs you do which probably don't need to be done at all. This list is sometimes quite difficult to make on your own and you may need some help with it. Too many managers unconsciously create unnecessary work for themselves, and therefore, for others. They see their job as filling in time. Are there some jobs you could stop doing?

Give some parts of your work away

An effective manager asks of every piece of work that comes up, 'Who below me could handle this?' A manager is not worked out of a job this way – but is worked into the *right* job. A manager may be rid of routine administration and do more on planning, liaison with other divisions or the more effective development of the subordinates.

Give your in-basket to your secretary

Do you spend too much time rummaging through your in-basket? Are papers brought to you when you want them or do you let others push their expectations onto you when they want to? Are you somehow seduced into thinking that a full in-basket means you are working at making the right decisions? It is very likely indeed that your secretary has all the capacity necessary to maintain your in-basket for you, let you know what is in it, and make many decisions concerning it. Why not put it to a trial?

Remove your desk from your office

This may seem to be a dramatic proposal, and it is. When you read Chapter 14 you will see what happened to a CEO when he did just this. About the only bad outcome from having a trial at removing your desk is your red face when you decide to put it in again. The modern and ancient desk for managers has no real function except to distance one from visitors to the office and, for the very dim manager, to give an aura of self-importance. Look around your office now and think what could easily be moved out. Yes, most of it. You will have a shock when you come in the next morning when you find there is no desk and no comfortable in-basket. You will have to start thinking what your job really is rather than thinking the in-basket should drive you. It will not be there to do it.

RECOMMENDATIONS FOR CHANGES IN YOUR BEHAVIOUR

All the recommendations given in this chapter involve some changes in your behaviour but recommendations in this section concentrate on what are generally considered the self-behaviour changes rather than management changes. The recommendations include:

26   Make a risk-taking list
27   Experiment with new behaviour
28   Write a letter to yourself about what changes you will make
29   Walk the shop
30   Investigate ways to change your technology

Make a risk-taking list

A few managers are imprudent and take too many risks. This, however, is the exception. Most managers do not take enough risks. Some managers with a good level of performance do not take enough risks simply because they want to maintain the existing level of performance with some certainty rather than attempting to get higher performance through some risk-taking. So, make a list of what risks you might take and think about whether you should make some decisions concerning them. Some advice from someone who knows you and your position would be helpful.

Experiment with new behaviour

Do you hold too many meetings? Do you hold too few meetings? Do you put relationships first? Or do you put tasks first? Do you spend too much time behind your desk in your office or too much chatting over tea or coffee? Do you make plans that are too detailed or do you make plans that are not detailed enough? Make a decision to experiment with some particular change in some particular behaviour.

Obviously, the best behaviour to start with is that which will not lead to a serious lowering of output if the behaviour change turns out to be incorrect. Another criteria for choosing which behaviour to start with is how soon you can get feedback on the results of your change.

Write a letter to yourself about what changes you will make

Write a letter to yourself and, on the envelope, identify one or two dates on which it should be reviewed and the date the contents might be evaluated. This letter will concern things that you think you should do. This chapter provides many such ideas and you will have many more of your own. The purpose of writing the letter is to encourage you to think about changes more than you might otherwise and to give you a chance for self-review. The output-oriented manager is candid about effectiveness in self and others. This manager, quite routinely, differentiates and uses such concepts as apparent effectiveness, personal effectiveness and managerial effectiveness. Based on your understanding of this book, you now have a good idea of what effectiveness is. As indicated in Chapter 3, a good method of improving performance is to obtain or give feedback on performance. That is what being candid about effectiveness leads to.

Walk the shop

Do you get out of your office enough? Do you regularly walk the rounds? Do you make plans to do it very frequently? One CEO of a 35,000-person company spent forty days one year in having face-to-face meetings with groups composing every employee in the company. Yes, it was thought to be that important to achieve a higher output. The idea was clearly the correct one. If that CEO could spend that much time, how much time might you spend? Climate is becoming to be seen more and more as an important variable in improving performance in organizations. Walking the shop quite definitely creates a higher output climate.

Investigate ways to change your technology

Briefly, technology is the way work can be done to ensure that effectiveness results. Within limits, a manager is able to change technology – that is, able to change the things the manager places emphasis on. This then presents one of the most important opportunities to improve effectiveness. Some authority is needed to do this, of course, and it is more likely to be found in managers at the top of the organization or in firms that have a deliberate policy of position flexibility. Effectiveness areas are particularly susceptible to change when the job is new, or the manager is new in it, or when a crisis has developed, or when managers operate as a team and are thus willing to engage in flexible job-trading. Some of the many things that a manager can consider when modifying the technology are:

- Emphasizing either task or relationships
- Emphasizing one of planning, directing or administering
- Being either basically an inside or outside person for the department
- Working with more or fewer subordinates

READING

Here are some recommendations concerning reading. Recommendations from authors concerning reading may well be suspect in some quarters. The simple point is though that the author, in particular, knows what goes into a book and how much a book can be helpful if properly used. You are invited to consider these:

31 Re-read this book
32 Get your superior to read this book
33 Get your co-workers to read this book
34 Get all of your subordinates to read this book
35 Give a talk on this book
36 Subscribe to, or obtain, on a regular basis, a new management magazine
37 Compile a 'Books to Read' list
38 Obtain a management article abstract service

Re-read this book

The ideas in this book have, literally, greatly magnified the effectiveness of thousands of managers. The ideas can do the same for you but only if you learn them well. Do read this book again.

Get your superior to read this book

Life is much easier when your superior is on your side. You have probably never asked a superior to read a book before. Ask your superior to read this one and to discuss with you what could happen next.

Get your co-workers to read this book

Have you ever recommended a book to a co-worker? Probably not, except in passing. Why not let each of your co-workers know what you think of the book and where they can get a copy. It might convince them if you told them of some behaviour changes that you have made based on reading it. Do not be too concerned if, like most co-workers they say about the changes you made 'Well, it's about time – why did you need the book anyway?'

Get all of your subordinates to read this book

You can directly influence your subordinates to read this book. If you think the book can help you, then it will help you much more if they all read it.

Give a talk on this book

Giving a talk on outputs is no substitute for reading a book on outputs, though it helps. Giving a talk on this book will greatly help you to integrate the ideas in this book with the good ideas you already have. It would also help others begin to think more like you in terms of increasing higher output orientation.

Subscribe to, or obtain, on a regular basis, a new management magazine

Is there a magazine, or possibly several, which you have often thought of reading regularly but have not yet started? It would be a good idea to make a list of these and develop some method of seeing that they come to your attention each time a new issue comes out. A good way to do that, of course, is to take out a subscription. With your desk out of the office you will have more time for reading and reading will help you improve your output orientation.

Compile a 'books to read' list

You have heard about many books which you have not read. The average book on management takes about eight hours to read. Is there any reason why you could not make a commitment now to read several books over the next twelve months?

Obtain a management article abstract service

It is a very good idea to subscribe to some form of management article abstracting service. Your business university library may be able to suggest one. In the author's opinion, the best by far is ANBAR Publications Limited, Circle House South, 65-67 Wembley Hill Road, Wembley, Middlesex, HA9 8DJ, UK. They abstract articles in the following five areas: Accounting and Data Processing, Management Services and Production, Marketing and Distribution, Personnel and Training and Top Management. The selection of abstracts are published for each of these areas every six weeks. One of the most useful features of the service, for some countries, is that subscribers can obtain the actual article from ANBAR at a moderate cost. The author has been using ANBAR for many years and heartily recommends it for managers who want to be better informed.

TIME MANAGEMENT

Here are some recommendations that will help you manage your time better. The thrust of the recommendations is to persuade you to analyse how you spend your time. When you do this, what you need to change will become obvious. Time management starts with a heightened awareness of time, how much time is available and how it is being spent. Some managers have found it useful to undertake a study of their own use of time. They are almost invariably surprised at the results and the lack of effective management displayed. Effective managers need to learn how to create massed undisturbed time and distributed undisturbed time. Massed undisturbed time is particularly useful for projects that involve thinking sequentially such as writing a report or book. Small blocks of distributed and undisturbed time are useful for clearing the desk of the accumulation of notices, memos and travel claims to sign. An obvious short-term way to create mass undisturbed time is by coming in three hours early or doing work at home. This may lower effectiveness in the long run, so other methods may have to be used. One such method, and there are practical limits in many jobs, is simply to make oneself unavailable on certain days or between certain hours. Most daily interruptions, for many managers, are on relatively trivial matters. As each interruption occurs a manager should ask, 'How could this have been avoided?' and then modify the decision or information system so that such interruptions either do not occur or at least are minimized.

The recommendations are:

39 Start keeping a time record on how you spend your time each day
40 Study how you spent your time for a given past period
41 Compare your time diary results to your effectiveness areas
42 Plan to structure your time use differently

Start keeping a time record on how you spend your time each day

Managers who keep a time record almost invariably report how surprised they were at the results. Completing such a time record need only take a few minutes a day and for some, might be done by the secretary or obtained from an appointment diary. You are asked in this recommendation to spend very little time indeed, at studying an important way in which you behave as a manager. It is suggested you keep your diary for about two weeks.

Study how you spent your time for a given past period

After two weeks or so, make some kind of analysis of how you spent your time. Many bases of such classifications exist and it is best for you to create your own to suit your own situation. You may well want to analyse your time diary in several different ways.

Compare your time diary results to your effectiveness areas

As a minimum, compare your time diary to each of your effectiveness areas. Specify as precisely as possible how much time you spent on each of your effectiveness areas over the two-week period. These results may well make you think about changing your use of time in your intent to become an output-oriented manager.

Plan to structure your time use differently

Your analysis will be of little value if you do not make a plan to change the way you spend your time. So, make such a plan and develop some method of giving yourself feedback as to how well you are keeping to it, and if not, why not? You will find it motivating in making this plan to think about all the things you have not got around to which you could now if you get control of your time.

TRAINING AND DEVELOPMENT

Not all managers are in control of time and money needed to take additional training. Some are, and others can often obtain it through good situational management. The world is chock-full of a wide variety of training courses. Some that last a day are useful and some lasting several months are useful. Think about those aspects of your job which you could do better if you had just a little more training in them. In a well-designed training course if does not take long for a manager to learn a great deal. Some excellent training courses last only three hours. These are a bit hard to find but they do exist. As a start, you might want to look around and find out just what is available in your general interest area.

Here are some recommendations concerning your training and development. They include:

43   Make a training and development needs analysis of yourself
44   Investigate what training is available to you incompany
45   Investigate what training is available to you outside your company
46   Make a training and development plan for yourself covering one to three years
47   Investigate the Managerial Effectiveness Seminar

Make a training and development needs analysis of yourself

What knowledge or skills do you need to make you an output-oriented manager? Start by making a list yourself and ask others who know you and who know about training.

Investigate what training is available to you incompany

What training can your company provide? Even very small companies have access to a wide variety of training. The astute personnel department or training department has a good knowledge, or can obtain details of courses not now offered incompany but which could be if a sufficient need emerges. Several universities have what they call 'Corporate MBA Programmes' which are the conventional two-year MBA programme done on an incompany part-time basis. If this can be accomplished then most other things can. You may reasonably assume that anything you need to know or anything in which you need to have a higher skill, can be provided on an incompany basis should the company see a sufficient need and also believe that there would be a reasonable cost benefit for the company.

Investigate what training is available to you outside your company

You may well know, from the number of brochures reaching your desk, that there is a great deal of training being offered to managers generally. Obviously, some courses are better than others. As a start point, however, it is better to see what is available and then only later try and evaluate one against the other in terms of them suiting your purpose. Obviously, your personnel or training department can be of direct help.

Make a training and development plan for yourself covering one–three years

For how many days a year do you think you could profitably obtain some benefit from training, and which you might reasonably expect to obtain approval for? Using this as a base and your knowledge obtained from the two previous recommendations, create a training and development plan for yourself.

Investigate the managerial effectiveness seminar

Chapter 10 describes the Managerial Effectiveness Seminar. This seminar has been conducted and improved for over twenty years and is the main training method to instill the ideas in this book in managers. As a minimum, it would seen that you owe it to yourself to learn something about it and its availability to you.

FUNDAMENTAL QUESTIONS

Here are some fundamental issues which managers consider from
time to time. You are invited to consider all of them. You are not
required to make a 'yes–no' decision on each but are encouraged to
think about them. They are:

  Decide that you want to become more effective
  Consider changing your job
  Consider your future
  How can you improve your superior's effectiveness?
  How can you improve your subordinates' effectiveness?
  How can you improve your co-workers' effectiveness?

Decide that you want to become more effective

It is natural for a manager to say, 'Of course I want to become more
effective.' However in practice, every manager is not always prepared
to make the effort to become more effective. One manager may
simply want to mark time until retirement; another may be in the
wrong job and any additional involvement would be unpleasant;
some are simply lazy and not inclined to do their best in contributing
what they can. Managers must be sure that they really want to
become more effective before they read about how to do so. So, do
you want to become more effective?

Consider changing your job

Once they have looked closely at what a job really demands, some
managers decide that they are in the wrong job. Sometimes everyone
knows it and sometimes no one does. There is a big difference
between having daily deadlines or not, between supervising professionals and supervising hourly-paid workers, between system
management and selling. It may be that the job is too demanding, not
demanding enough, too boring or involves you in things you would
simply rather not do. When one has seen hundreds of managers at
work, it takes very little skill to pick the ones who are in the wrong
job. They simply are out of touch. They get no pleasure out of it.
They spend all the time they can doing routine work and avoiding
decisions. They are more to be pitied than blamed but they cannot be
ignored. Perhaps the salary attracted them and that; together with the
pensions scheme, now has them locked in. Perhaps the job demands
changed while they were in it. Perhaps through their own low

sensitivity they did not know what they were getting into. A common example of this is the professional who gets promoted into managing fellow professionals. The ideal solution to being in the wrong job is obvious. The majority of managers who move from, or are moved from, a position in which they are performing poorly, turn out to be more effective and have higher job satisfaction in the new position.

Consider your future

Whether or not the organization has a career plan for you, you should have one of your own. You need to sit down annually and plan where you expect to be in ten years' time. A good start is to list the ages of all your family, your estimated personal wealth, your position, your salary and your accomplishments. Then fill in the ten-year gap with what it is necessary for you to do in order to achieve your plan. The future can simply occur or it can be invented. You can see yourself as a cork bobbing on an ocean of fate or as someone with your hand on the tiller in a fresh breeze. The way you see yourself as an effective manager must be understood if you are to invent your future.

How can you improve your superior's effectiveness?

Most managers would like to be able to influence their superior in some way. There is no better way for a manager to gain such influence than by amply satisfying the superior's expectations. This usually involves the manager directly in becoming effective and at the same time making the superior more effective as well. If your own subordinates could take action to improve your effectiveness then presumably you can do the same for your superior. You are unlikely to do much in the way of changing the style, but you can make the superior more effective. This is particularly possible if the status and power differential between you is low, and if the superior's job is much interwoven with your own and therefore more dependent on you. A superior may also be influenced by using an indirect approach by getting someone else to provide ideas. This influence may be exerted by another manager, a book or article, a consultant or a course. The written word is a much underused influence, yet it is particularly helpful in the low influence situation which a subordinate is often in.

How can you improve your subordinates' effectiveness

By improving effectiveness of your subordinates, the effectiveness of the manager is also improved. Perhaps the best single test of a manager is the effectiveness of subordinates. As a minimum this would be expressed by the capacity for one or two of the subordinates to step into the manager's shoes. The most effective way of making subordinates more effective is by giving them challenging responsibilities early in their career. The more challenging the responsibilities, the more effective the subordinate is likely to become. Effectiveness areas for subordinates are crucial. While the development of managers can be furthered by formal courses, 95 per cent of all real management development goes on in the context of the superior/subordinate relationship. The quality of this relationship determines effectiveness. The superior has by far the most influence in structuring it. A subordinate does not have to model managerial style on the superior in order to become effective. The younger ones tend to do so especially if the superior appears to be effective, has upward influence and gives them support. Managers usually accept or even welcome such modelling; but the real skill is in recognizing, accepting and managing differences. Managers can be effective in different ways. To force a subordinate into the manager's mould may not work or be necessary. A superior is not running a game called, 'How to be more like me' but instead must demonstrate that subordinates should meet their effectiveness areas, not to please the superior, but because their position demands it.

How can you improve your co-workers' effectiveness

Co-workers are usually open to influence at meetings which they attend with you. Managers should therefore think of starting meetings with one of these questions: 'What is the objective of this meeting?' 'How will we know if it has been effective?' 'Do we need it?' 'Can we conclude it in 15 minutes?' To do this out of the blue is not always to be recommended, but managers should get around to it as soon as they can. Over time, it is a relatively simple matter for an effective manager to raise the aspiration level of co-workers by sharing with them the past successes and failures; by describing things as they really are, and by suggesting that standards could be much higher and, by personal example, can show that this is what the manager intends to do.

OTHER CHANGES FOR YOU TO DECIDE

These recommendations may well have triggered other ideas of your own. It might be a good idea to list them.

Action checklist

Here is a list of the 47 recommendations.

● Against each is YES ? NO

For each recommendation circle one of these three to indicate that you plan to take some action on it in the reasonably near future, or you do not know, or you have decided not to. If for any recommendation you feel you are already doing it or have done it before and are satisfied that you do not need to do it again then circle YES.

Make a list of all of those for which you have circled YES and put the list into some time frame. The time frame might be immediate, in a few weeks, or some other set of timing that seems satisfactory to you.

MY REACTION TO THE RECOMMENDATION

A. *Basic recommendations*

1.	Decide your effectiveness areas	YES	?	NO
2.	Decide your measurement areas	YES	?	NO
3.	Determine your authority areas	YES	?	NO
4.	Create your job effectiveness description	YES	?	NO
5.	Burn your existing job description	YES	?	NO
6.	Decide your objectives	YES	?	NO
7.	Establish your resources	YES	?	NO
8.	Create your first objective planning form	YES	?	NO
9.	Create an objective planning form for all of your measurement areas	YES	?	NO

B. *Meetings with others about effectiveness*

10.	Meet with your co-workers and superior together on effectiveness areas	YES	?	NO
11.	Meet with superior alone on effectiveness areas	YES	?	NO
12.	Meet with all of your subordinates together on effectiveness areas	YES	?	NO

13.	Meet with your co-workers and superior together on JEDs	YES	?	NO
14.	Meet with your superior alone on your JED	YES	?	NO
15.	Meet with all of your subordinates together on JEDs	YES	?	NO
16.	Hold a one-to-one with each of your subordinates	YES	?	NO
17.	Hold a one-to-one with each of your co-workers	YES	?	NO

C.   *Improving your decision-making*

18.	Make a list of your decisions outstanding	YES	?	NO
19.	Make one or more decisions now that you have been postponing	YES	?	NO
20.	Analyse your past decisions	YES	?	NO
21.	Make a decision list with timings	YES	?	NO

D.   *Giving work away*

22.	Stop doing some things	YES	?	NO
23.	Give some parts of your work away	YES	?	NO
24.	Give your in-basket to your secretary	YES	?	NO
25.	Remove your desk from your office	YES	?	NO

E.   *Recommendations for changes in your behaviour*

26.	Make a risk-taking list	YES	?	NO
27.	Experiment with new behaviour	YES	?	NO
28.	Write a letter to yourself about what changes you will make	YES	?	NO
29.	Walk the shop	YES	?	NO
30.	Investigate ways to change your technology	YES	?	NO

F.   *Reading*

31.	Re-read this book	YES	?	NO
32.	Get your superior to read this book	YES	?	NO
33.	Get your co-workers to read this book	YES	?	NO
34.	Get all of your subordinates to read this book	YES	?	NO
35.	Give a talk on this book	YES	?	NO
36.	Subscribe to, or obtain, on a regular basis, a new management magazine	YES	?	NO

37.	Compile a 'Books to Read' list	YES	?	NO
38.	Obtain a management article abstract service	YES	?	NO

G. *Time management*

39.	Start keeping a time record on how you spend your time each day	YES	?	NO
40.	Study how you spent your time for a given past period	YES	?	NO
41.	Compare your time diary results to your effectiveness areas	YES	?	NO
42.	Plan to structure your time use differently	YES	?	NO

H. *Training and development*

43.	Make a training and development needs analysis of yourself	YES	?	NO
44.	Investigate what training is available to you incompany	YES	?	NO
45.	Investigate what training is available to you outside your company	YES	?	NO
46.	Make a training and development plan for yourself covering one–three years	YES	?	NO
47.	Investigate the Managerial Effectiveness Seminar	YES	?	NO

PART IV
Case Studies

Introduction

The Reddin Organization has helped several hundred organizations become more output-oriented. These vary from the very small to the very large. They cover, as might be expected, a wide variety of different types of organization such as production, banking, government and social service. In virtually every case the first step in improving output orientation was that the entire top management participate in the managerial effectiveness seminar which is described in Chapter 10. This section contains a reasonably rich and diverse account of the experiences in several organizations, the method they used and some of the internal documentation they produced to help themselves become more output-oriented.

The four case studies provided in this section have quite different objectives. The first describes a large organization which used the ideas in this book to create a highly profitable change. The second one demonstrates how a CEO of a small orgainization can create all the changes needed and make a superb success of it.

The next case discusses how a multinational took an opportunity, before becoming more output-oriented, to take a really good look at itself in an objective way. The last case shows how IBM has made extensive use of these ideas.

13 How a large organization uses these ideas

Reviewing your subordinate managers' progress three times during the year is ABSOLUTELY MANDATORY FOR EVERY MANAGER.

Our system rewards managers mainly on the basis of ratings of their overall performance against all their EAs particularly their performance against their objectives.

The organization considered here is Westpac Banking Corporation. It is the largest bank in Australia, and one of the largest in the world, with over 35,000 employees. The organization accepted the ideas of outputs fully and used them for a basis for many systems. This chapter describes what the bank actually did. It took a great deal of hard work and some time to accomplish all this.

As this book goes to press over 1700 managers from the CEO down have completed the 3-D managerial effectiveness seminar as described in Chapter 10. There have been about fifty team meetings starting with the top team and moving downward through the organization and several large group meetings addressing such issues as reorganization, changes in personnel policy and how to make a merger effective. As seen by the bank the environment was changing rapidly and was about to change even more rapidly. A government commission was expected to propose that foreign banks could enter the market, as it did, and this would produce an even greater need for a flexible response. That, together with a new CEO with deeply held views about output orientation, led to the start of this organization development programme which has been described as the largest and most successful in the world.

This chapter is based, in the main, on an internal booklet distributed by the bank with the title *Managing for Results – The Westpac Management System*. It is also based on a talk given by Bob White, CEO of Westpac Banking Corporation, to a meeting of the International Monetary Conference held in Boston. A contribution was also made by Geoff Thompson, New Zealand General Manager and Ross O'Brien, Chief Manager, Personnel and Support Services.

At the outset of the programme the bank's annual profit was $100 million. Some senior managers were somewhat embarrassed with how high it was. After some years the profit increased to approximately $800 million. Obviously, it would be impossible to attribute a percentage of variance in the change of profit to any particular thing. Without question, the critical element was the new CEO. However, there is a widespread view in the bank that the output orientation programme did help a great deal. Looking at the increase in annual profit it is clear that the cost-effectiveness of the programme bordered on the enormous.

All material marked with bullets is taken directly from an internal document '*Managing for Results – The Westpac Management System*' used by all managers. Other material is direct quotes from Bank Offices.

THE EMPHASIS ON JOB EFFECTIVENESS DESCRIPTIONS

It is evident that the bank gave central importance to job effectiveness descriptions.

- Every managerial position in Westpac is described in terms of its output requirements. These descriptions are called job effectiveness descriptions or JEDs.
- A Job Effectiveness Description, or JED, is a description of a managerial position using output terms. It comprises a manager's effectiveness areas and their accompanying measurement areas and authority areas.
- Your JED provides anyone who has little or no knowledge of your job with:
  Effectiveness Areas: a list of the results you are required to achieve through your daily work (your outputs).
  Measurement Areas: a list of the ways in which your outputs are measured in your progress reviews and when you are being appraised.
  Authority Levels: the levels of authority allocated to your position and thus what actions you can take and what decisions you can make without referring to your superior.
- Your JED is very important because it helps you think of your job, and those of your subordinates, in terms of outputs. It is an essential part of Westpac Management System because it is the basis upon which your objectives are written. Your planning **starts with your JED.**

- Your subordinate managers' JEDs should be reviewed, updated and confirmed annually, at any restructure and on any change of incumbent in a job. This should usually be done at a team effectiveness review or normal team meeting.
- Use of a JED helps us think of our jobs and those of our subordinates in terms of outputs, rather than the things we do, which are inputs.
- Our JEDs are the first link in a chain that leads to the rewards we receive. The full process looks like this:

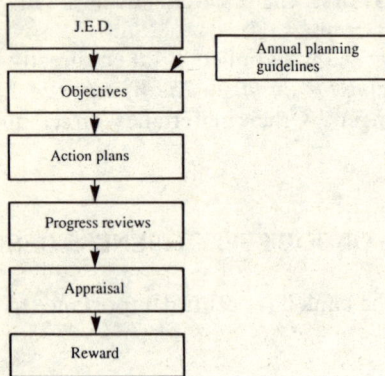

```
            ┌─────────────────┐
            │     J.E.D.      │
            └────────┬────────┘
                     │          ┌──────────────────┐
                     │          │ Annual planning  │
            ┌────────▼────────┐ │ guidelines       │
            │   Objectives    │◄┘
            └────────┬────────┘
                     │
            ┌────────▼────────┐
            │  Action plans   │
            └────────┬────────┘
                     │
            ┌────────▼────────┐
            │ Progress reviews│
            └────────┬────────┘
                     │
            ┌────────▼────────┐
            │    Appraisal    │
            └────────┬────────┘
                     │
            ┌────────▼────────┐
            │     Reward      │
            └─────────────────┘
```

If you want to get rewarded, start with a JED.

Exhibit 13.1   It starts with the JED.

- Two particular aims of these reviews of JEDs are:
  To ensure that the EAs of your subordinate managers are complementary and do not overlap or underlap.
  To make sure that your EAs incorporate those of your subordinate managers and that your EAs are incorporated in those of your superior. This helps ensure that your EAs complement those of the other managers in Westpac.

Effectiveness areas (EAs)

- Your EAs must not overlap or underlap with those of the other managers at your level. Overlap is when two positions are accountable for the same output and underlap is when no position has assigned the accountability for an output.
- Your EAs must incorporate those of your subordinate managers and your EAs will be incorporated in those of your superior.

This helps ensure that your EAs complement those of the other managers in Westpac.

- Avoiding overlap and underlap and ensuring that EAs are complementary is an essential part of the regular reviews of your team's JEDs.
- Although your EAs must incorporate those of your subordinate managers, you may also write additional, personal EAs (and objectives) if you wish.
- EAs should be written in one to four words. Avoid the use of words such as 'increase', 'maximize' and 'satisfy' and any quantities or timings. Otherwise the EAs will become measurement areas or objectives.

Measurement areas (MAs)

- A measurement area is a statement of how an output described by an EA will be measured.
- At least one MA should be written for each EA.
- It is important that your MAs be agreed and clearly understood by you and your superior. These agreed MAs will be the only measures used in your objectives and will be used when your superior reviews your progress towards, and appraises your performance against your objectives.
- Choosing the best possible MAs is important if we are to use the Westpac Management System effectively.

SYSTEM LINKAGES TO THE JED AND OUTPUTS

As indicated in Chapter 11, many in-company systems can be linked to the JED and outputs. The list provided there included:

- Basic corporate philosophy
- Management information system
- Objectives
- Appraisal
- Budgets
- Job specification
- Selection
- Job evaluation
- Organization design
- Teamwork
- Rewards

This is what the bank did about each.

BASIC CORPORATE PHILOSOPHY

The basic corporate philosophy is best summed up in these statements.

- The bank's output statement is: 'The competitive servicing of customers' needs.'
- The output statement highlights our customers' needs as the most important factor in our corporate life. It recognizes the fact that we could not exist without our customers.
- Our output statement means that we must change from a bank driven by our own concerns to one driven by our customers'
- Our output statement means that we must change from a bank driven by our own concerns to one driven by our customers' needs. For example, we must learn to be more influenced by our customers' requirements than by the requirements of our trading bank computer system or the fact that we have a branch network.
- Our output statement gives direction to the many changes occurring in the bank. It guides our major product and market strategies and should also help in many day-to-day management decisions.
- The importance of our output statement is reflected in the fact that every submission to the bank executive committee must include a Customer Impact Statement.
- The bank has four medium-term output statement goals:

  1. being better at understanding the financial needs of our customers so as to produce the right products for each customer segment;
  2. being better at providing a total financial management service to our customers;
  3. being better in the customer service orientation of all our people, particularly their friendliness and helpfulness;
  4. being an organization which encourages excellent performance by its managers.

- The achievement of these goals is critical to the future success of the bank.
- The achievement of these goals requires the contribution of all bank managers. Managers are expected to explain the goals to their team members and to set them an example by their efforts **towards achievement of the goals.**

MANAGEMENT INFORMATION SYSTEM

With the bank's emphasis on outputs and the JED the management information system obviously had to be organized around outputs. For a while, two systems were, in fact, running; one based on the prior method of inputs and the other on the emerging method of outputs.

OBJECTIVES

Every manager in the bank, there were about 3000 of them, had to have very carefully set and reviewed objectives. The objectives were, basically, on an annual basis and reviewed quarterly although this varied with the nature of the work being done.

Characteristics of good objectives

- The four characteristics of good objectives are:
  1. *Measurable*: objectives must include a quantity and be easily measurable. If a result can't be measured, then there's no point in trying to achieve it because no one will know if you do. The measurement areas used to make your objectives measurable are recorded in your JED.
  2. *Specific*: objectives must describe the results you plan to achieve as precisely as possible.
  3. *Time-bounded*: objectives must specify the dates by which results will be achieved or the periods during which results will be achieved.
  4. *Challenging*: objectives should be pitched at a level that will provide a sense of accomplishment and develop your managerial skills. However, they should not be so difficult that they are beyond your abilities and should not be outside your authority levels.
- Your objectives must be directly linked with your JED. They must correspond to your effectiveness areas, use your measurement areas and be within your authority levels.
- Your objectives should reflect your most important EAs. Line managers should write objectives that are market-centred and focus on the success of their business. Administrative managers should write objectives that are user-centred and affect the quality of the service they provide.
- As stated, objectives must be consistent with the annual planning

guidelines. Any objectives that are not consistent will have to be altered.

● After you draft your objectives, they are negotiated with your superior and between two and eight are agreed and recorded on your appraisal form.

● The role of the superior at objective-setting discussions is very important. It is the superior's responsibility to ensure that the objectives are good ones and reflect the most important EAs. This is done by comparing them with the objectives of the other managers in the team and, if necessary, negotiating with the manager to change them. Therefore, negotiating skills are very important.

● Most managers find it necessary to require their subordinate managers to accept additional objectives during the year; for example, because of new policy decisions by general management. These new objectives are recorded on the subordinates' appraisal forms and because of the additional workload involved, the priorities placed on them and the time required to achieve them are taken into account in appraisals.

● Having objectives that have been agreed with your superior, and agreeing objectives for your subordinate managers, is ABSOLUTELY MANDATORY FOR EVERY MANAGER.

Obtaining the right degree of challenge

● Many managers find it difficult to obtain the right degree of challenge in their objectives.

● You can also say in retrospect that if all your subordinate managers achieve all their objectives, then they may not have been challenging enough. And that if none of your subordinate managers achieved any of their objectives, then they were probably too challenging.

● The biggest problem in negotiating and agreeing on this degree of challenge is to obtain consistency across the different areas of Westpac. Consistency is critical if our performance appraisal and reward system is to work properly. As yet we have no effective means of measuring this degree of challenge and so we must rely on the experience of, and communication and peer group pressure between senior managers.

● Some lower level managers have also reported that it is difficult to obtain a consistent degree of challenge in the objectives of their subordinates, even when their subordinates' jobs are similar. As stated in the text, managers must negotiate this degree of challenge with their subordinates. It is suggested that the negotiation takes place in a team meeting where team members can bid for 'shares' of the team's objectives until their combined objectives are adequate for the team's objectives to be achieved. This provides a comparison of the degree of challenge provided to each subordinate and places peer group pressure on them to accept appropriately challenging objectives.

Subjects of objectives

- The subject of your objectives (that is, the things you plan for) are described by the EAs in your JED. Each objective must correspond to an EA.
- Because your EAs must complement those of the other managers around you and must not overlap or underlap, this will ensure that your objectives are complementary and don't overlap or underlap.
- As your EAs must be within your authority levels and the limits of your accountability, so too must your objectives.
- Each of your EAs should represent an important or significant part of your job. Your objectives correspond to the most important EAs and should affect the success of your business if you are a line manager or the quality of the service you provide if you are an administrative manager.
- Your objective must be consistent with the annual planning guidelines.

Reducing forecasting errors

- Forecasting errors have been reported as a problem by some line managers whose measurement areas involve forecasts of business conditions. Some administrative managers also find forecasting difficult because the service they provide takes the form of projects that require considerable time to complete; and an increase in demand for these services can considerably deplete their staff resources.
- It must be understood firstly that objective-setting always involves forecasting.
- Secondly, forecasts twelve months ahead are always inaccurate to some degree. In extreme cases, managers can find after a few months either that they have already achieved their objectives or that achievement will be impossible.

- One consideration when you find forecasting errors a problem is to make sure you are planning for the right things. Your objectives must correspond to your most important EAs and be within your authority levels. This ensures that you have adequate authority to compensate for changes in the environment and achieve the results you have planned for.

Examples of objectives for regional managers

- Complete regional market analysis (in Network Design regions, with district marketing teams) by end of October.
- Within the personal customer market segments identified, increase product sales as follows:

Term Deposits under $50,000	20 per cent
Advantage Saver	60 per cent
NBI Deposits	10 per cent
Personal Loans	35 per cent

  on previous year by end of September.
- Increase the number of customers in seven commercial market segments as follows:

Doctors	50 per cent
Solicitors	70 per cent
Accountants	45 per cent
Real estate agents	50 per cent
Dentists	35 per cent
Newsagents	60 per cent
Grocers	55 per cent

  by end of September.
- Increase annual average bill acceptance line outstandings by 75 per cent on previous year.
- Increase total charges and commissions collected during current year by 15 per cent on previous year.
- Increase the annual average interest rate on advances, after allowing for changes in market rates, by 0.2 percentage points on previous year.
- Reduce personal loan write-offs to less than 2 per cent of outstandings by end of September.
- Amalgamate two branches without losing business by end of September.

Annual plans

- Annual plans commit us to achieving specific results using the resources we have allocated. They focus on the group's sales, income, expenditure and profit. Branches, districts, regions and divisions all make annual plans and these are combined to make a group plan.

- The annual planning process starts with guidelines that are prepared by general management on the basis of the first year of the medium term plan. The annual planning guidelines consist of 'where we want to go' statements.

- The second step in the annual planning process is for managers to write their own objectives and negotiate and agree them with their superior. It is essential that managers' objectives at all levels be consistent with the annual planning guidelines.

- Finally, these objectives are combined to make a group plan that consists of 'where we want to go' statements and supporting budget commitments.

- Thus, our annual planning process is interactive and emphasises negotiation. It is partly 'top-down' and partly 'bottom-up'.

- Because all the objectives agreed in the annual planning process are interrelated, the timing of their preparation is important. Any deadlines given must be adhered to.

- The most important parts of our annual planning process are the objectives of our line divisions. A major feature of the process is that our group plan is a combination of individual managers' plans, so that the things our group does are directly related to what individuals do.

APPRAISAL

While appraisal was always made formally of all objectives set, the emphasis was on progress reviews and performance counselling. It is better to avoid things that one does not want to happen rather than just comment on them at the end.

Objective of appraisal

- The objective of our appraisal and reward system is to improve the performance of our people, so that Westpac's performance is improved.

- Progress reviews and appraisals provide us with feedback on our performance, which helps us to improve it. Everybody needs continual day-by-day feedback to maintain their enthusiasm and feel part of a team. Progress reviews and appraisals add to this by providing us with comprehensive, structured feedback.

Managerial appraisal form

- Our managerial appraisal form recognizes and rates our performance, highlights our development needs and identifies our potential for other managerial positions.
- The following comments are provided to assist appraisers when they use the form, and are to be read in conjunction with the instructions on the form:

    Performance Against Objectives: It is important to comment on whether the objectives were achieved, the degree of challenge in the objectives when they were agreed and the circumstances during the year which influenced the achievement of the objectives. These circumstances are usually so significant that the subordinate's performance cannot be rated solely on the basis of whether the objectives were achieved.

    If you have required the subordinate to accept additional objectives during the year, then comment on the priorities placed on these objectives and the time required to achieve them.

    Overall Performance: A rating of performance against all EAs, particularly performance against objectives. If you think this rating doesn't adequately cover your subordinate's performance, then you should comment and explain.

    Assessment of Skills: Under each rating constructive comments are required on the subordinate's strengths and areas for improvement.

    Personal Profile: Comments should be candid and constructive.

Further comments on appraisal

- At the end of the year managers appraise the performance of each of their subordinate managers.
- As with progress reviews, the main purpose of appraisals is to improve the performance of your subordinate managers. Again, it is your subordinates' performance that is appraised, not their personality.
- Appraisals must be face-to-face because, as with progress reviews, this is the most effective way to improve your sub-

ordinates' performance. In addition, appraisals directly affect managers' bonuses and future career progress.

- Appraisals are mainly based on performance against objectives. They take into account whether the objectives were achieved, the degree of challenge in the objectives when they were agreed and the circumstances during the year which influenced the achievement of the objectives. These circumstances are usually so significant that a manager's performance cannot be rated solely on the basis of whether the objectives were achieved. When managers have been required to accept additional objectives during the year and their workload has consequently increased, appraisals take into account the priorities placed on these objectives and the time required to achieve them.
- Secondly, appraisals take into account managers' overall performance against all their EAs.
- Appraisals should contain no surprises. All aspects of your subordinate managers' performance should have been discussed previously at one or more of the three reviews of progress.
- One section of the managers' appraisal form asks you to assess your subordinate managers' various work skills and requests development plans for any areas that need improvement. It is suggested that you complete this section of the form at a progress review, and confirm it during appraisal, so as to spread your workload.
- Appraising your subordinate managers' performance face-to-face at the end of the year is ABSOLUTELY MANDATORY FOR EVERY MANAGER.

Performance counselling

- Performance counselling is an important part of the process involved in quarterly progress reviews and annual appraisals.
- Counselling allows subordinates to find out exactly how they are currently performing in the eyes of the manager who will appraise them at the end of the year. Unless counselled effectively, highly effective subordinates can believe that their manager is dissatisfied with their performance, while ineffective workers can believe they are performing at highly satisfactory levels.
- The main objective of performance counselling is to improve the performance of your subordinates. However, achieving a lasting change in your subordinates' behaviour is often difficult.
- Performance counselling is a specialized skill. Few managers in

any organization can be described as excellent performance counsellors and they normally undertake extensive training and regular practice. Many managers in Westpac consider themselves to be and are in fact excellent interviewers but this does not make them good counsellors.

● In all, there are four objectives of performance counselling:

to help your subordinates do their job better by encouraging them to excel;

to give your subordinates a clear picture of how well they are doing at present by showing sincere appreciation;

to build a stronger, closer relationship with your subordinates by listening, accepting feedback and eliminating misunderstandings;

to develop practical plans for improvement and to launch projects designed to use your subordinates' total capabilities more completely.

● When you develop a plan to improve a subordinate's performance, you should follow three steps:

1. Identify the factors affecting your subordinate's behaviour.
2. Determine the possibility and probability of change.
3. Influence by convincing your subordinate of the need for change.

● Current behaviour science research suggests a positive approach works best for improving performance. The use of punishment and fear can temporarily change the behaviour of some subordinates but rarely results in a positive attitude towards work and can result in undesirable side-effects such as increased absenteeism.

● Behaviour change brought about through positive reinforcement and feedback, such as praising sound performance and suggesting ways to improve poor performance, is more likely to be lasting and self-perpetuating than that brought about through fear.

● The basis of this positive approach is to encourage your subordinates to improve their performance. It works with everybody, from the best performer to the weakest.

● Further, it is accepted by researchers that managers of superior performing teams rate highly in the skills of maintaining personal communication with the individuals in their teams. Because each subordinate is different and has individual attitudes, the best method for communicating with and influencing each subordinate will vary.

BUDGETS

A major change in the bank's accounting system was made in its move from input accounting to output accounting. This proved to be one of the most difficult exercises to undertake and some specialized outside assistance was used.

JOB SPECIFICATION

The bank no longer has a job specification independent of the JED. For them, the JED is the job specification.

SELECTION

While the JED is used as an important selection tool, it is not used very often. The reason is that the bank hired relatively few managers from outside. Over 95 per cent of the top 3000+ managers joined the bank as 'cadets' at the age of fifteen. There is a JED for this position, of course.

JOB EVALUATION

About half-way through their programme of change to becoming more output-oriented, the bank used the Hay Job Evaluation System for the top 100 or so managerial jobs. (They would have used the Reddin Output Method but that method was not then designed.) Naturally, the bank insisted that the Hay consultants thoroughly learned about outputs and that many of their type of job descriptions were modified to match the JEDs.

● Managers covered by Hay System complete Job Dimension Reviews, which expand on the descriptions of the output requirements of their jobs in their EAs. The information contained in Job Dimension Reviews is scored using the Hay evaluation method. The scores are based on evaluations of the know-how and problem-solving requirements of the jobs and their level of accountability, and reflect the size and relative importance of the jobs to Westpac. The scores are used to determine market-related salary ranges for the jobs and managers are placed within the salary ranges on the basis of ratings of their overall performance.

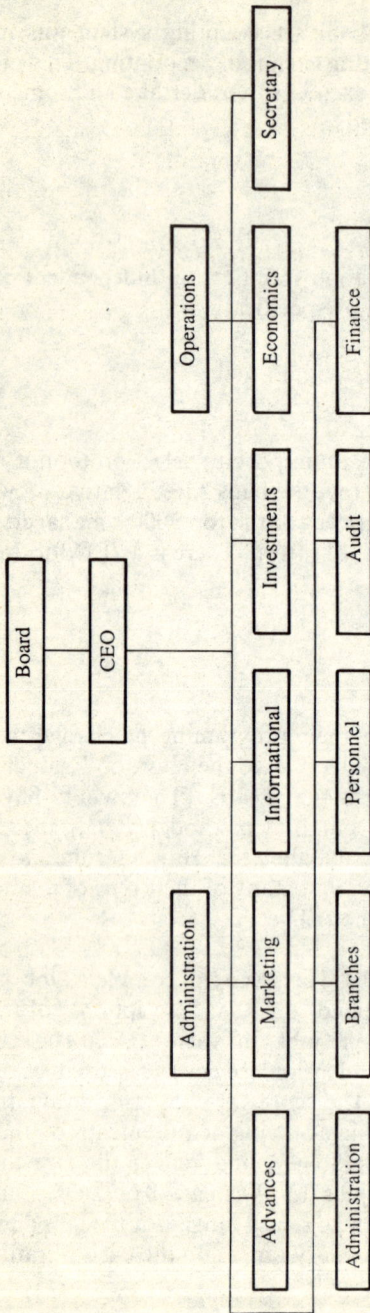

This is a staff-run organization. There are no line managers at the top except for the CEO.

Exhibit 13.2 Westpac before the change.

ORGANIZATION DESIGN

Very early in the programme of changing from inputs to outputs orientation, the bank went through a major reorganization structuring. The previous structure is shown in Exhibit 13.2.

This structure shows a high degree of staff control and virtually no one having any authority. It is also very input-oriented. In a period of only three days the bank moved then to an output-oriented structure as shown in Exhibit 13.3.

Over the next few years the bank made changes in this top level of management almost every year.

The resulting restructure achieved many objectives including:

- Moving more power from staff to line positions.
- Removing a layer of top management which permitted line general managers to report direct to the CEO.
- Reducing the numbers in the top team.
- Moving more responsibility downward to as close to the action as possible.
- Becoming more customer-oriented.
- Greater concentration on strategy and planning.

TEAMWORK

The bank placed a great deal of emphasis on genuine teamwork based on shared outputs.

- Westpac is structured as many interlocking teams. All managers are members of their superior's team and, if they have subordinates, are top man or top woman of their own team.
- Teams are an effective and natural way of:
      communication
      gaining commitment
      achieving results
- One benefit of teamwork is that is improves the performance of all the team members. Teamwork must not be neglected if we are to make the best use of our people resources.
- The basis of teamwork is simple – it is talking with people. Managers are expected to talk with other managers, their subordinates and customers. If we all talk with each other more often, then better communication, understanding and co-operation will follow.
- In Westpac, much of our communication should take place and

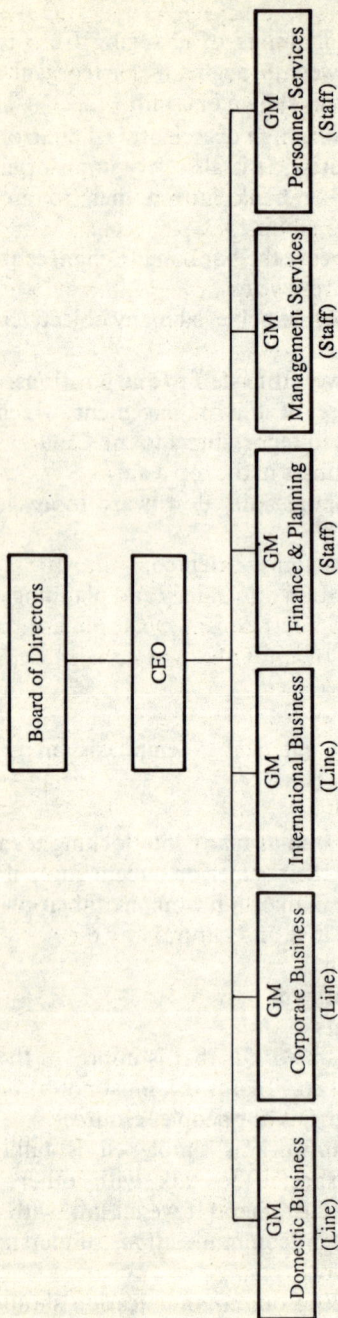

This is a line-run organization with competent staff support.

Exhibit 13.3 Westpac after the change.

many of our management decisions should be made in team meetings. Managers are expected to actively contribute to their teams.

● Managers with subordinates are expected to know each of their team members' competency levels and aspirations and to assist them to be more effective. This involves performance counselling of your subordinates.

● Managers are also expected to ensure that their team members are trained to use the Westpac Management System appropriately.

● All teams are expected to meet regularly. The appropriate interval will vary for different teams but should not be less than once every two months.

● Team meetings can be used for:
    reviewing and updating JEDs (and Job Dimension Reviews, if appropriate)
    discussing and agreeing objectives and action plans
    reviewing progress
    exchanging information
    training
Each meeting should normally be used for several or all of these purposes.

● It is important to communicate to team members all decisions that will affect them. Otherwise, their commitment to the decisions will be reduced.

● As stated, the use of team meetings to ensure that members' EAs are complementary, without overlap or underlap, is also important.

● Team meetings should always have objectives and agendas and the effectiveness of meetings should be regularly reviewed.

● There are techniques for developing teams and for improving their effectiveness in meeting their objectives. Two important processes are the Team Effectiveness Review and the Team Role Laboratory.

REWARDS

The current reward system is described this way.

● Westpac's reward system for managers consists of salaries, annual bonuses and other benefits. Our system rewards managers mainly on the basis of ratings of their overall performance against all their EAs, particularly their performance against their objectives.

- Managers' salaries are either prescribed in industrial agreements or, starting this year, based on the Hay system of job evaluation and salary administration.
- Whether individual managers move over time to more highly paid senior positions, with more demanding EAs, will increasingly depend on their track-record of objective achievement and performance against EAs. Also taken into account are managers' location preferences; and any strengths or weaknesses in their skills, as all positions have specific skill requirements.
- Annual bonuses are distributed to some managers who achieve superior ratings of overall performance, compared with other members of their team or peer group.
- Other benefits are related to responsibility and performance.
- Thus, our rewards are the final link in a chain that starts with our JEDs and the objectives we set.
- Future changes in our reward system will be designed to ensure that the highest rewards go to the highest achievers. This will support our driving force goal of encouraging excellent performance by managers.

14 How a small organization uses these ideas

> The company wasn't going anywhere and I couldn't figure out why. I put the company in for analysis and it came out that it was being run by an autocrat who was killing his own company, had surrounded himself with input people and was destined to fail.
>
> Without taking that seminar when I did and then implementing the ideas of outputs, it is extremely likely we could have gone bottom-up.
>
> Colin Ward

After participating in an output seminar based on the ideas in this book this managing owner of an air conditioning installation firm with about eighty employees made many changes. He decided to base his firm on outputs, get rid of his desk, hold team meetings as described in Chapter 6 and to change many things. Change is slightly nervy but he had the nerve. Profits doubled the next year, and then doubled the year after. He has now secured his family fortune. He took a risk and it succeeded. He wrote this letter to the person conducting the seminar.

A LETTER FROM A MANAGER

Dear . . .

You are on my mind as my desk is just being moved to my accounts manager's office, and I am trying to adjust to my new executive surroundings.

Actually, the cheapest part of the output seminar I attended was the seminar fee for since then I have spent $5000 refurbishing my office to my new output style. I have had a three-day live-away team meeting with my seven top executives and they have had one-day team meetings with their groups.

You mentioned when I phoned you on my decision to rid myself of my desk that you don't always get feedback on results and that's a pity for the changes that have taken place here in the last month are nothing short of miraculous! I went to my team meeting with seven individuals and came back with a committed team and the message has flowed on.

Tomorrow I have a one-day final review of all the effectiveness areas and measurement areas and the twelve-month plan for each executive and then we start the new year – a new, revitalized, re-organized and committed company: Your seminar showed that we were headed for trouble because of inbuilt and growing stagnation which was stifling our real purpose and marketing objectives.

There is a time and tide in the affairs of all men and I'm grateful I was ready for the message I got from you and your beautifully planned and deeply thought-provoking seminar which can give such quick and concise indicators and where I have proven that the disciple's message has just as much effect as the master's.

Thank you and I am sorry I am not in the business of selling output orientation for it is a message I could really move along.

Sincerely,
Colin Ward
Atlas Air Australia Pty. Ltd

A SUBSEQUENT TALK TO MANAGERS

Based on receiving the above letter, the writer was asked to talk to a group of senior managers attending an output seminar. This account is as related by the CEO himself with some minor terminology changes.

I will just feed you some facts and you can see if they are useful or not. I am very grateful to be invited. Our company isn't a big company and I'll give you some background on that.

Our particular group started some 15 years ago in the true fashion of husband and wife team, and $300, and we were in the air-conditioning field. When you haven't got any money you have to put in a lot of time, and we pursued that course. We grew to a point where we had about $5.5 million turnover.

We went into the credit squeeze and lost $400,000 – nearly lost our house and nearly lost everything that we had through the tradition of payment within our system, where builders obtain stage payments and if they go broke they take you with them. But we survived out of all that, coming down from 120 to 50 people and from $5.5 million turnover to $3 million and we restarted.

We then sold 15 per cent of our shares to an Italian group that we represented here and in South East Asia, New Guinea and New Zealand and we were formally looked upon as part of their international group, so that our company was now back to six million turnover. We rose to 80 people, but were certainly a very different profit-oriented company from what we were earlier, broader-based with different products, but while we were all that I was very conscious of the fact that we were not making any real growth. I was conscious of the fact that I had pushed and pulled and I was very proud of my company. I thought I was reasonably intelligent; I travelled overseas twice a year; I am observant; I read and if someone asked me about my company I would have said that 'Well we'd got a great company' but we were not really making real growth we were just keeping pace with inflation and this worried me.

I knew there was something wrong with my company. We sort of restructured and did a few things. Finally, I looked in the mail and there was this Institute of Management booklet. I have always been too busy to go to seminars and you know, who wants a lot of these seminars which have sort of trite people that stand up in front of you, who say the same sort of language and the same sort of talk? You finish and there has been no impact.

So I enrolled for the output seminar that you are doing now and sat over yonder. I didn't really know what was in front of me other than the idea of outputs, but I had an open mind. I had need of change – for some reason or other despite all our hard work and relative success, I was not happy about the way our company was going.

Then we started to do what you are starting to do – we began to get a common language, an output language. By this time you had either made up your mind that you sort of understand it and you like what it's saying or you don't. You are rejecting it or you are open to it.

Our seminar work team got along quite well. Sitting at the same table was a member of the top team of a 35,000-person bank and the national CEOs of Digital and Olivetti. We started with a good output analysis case study session. When we had finished we had a little time so I said, 'Look, why don't you guys help me. My company is the smallest of the group. Wouldn't you like to feed my company in as case study number seven which we have the opportunity to do?' And we did.

My company came out to be a company with a completely input style, which was quite different from what I believed my company to be. As an individual and as a person dedicated to the company I would have told it quite differently.

So then I had the opportunity with this work group, and they were very kind to me, to look at the executives. I had one deserter and four bureaucrats in a group of eight senior executives, including myself. A lot of meetings that I thought were participative were not, as it turned out. I ended up to be an autocrat and I guess after a fashion, when I got over my initial reaction, I was. I guess a lot of guys who start a business off have to be autocrats and highly task-oriented to succeed. The four bureaucrats and the deserter were worrying also.

When I started to think about my company climate I realized that it was in fact choking and was going to wither and die with a current inflation rate of 12 per cent. So armed with all the seminar messages and books that you've got, I went back home to my group. I called them in and said, 'Look, I have just finished a seminar. OK, you can say I am enthused about it and I like the output message. There is a real message for us. Now I realize that I have been calling you in and talking with you, but the decisions were really pre-made and I have been handing tablets down from the mountain and saying what's great, while you have been sitting there anticipating the decision', which was true but I didn't believe it. I thought I was one of those fair, wise, tolerant, thoughtful people that you keep hearing about.

Then I said, 'If you are interested and want to be a senior executive of this group, I would like a commitment and in turn I will make a commitment to you. To do that, I want you to give up a weekend of your time. That's your commitment for starters. Not in the company time, in your time – still the autocrat in me!' You have got to give something to get something, so I asked them for their own time. I said that we would go away and discuss the company in a way that it had never been discussed before. I felt the company needed change and with an output style I now had a formula. I now had a common management language that we could use. If after the meeting they did not want to be part of this, or if they felt the company would not benefit from it – at least we would have spent three days discussing it. I actually did give them the Friday, let's be fair about it.

We arrived for the weekend meeting. Eight people with a fairly tight schedule. There was a lot to go through and we started with an anlaysis of some of the case studies this seminar provided. Then we came to study ourselves. This was the first time, I guess, that they had ever been asked to comment in open honesty and candour on their own company's objectives, level of resistance, existing level of outputs as shown by effectiveness areas and measurement areas and how to make it higher. Previously I was always doing the planning and doing all these other things myself . . . if they were done at all.

Then they had the opportunity of analysing me as a CEO. They gave frank comments on my style, my effectiveness areas and my effectiveness. They were really given the opportunity of analysing me along set terms which were impersonal. I think the main stress here is on the top person, as they must be ready to accept honest criticism and the fact that they can be wrong. Then, of course, we analysed the seven senior executives of the company, which was them. We had a room that we had hired that we could stick paper all the way round.

Then they analysed the company and found, much to their shocked horror that it was an input climate – eight out of eight agreed that it was input.

We then asked everyone to write their effectiveness areas – the first step in becoming output. When a person joined out company we gave them exactly what this seminar talks about – a job effectiveness description but for us it turned out to be an input job description. We looked at all the advertisements that we had placed for staff over the past 12 months. They were all inputs. They were not output and objective advertisements; they were input advertisements. Which is why we were not getting top staff, I guess. This was a revelation to all of us in the room. Then when they started to write their effectiveness areas some of them were – in fact – total inputs, as they put them up in what they believed to be, and I believed to be, their areas of effectiveness. So we sat down and rewrote them.

First we wrote the effectiveness areas of myself as CEO. We all agreed on what my job was and what my area of effectiveness was. Everyone doesn't have to come in at eight o'clock because I did and they didn't have to stay until seven o'clock because I did. And I did not have to keep proving to them that I could be first in and last out for the rest of my life. We did not have to keep proving to one another – we had to be effective. That was a great release of tension for all.

They then raised all of the areas that caused them consideration and problems, even to the point 'Could they select the colour of their own car?' Some things were simple; but for them important. Some were big things. So if you would like to call it a grievance-and-an-open-honesty session, we went through that, to clear many of the blockages. We then agreed each person's effectiveness areas looking for overlaps and underlaps. This took all day and a lot of serious thought. They would be working next day so they were supposed to stop at 5 but they were so keen they went on until 6.30.

It was a hard day, a hard three days, because they were tense days with some of them, including me, hearing things they did not want to hear. We got through that and we all walked out with new effectiveness areas, new objectives and a new planned company climate that we committed ourselves to. We were to be an output company, suited to our size of company and the industry that we were in. We all mutually agreed on that – one vote, one person. Now I don't carry any more weight in those output team meetings than they do, because now I'm just another cog in the top management group.

We then agreed to have monthly team meetings. Most management improvement schemes fail because they don't have effective team follow-up meetings. No feedback and review. They have floating little groups and after a while they get soft at the edges and die. We agreed to hold these review meetings away from the company, we hire a motel room from 8 until 5. Each person would be able to discuss their effectiveness areas and they would be judged on a budget, which they agreed to, set previously under this new scheme. I had set it with them, sitting on the other side of the table, so they were a committed group.

We then left our meeting place having achieved a tremendous thing. Tensions had been eased and role behavioural clashes had disappeared, because people realized why they were having them. My relationship with my top staff had improved considerably. Because I was the leader I was dominant and I did want them to move when I made the decision. The timing was my timing and the company revolved around me. And yet on the other side of me, I was trying to be people-related and nice, as well as all the things that autocrats try to do to keep people together. The seminar calls them hypocrites, but I couldn't quite face up to that. But the thing is we did leave as a very hard core and a better-formed group.

I then came back to my company and removed my desk. Now when this seminar made the invitation to us as undoubtedly it will to you, or has, to take away our desks, suggesting we sit on them and be photographed for the local newspaper, being carried out of our office on them – I thought well, you know this sounds good. I wouldn't mind a bit of public relations.

Then I thought, well I won't go into the publicity, but I will do what output suggests because if I am serious about change, I have to be committed to it. Why is my company input-based? Why are we over-systemized? When we added up the pieces of paper we had 120 forms. We had some of those policies written in times of survival some years ago which people still trotted out when it suited them. They flicked through the book and quoted 'You said this then, that you could do this.' So we decided to rip all these things up and keep the ones that were valid and effective and get rid of those that were now ineffective and out of date.

But to return to the desk. I looked at it for a long while. I was a guy who had worked from a long apprenticeship. Part of the status symbol was to have a beautiful desk in a nice office, an attractive secretary and a few phones and sort of feel as though one was superior. It was a magnificent looking desk, black leather on top, looking like it was worth several thousand dollars. It had a drawer in the bottom where I had my secret files on salaries and performances and a few other things. I looked at it and said 'Well, where should this desk be?' The group said it should be with the most effective bureaucrat in this company. 'Who was that?' Answer, our Finance Manager. Great! So out of my office it went, round the corner into the Finance Manager's, who happens to be a woman. She sat behind it on the big swinging chair and she said, 'This is beautiful. I can have my in-tray there and I can have my files here. Thank you.'

I walked back to my empty office and I thought 'Bloody output orientation has done this to me, what am I going to do?' So I called in a friend of mine, who is an interior decorator and explained what I wanted to do. I wanted to get out of the office. I didn't want an in-tray, I wanted change and the change had to be permanent as far as I was concerned – I wanted to commit myself. So she bought for me some U-shaped little modules of Italian brown velvet; a little lounge suite that you push together, very nice. Also a great big coffee tale, very deep and very long and the height where you can write if you want to Then I got this little work station on the side of a smaller table that fits in the corner where the phone sits – and that's all there is.

Next I called in my private secretary and said, 'Margaret, you're great. But do you know what – I haven't been using you as a private secretary, have I?' She said, 'No.' 'I have been using you as a typist, haven't I?' She said, 'Yes.' 'So would you like to take all of my private files and put them in your office?' She said, 'Yes, I would.' So out came all the secret stuff and went into her drawer. Out went the library and I said that when I wanted a book I'd press a button and she could bring the book in for me. She said, 'Love to.' All of a sudden I had a private secretary.

In came all the new furniture, which cost me 5000 bucks, but change you've got to pay for and you know you get what you pay for. There I was – seated in this new office lined with wood, and glass down at the end so I could see myself. A little bit of an autocrat. No desk, no in-tray. I sat and thought, 'Where do I put my pencil?' 'Where do I put my pen?' 'Where do I put all the things I have accumulated – calculators and things?' I didn't have a place to put things and that's when the output change started to take place. I either had to get a place to put them in or I had to delegate, so I delegated.

Now I go and sit with my executives in their office and we use my office as a general board room. If any of the senior executives have someone of importance they want to impress with Italian furniture and glass, they can use my office. It is now not the domain of the CEO. When I am there I use it – but now I am out of the office. Now I am working to my job effectiveness description. Last year I was able to visit Israel, Stockholm, Italy, Singapore and Malaysia.

No one worried about me because I was out doing my bit – I didn't have to account to anyone that I wasn't in the office, and they didn't have to worry that I was watching them over my shoulder. They knew that we would all have to stand up and be counted at the monthly review meeting.

At these monthly meetings we have a complete reappraisal of the budget achievements which is fairly normal. We also have a complete reappraisal of our adherence to our agreed outputs and if they should be changed. It can only be changed with a group meeting – not just by me. Admittedly I've got the flexibility at a one-to-one meeting, but now I am committed I want this thing to work and I want them all to carry on the message of outputs.

I went to a board meeting in Stockholm, and I introduced the ideas of outputs to the International Group – a young Italian company now based in Luxembourg, financially, but with Italian bases and new factories in America, Spain, Austria and Ireland. They are in a state where frankly they are bogged down. They need help. Talking with the founder and CEO I truly felt like a disciple. I said, 'This is what you need.' Then I went into my briefcase and out came materials on output orientation that I had with me. He said, 'What's that?' I said, 'This is what's made me so different. This is what has given my company a new revitalization. This is why I can be here not worrying about whether this or that has been dealt with, because I trust my staff. They know I trust them – they've got known effectiveness areas and objectives and I've got known areas of effectiveness with objectives. This is what you need.'

In Stockholm they had their first team meeting, so the message – the still pure message – is now flowing into an international group. The CEO has got his 16 top executives around the world on output orientation.

Next weekend we go on our strategy meeting. They are all studying their pre-work and we go away for Friday, Saturday and Sunday. For the first time in our little company we will be discussing a five-year strategy plan. I've always shunned five-year strategy plans because anyone can sort of extend figures – you don't have to be real clever. But if you start to do a serious one it is indeed a mammoth task, as you know. All the inputs and ramifications of what is going to happen to you in five years just on 12 per cent inflation. And doubling your turnover, new premises and types of staff and utilization of all your facilities and resources. However, that's one of the things we will be discussing at our next meeting, and we will be bringing our new job effectiveness descriptions and checking them because they could have changed. We will be going over the whole thing again – setting ourselves up for our next year. That's what's happening next weekend.

So what can I say? I don't often do commercials and I'm not being paid for this one, but I do feel so enthused about it and it has liberated our company so much. That is why I wrote the letter. It's nice to get the feedback that outputs are creating change; that some people do not just walk out of that door and say 'Gee! outputs are good' and then go off to the next seminar. It must help to meet someone who says, 'I have put the pure written word to the test and it's surviving.' We're not living in some unreal world and the people I work with don't have to do what I tell them to do. If they don't like it, six or seven votes against one beats me. That's the end of the story, so really I owe the idea of outputs a great deal. I owe the Institute of Management a great deal because without them I wouldn't have come on this seminar with its very true message. It's a wonderful message of integrity. Starting from here 12 months ago my company has doubled its profit. If someone makes a statement that they have doubled their profit I always look at them rather sceptically, but we are talking inhouse here and that is exactly what we have done.

I am now managing by consultation. I only see some of my senior executives once a month at the one-day team meeting because I am a task-oriented person and I am involved with my output. Now when they want to see me they just buzz through and sit in the lounge next to me, not over the other side of the former desk. I sit next to them; I look into their eyes and we communicate because we are right next to one another – and it's all right with your secretary, too!

Gentlemen, I won't bore you but I do thank you for the chance of giving you the message. It is obviously a different message from that of a very large company, where their team meetings might involve hundreds of people. I only had eight and because of our size I have been able to move fast and it has made a tremendous difference. I shall be very interested when next the group re-cast their votes on what sort of company we have. Has it moved from inputs to outputs or hasn't it?

The session moved to question and answer.
Question: Who were the seven other people?
Answer: They are my top team. I might add too that since we introduced outputs they have taken the message. They have set out output-based teams with their next line of management. So I gave the message to my top team and they have now set up outputs with their

group. We are now down to supervisor level, that's where we are. They hold their monthly meetings away from the company too and they have found the same freshness, candour and honesty coming out on feedback and relationship with their people – so in our company in 12 months we have achieved not just the top team, we have now gone through our whole management layer.

Question: What are your Effectiveness Areas?

Answer: Well, basically, the number one is to give the shareholders profit return on investment. This is my number one. To make the company profitable based on an agreed shareholders' return, bear in mind I have an overseas shareholder now as a partner. My output is to look for new products, because at this particular stage we are broadening our profit centres; and to investigate the world for new products that dovetail into the way I want future strategy on profit centres; to maintain international corporate image from a profitability point of view. As you know, when you are dealing with the Chinese, when you are dealing with the Israelis, you have to deal very personally with them. The rules that apply here don't apply to many of our trading partners overseas and so I do spend, as I say, six months of the year travelling at this particular time of my life. When all this is set up, I'll be in a position to delegate quite a lot of those trips to other people. Of course, if I keep doing this it will have detrimental effects upon my marriage, which I don't want to happen, but it is an agreed thing which my wife is involved with. She knows why I am going and we have the board meetings at home now to keep her involved. She is aware of the reason I am going to Israel, why I am going to Singapore and why I am going to New Zealand and Italy, and why I should attend board meetings. I want better deals, and I want to try to unravel all of the problems that happen with telexes between us and Italy, because again we are all different people and that takes a lot of personal dealing at top level. It is something at this stage, that I have to do – it is part of my job, if I want to be CEO of my company and it wants to import goods from overseas, I have to be there. It is as simple as that, policies and so forth for the company. I didn't bring anything in writing with me, I just prefer to talk with you *ad lib*, but I can assure you that everything we do now is double checked in writing when we've said it and then we get a bound little copy of all of our agreed job effectiveness descriptions, so that we can look at them if we want to refresh our memories of the company structure, which they comment on and help form.

Question: I've been wondering is there any problem with approaching a union official with this output scheme?

Answer: That's when I become an autocrat again. Actually, we are a non-union shop. We are union by membership, non-union by the fact that we have profit-sharing within the company. I think this is one of the things that output orientation brings out as a link-back reward system. All of my senior executives are on a profit-sharing basis on the achievement of the areas of effectiveness and objectives. The company has a holiday unit where we give them free holidays, and a few other things that small companies can do that are tax-free incentives, so we try and keep our people happy, which output orientation is helping us to do. We have far better relationships with our people, who are I think more loyal to us than to some union boss, which is the way we have got to be, because the union is going to kill us. I don't know if there is any union official here, but that's my honest opinion, so we are non-union in effectiveness.

Question: How about measurement of support things such as finance/personnel?

Answer: Well, the finance world is a difficult one. The only way we can judge our financial department is that, number one, we get our monthly profit and loss on time, we get our balance sheets on time. We have set dates for our board meetings and that division has got to conform to that effectiveness feedback time, that the statute returns are put in on time. We want to be in there by September, to have a deadline date of being to the bank with our printed audited reports by the 30th September. It's fairly hard going for any company. We have monthly review meetings on outstanding debtors and the whole trend of business, which is at a board meeting, plus the fact that we play it through our profit and loss accounts to each individual top team manager, which never happened before. So they now give a divided share of administration costs and they have to have that for the monthly outputs review meetings. The accounts department has to perform and then I have got the accounts manager tied in to an overall percentage of her co-workers, her peers, that she has to support. When they achieve budget objectives she gets an overriding bonus on each of their achievements, which is the only way we can do it because, as you say it is very hard to set a profit centre for them. There are some, but it is very hard to measure them, so we are giving her an overriding commission. This gives her a chance to go around and say, 'Look, I have given you these things, we have got to do this. How are things going?' She is interested and so is the whole department that is centralized, as most finance departments are. We find now that each manager is going along and saying, 'Gee, my administration costs have gone up.' They are worried and they are involved, whereas before they didn't care. Now they are fighting for percents because they want to sit at the review meeting and say, 'I have been profitable and I am going to get my bonus and I am going to be effective in my outside selective area of outputs.'

Question: Are your franchises part of all this as well?

Answer: No. They are straight-out distributors, but when you say, are they part of it?, previously my national manager for computer air conditioning would go out and he would just do a traditional job. Now he's gone out and said, 'Listen, if you want to be the distributor this is a very important state to me, you represent a large per cent of my budget. Do you realize what a wonderful thing you have got going for you? Now look, where is your plan? I want an output plan with objectives from you.' He is now carrying the message over to the distributors by asking them questions, and putting it to them: 'I want a complete plan, a marketing plan within one month. If you want to reassure this, we have got to work together as trading partners and I want to help you. I don't get any feedback from you. I have got to come down and visit you and you are just a typical distributor. I want to tell you it's not good enough. I am now looking at terms of outputs. Let's have a look at this, let's look at your objectives.' Now, of course, he has changed his attitude, he is beginning to change the attitude of our distributors without them knowing what they are doing, just by putting the questions and taking a more positive involved attitude, which is why my profits increased by 100 per cent.

Question: While I've often seen high profit return from changing behaviour like this, did most of that 100 per cent increase in profit come from this change within your control, as a result of these things you've told us about, or was half of it outside?

Answer: More effectiveness I think was the answer, in one area for instance, the air conditioning manager who up to that point was carrying my message all of a sudden said, 'Do you know what? Our costing is wrong.' 'Is it?' 'Yes, I've been doing it one way because you did it that way, and, I thought I wouldn't offend you, but we are losing money. I can make you more money.' 'Can you? Show me, you bring it back.' This guy is like a flower, you pour water on him and it starts opening and opening. He's changed the whole costing philosophy. He's changed the call priority rate to people, he's changed the method of designing brackets and systems so that we design off the site and go on the site with brackets and so forth. He has assisted me with research and development – we've got four new products this year. I won't give myself a plug, but we've got a wonderful air conditioning system, a do-it-yourself home air conditioning, and it's really something, but I was free to search that out, and this guy wants to help me, and I was able to do a job where my talents have been suited. Instead of worrying about everyone, carrying the weight of the whole company on my shoulders and going home having a nervous breakdown, stiff neck, palpitating heart, and all the things we have under stress, now I don't have all those very much and these guys are wearing it with me. They are sharing the burden and it's been a combination of just being more effective and profit conscious whereas before they were just workers.

EPILOGUE

The success continued for this output company. Here is an article that appeared in the dominant national financial newspaper a few years after the talk was given.

Atlas reconditions the attitude to success

By Richard Hefy

The managing director of Atlas Air, Mr Colin Ward, wants other managers to hear the story of his company because 'there's a lot of doom and gloom out there and we need some success stories'.

Atlas Air, which manufactures air conditioners for computer installations and, more recently, for office buildings, is about to merge with a larger company in an estimated $5–15 million deal.

As well as giving Atlas Air much needed injection of funds for its ongoing development programs, Mr Ward said the deal would make him 'financially independent for the first time in his life'.

But for the fiercely patriotic entrepreneur, the merger has the added benefit of giving funds to advance the technology Atlas has pioneered.

The company was set up in 1964 as a husband-and-wife operation with 'enough capital to last three months'.

It installed air conditioning units and on the suggestion of IBM, began to specialize in computer mainframe cooling – a business which later burgeoned. Later the company began designing and manufacturing its own units. It was up against major international competition which included Liebert (a $200 million company) and Siemens (the giant German multinational).

'I think they dismissed us as a joke when we started,' Mr Ward said.

According to Mr Ward, a large measure of the success of Atlas can be attributed to a business technique known as the output system pioneered by Professor W.J. Reddin. Mr Ward attended an output seminar when Atlas was languishing.

'The company wasn't going anywhere and I couldn't figure out why. I put the company in for analysis and it came out that it was being run by an autocrat who was killing his own company, had surrounded himself with input people and was destined to fail.

Previously nothing moved in this company unless I knew about it. That is how most small companies start out and that's why most managers can't expand their own companies.'

The crucial part of the success of the system was sticking to it, according to Mr Ward.

We have hung in there and made it a part of our culture,' Mr Ward said. 'Other companies use it as a veneer and that's why things like management by objectives usually fail.'

Atlas has 12 division heads all of whom are now individually accountable and must meet goals on a monthly basis. As well, the company has a system of profit sharing for each of its managers.

According to Mr Ward, one of the most important secrets of the system is the free flow of information.

'They [Atlas managers] are better informed than most board members,' he said.

Its South-East Asian branch is based in Singapore, and Atlas has recently broken into the Chinese market and has been officially recognized as a supplier to the Chinese Government.

Turnover now is about '27 million' and Mr Ward said the company was on schedule to achieve this year's target of $35 million, about 25 per cent of which will come from exports.

But the area of greatest potential growth for the company is its recently released modular office air conditioning system.

The system is said to be a world first and cost an estimated $2 million to develop.

Further plans for development with its new partner include the development of the first commercially viable gas cooling system and the setting-up of a factory in India to facilitate entry into the booming computer market there.

Financial Review
8 December 1986, p.30

15 A multinational examines itself

It is now possible to determine accurately the degree of output orientation in an organization, to identify the stronger points and to see what weaknesses need to be changed. An 80-item survey, the *Organization Output Survey*, has been designed to do just this. The Survey consists of eight scales, each with ten items to which the respondent replies 'yes' or 'no'. Some organizations use it annually as a measure of the degree of output orientation being obtained. Some have used it for several thousand managers.

This chapter will describe the survey, and several of the items composing it, and give actual results from one large multinational. Together, these will give you an opportunity to think about what you may want to measure in your organization as a whole, or in your part of it, it will also provide you with an opportunity to test your ability to make a diagnosis of what is wrong and right concerning outputs in a particular organization using the survey data provided here.

THE ORGANIZATION OUTPUT SURVEY

The eight scales of the survey

The survey measures eight characteristics of organizations. These characteristics have a scale consisting of ten items. The eight scales are:

Effective Linking with Superior
 The degree to which the superior is seen as using outputs and effectiveness as a major means of managing.

Effective Linking with Subordinates
 The degree to which oneself is using elements of outputs and effectiveness with subordinates.

Effective Linking with Co-workers
 The degree to which the relationships with co-workers facilitates the output process.

Effective Position Design
> The degree to which one sees one's own position as clearly and appropriately designed.

Resources to Position
> The degree to which there are sufficient resources available to perform effectively.

Climate for Output Orientation
> The degree to which the climate is ready for output orientation.

Benefits of Output Orientation
> The degree to which output orientation has potential benefits.

Effective Management Information
> The degree to which the management information system is adequate. (This scale is given in full in Chapter 13).

(See p. 69 which gives the ten items composing the Effective Management Information scale.)

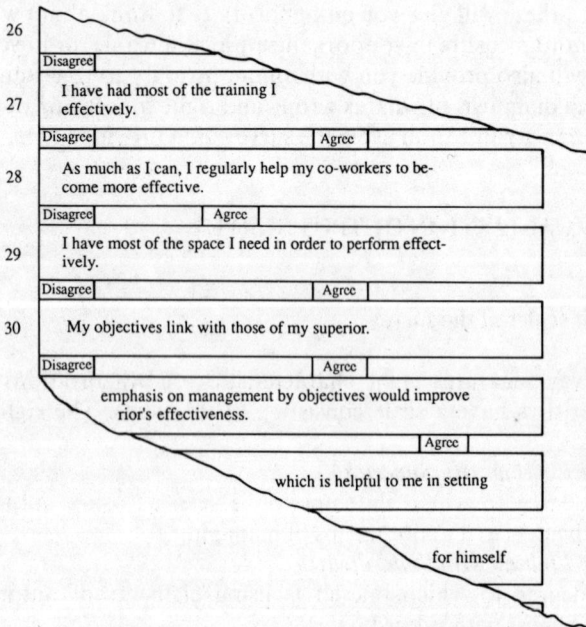

Eighty such items cover most aspects of output orientation.

Exhibit 15.1   Illustrative items from the organization output survey.

Basis for norms

A survey is of little value unless there is some form of baseline comparison that is realistic. With no such baseline on a 'yes-no' questionnaire, the assumption is that 0 is low and 100 is high, little else can be assumed. The norms given here for the survey are based on a wide variety of large and small companies and thus represent what might be seen as a reasonable organization average. Without such there is no way of knowing whether 52 per cent agree to an item such as, 'Most of the job related information I receive comes in good time' is good or poor.

Format of survey

The format of the survey is along these lines with the 80 items being numbered and an agree–disagree response requested (see Exhibit 15.1).

Continual update of norms

Users of the survey are asked to provide information on the percentage of their respondents who replied 'yes' to any item and in this way, norms are continually enlarged and improved.

Survey uses

The survey is used by the Reddin Organization to obtain a diagnosis on the state of affairs in a company and to provide ideas on what things could be changed that could produce the greatest leverage in effectiveness improvement.

THE MULTINATIONAL'S SURVEY

The organization referred to here as 'multinational' is a European firm with extensive manufacturing facilities at several locations in Europe and in over fifteen countries outside Europe. The total workforce is over 50,000, about 30,000 of whom are in Europe. Those completing the survey include 116 managers outside Europe. The survey was conducted several years after the implementation of a formal MBO programme which was thought to be based on outputs and which was seen as effective. The firm worked to integrate more of outputs and more of teamwork into its programme and a still high level of candour. It commissioned the Reddin Organization to conduct a survey preparatory to a one-day meeting in which the future emphasis on outputs and planned change was to be decided. The 268 top managers completed the survey.

Your task for this chapter is to read over Exhibits 15.2 to 15.4

which cover the highlights of the strengths and weaknesses of the multinational, and to make your own assessment.

Exhibits 15.2 to 15.4 give three pages of a computer printout giving the survey results on the organization. Other pages of the printout gave particular scores on every item, one scale to a page, with each scale containing the ten items.

You may well see some inconsistencies across the scores. Nevertheless, these scores do represent what the individual managers, in aggregate, replied. They represent the reality as they see it.

Other diagnostic input

There are two additional items about this company which you may want to think about before you make your own analysis. These are:

● In-company feelings before the survey was conducted
● The overactive role of the management development advisor (MDA)

In-company feelings before the survey was conducted
In a document distributed by the CEO some time before the survey was conducted, the two following points were made. They gave the managers' perceptions of the system being used and the CEO's reaction to these perceptions.

The two criticisms levelled at the system give a fairly good indication of the problems in it. Aspects of these are picked up by the survey. Note that the CEO's reactions to them appear to be rather defensive. People were not being considered as much as they might be.

1. *This is a rigid system which will destroy flexibility and stifle initiative.*

   There is no doubt that any system wrongly applied can do this, but this is not an inherent characteristic of the system. Properly applied it should identify where flexibility is required and promote it. Furthermore, this encourages the widest possible constructive participation and channels initiative into those areas of most significance to the business.
2. *This is a mechanistic paper-intensive system.*

   Again this can be true if the purpose of any system is misunderstood. The system should promote the change necessary to achieve results and improvements and as such the paperwork involved is only a means to an end and should be kept to a minimum. Unless this is understood the mechanics and the papers can become the end rather than the means.

The overactive role of the management development advisor (MDA)
The company produced a thick guide to implementing their system.
A key figure in the system was the Management Development
Advisor (MDA). This was, supposedly, an advisory position with no
power. But look at the role provided for the position.

1.0   *Purpose of the MDA*
      The MDA's primary purpose is to help line and staff
      managers introduce our management system. Some organ-
      izations have attempted to introduce outputs without the
      help of advisors but this places a heavy burden on manage-
      ment to acquire on their own, expertise in our philosophy,
      methodology and disciplines which are essential prerequisites
      to adopting this style of management. Without an MDA
      managers would take much longer to operate within the
      framework because they have to learn from trial and error.
      If too much time is taken in getting the system working
      many of the benefits can be lost through frustration.

2.0   *Role of the MDA*
      Briefly stated the role of the MDA is to:
      1.   Assist managers in the formulation of their objectives
           – to act as a catalyst and counsellor.
      2.   Help prepare managers for their reviews.
      3.   Provide advice on all matters concerning the system.
      4.   Ensure that the company and unit key results areas are
           revised to reflect changing needs.
      5.   Help clarify joint responsibilities through the con-
           ducting of management matrix exercises.
      6.   Ensure that schedules are met – management guide
           agreements and reviews with the managers' supervisors.
      7.   Make the programme responsive to the needs of
           management.
      8.   Provide the necessary documentation to enable
           managers to carry on the programme.
      9.   Plan, control and monitor the progress of our system
           throughout the organization.
      10. Form an effective working relationship with the organ-
           ization's management.
      11. Ensure a thorough understanding of our system.
      12. Evaluate the effectiveness of our system.

Criticism of the role
There could scarcely be a poorer description of the proper role for
the management development advisor. The role takes the initiative
from the line and involves so-called knowledge workers or staff
experts where only line managers should tread. The definition of this

role as explained above flies in the face of anything we might know
now about authority. It is obvious that the MDA reported to the
CEO. Equally obvious, this happened because the CEO could not get
the immediate team as he wished, so, he added a hitman.

The organization's ten high scores on the survey

Exhibit 15.2 gives the ten highest scores the organization received on
the survey. The first item, 36, reads: 'I have a job description which is
reasonably up-to-date and accurate.' Ninety-two per cent of 268
people replying in this multinational agreed with this item. The
international norms revealed that only 41 per cent of managers do,
overall. A difference of 51 per cent is shown in the last column. Read
over these ten differences and consider the strengths of this
organization.

Item number	Item	This organization %	International norming %	Difference
36	I have a job description which is reasonably up-to-date and accurate.	92%	41%	51%
80	My co-workers and I discuss blockages between us and remove them.	80%	30%	50%
32	I have a job description which is helpful to me in setting objectives.	84%	46%	38%
52	Much of the job-related information I am required to produce seems to be of value.	92%	55%	37%
35	Most of the job-related information I receive is useful to me.	100%	73%	27%
68	My superior and I discuss any blockages between us.	82%	58%	24%
2	I have most of the staff I need in order to perform effectively.	92%	69%	23%
50	I can use most of the job-related information I receive.	88%	65%	23%
58	Change is easily introduced here.	70%	47%	23%
54	I am encouraged to interact directly with my co-workers without going through my superior or their supervisors.	92%	70%	22%

Exhibit 15.2   Your ten highest scores on the organization output
survey

These ten statements show, in order, how your organization most differs, in a positive direction, from others. They may reasonably be taken to show what your organization is good at.

The organization's ten low scores on the survey

Exhibit 15.3 gives the ten lowest scores the organization received on the survey. Read over these ten differences and consider the weaknesses of this organization.

Item number	Item	This organization %	International norming %	Difference
3	I have reached agreement with my subordinates on how their effectiveness will be measured.	36%	64%	-28%
7	Most of the job-related information I receive comes in good time.	52%	77%	-25%
28	As much as I can, I regularly help my co-workers to become more effective.	56%	81%	-25%
11	My objectives link with the objectives of those I work with at my level.	50%	73%	-23%
63	I have most of the information I need in order to perform effectively.	62%	85%	-23%
55	I have most of the specialist advice I need in order to perform effectively.	62%	80%	-18%
20	My subordinates participate fully with me in setting the objectives for their positions.	74%	92%	-18%
26	I can get most of the job-related information I need fairly easily.	58%	75%	-17%
49	Most meetings I attend here are productive.	48%	64%	-16%
61	I meet regularly with my subordinates to agree on their objectives.	50%	65%	-15%

Exhibit 15.3   Your ten lowest scores on the organization output survey

These ten statements show, in order, how your organization most differs, in a negative direction, from others. They may reasonably be taken to show what your organization is poor at.

The organization's scale scores on the survey

Exhibit 15.4 shows the organization's averages, compared to other organizations, on each of the eight scales of the survey.

Scale	This organization %	International norming %	Difference
Effective position design The degree to which one sees the position as being clearly and appropriately designed	82.8%	67.6%	+ 15.2%
Effective management information The degree to which the management information system is adequate	74.4%	68.9%	+ 5.5%
Effective linking with co-workers The degree to which the relationship with co-workers facilitates the output process	70.0%	66.1%	+ 3.9%
Climate for output orientation The degree to which the climate is ready for output orientation	74.8%	71.2%	+ 3.6%
Benefits of output orientation The degree to which output orientation has potential benefits	70.7%	68.3%	+ 2.4%
Effective linking with superior The degree to which the superior is seen as using outputs and effectiveness as a means of managing	65.1%	63.0%	+ 2.1%
Resources to position The degree to which there are sufficient resources available to perform effectively	77.6%	78.6%	- 1.0%
Effective linking with subordinates The degree to which oneself is using elements of outputs effective with subordinates	73.6%	78.6%	- 5.0%

Exhibit 15.4   Your scale scores on the organization output survey

This list shows, in order, the scales on which your organization is better (+) or poorer (-) than other organizations.

Your assessment

Based on your review of Exhibits 15.2 to 15.4, make a few notes on how you see this company and its degree of output orientation. The idea is to try to connect some of the higher scores with other higher scores, or some of the highest scores with lowest scores, and so on. Try to read something into the twenty items that are provided, and try and make some sense out of it all. It is a reality for an organization as seen by its members.

If you were a consultant what would you recommend this company do to improve things?

Some diagnostic comments on the multinational

Before reading these diagnostic comments, you might want to consider or reconsider your own based on your analysis of Exhibits 15.2 to 15.4

There seems to be indications that individual positions considered in isolation are well designed but these link fairly poorly to other positions, in particular subordinate positions, and link fairly poorly to such things as management information and resources.

The system they are using appears to work fairly well top-down but not so well bottom-up. This can be seen as an inconsistency because middle managers are in both positions. However, it is the superior who is most responded to, not subordinates.

A central problem is linkages with other parts of the organization. This is reflected in comments about co-workers, subordinates and information.

We can see that while a great deal of effort was made to clarify the individual position not so much attention was paid to making the necessary changes in the management information system.

There are several very low scores on management information system relating specifically to timeliness, amount and ease of obtaining.

It may be an overinterpretation of the data presented here but there seems to be an impression given that a fairly good system has been designed and the issue now is to make it work.

The request for this survey came, in part, because of an observed need to improve teamwork. In fact, this request came in response to

an article that was published by the author along the lines of
Chapter 6. It may be that they saw teamwork as a useful way of
getting a system to work better by providing linkages.

ACTION STEPS

1. This chapter was designed to put you in a diagnostic mode. It
    could be a very good idea if you got a few of your co-workers or
    subordinates or superior to review the information given here
    and to come up with a group diagnosis.
2. Consider whether you should make some survey of the system
    with which you are immediately involved.

GLOSSARY

Organization output survey: A survey designed to determine
the existing level of output orientation in an organization. It consists
of eight scales of ten items each.

16 How IBM uses these ideas

Here is the booklet prepared by a national subsidiary of IBM for their internal use in making their organization more output-oriented. Some ideas here are not covered in this book but are clearly related to the ideas in it. The term, effectiveness standards, used here is now referred to as measurement areas.

Performance Planning for Individuals and Teams

The purpose of this guide
is to provide a common framework
for performance planning.

2

PART I
UNDERSTANDING EFFECTIVENESS

1. Understanding Effectiveness
2. A basis for performance planning.
3. In search of Effectiveness Areas
4. Converting inputs to outputs
5. Examples of EAs.
6. How to write and test EAs.

PART II
A BASIS FOR ORGANISATION

7. The linking process
8. The delegation matrix
9. Making delegation work
10. Common EAs.
11. Mission EAs.
12. Link to PPC & E

PART III
PERFORMANCE PLANNING

4

PERFORMANCE PLANNING — OVERVIEW

PART I   UNDERSTANDING EFFECTIVENESS

The idea of Effectiveness Areas enables us to think about the job in terms of outputs and provides a sound basis for performance planning.

The first section is devoted to understanding Effectiveness Areas before we move on to their application to performance planning.

6
_____

UNDERSTANDING EFFECTIVENESS

EFFECTIVENESS IS THE EXTENT TO WHICH THE *OUTPUT*
REQUIREMENTS OF THE JOB ARE ACHIEVED.

EFFECTIVENESS AREAS (EAs)

THE KEY OUTPUT REQUIREMENTS OF THE JOB

OUTPUTS = RESULTS

_____ 7

UNDERSTANDING EFFECTIVENESS

There is only one realistic and unambiguous definition of Effectiveness: effectiveness is the extent to which a person achieves the **output** requirements of the job.

We aren't paid to be busy, for inputs, for bureaucracy or for mere activity. We are paid for output, for results, and activity is worthless unless it contributes to some desirable **result**.

This rather obvious point is the starting point for understanding effectiveness and for performance planning.

The first step is always to identify the most important output requirements of the job. These are called EFFECTIVENESS AREAS (EAs) and they are the key areas in which performance needs to be planned and controlled.

These effectiveness areas will provide the basic framework for the performance plan.

EAs can only apply to individuals or teams. In this first section we will consider EAs for individuals.

8
___

A BASIS FOR PERFORMANCE PLANNING

EFFECTIVENESS AREA (EA)	EFFECTIVENESS STANDARD (ES)	MEASUREMENT PROCESS	OBJECTIVE
The KEY OUTPUT REQUIREMENTS of a job	MEASURES OR INDICATORS of performance appropriate to each EA	The FEEDBACK SYSTEM which provides data relevant to each ES	SPECIFIC TARGETS which apply each ES

9

A BASIS FOR PERFORMANCE PLANNING

Performance plans need to include specific objectives. Effectiveness Areas are turned into objectives by using the idea of EFFECTIVENESS STANDARDS. These break down each EA to highlight the key performance indicators and therefore where objectives will be required.

Once we know the effectiveness standards the next step is to check out the MEASUREMENT PROCESS which will provide relevant and timely data for each ES.

Finally we agree objectives, which represent the specific levels of achievement required against each ES.

Note that objectives come last in the logic chain. While the idea of specific and agreed objectives is central to PPC & E, the other three ideas are the foundations for any objectives that are set. Only with a correct understanding of these foundations will the objectives be sound.

10

IN SEARCH OF EFFECTIVENESS AREAS

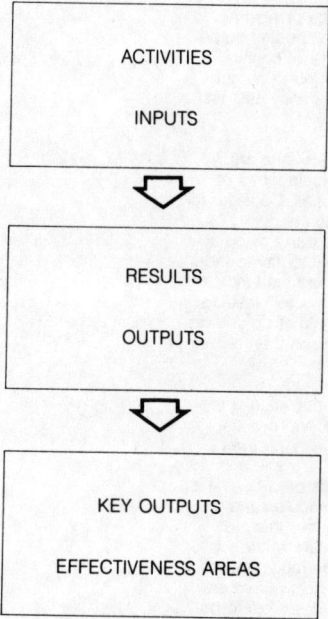

```
┌─────────────────────────────┐
│                             │
│          ACTIVITIES         │
│                             │
│           INPUTS            │
│                             │
└─────────────────────────────┘
              ▽
┌─────────────────────────────┐
│                             │
│           RESULTS           │
│                             │
│           OUTPUTS           │
│                             │
└─────────────────────────────┘
              ▽
┌─────────────────────────────┐
│                             │
│         KEY OUTPUTS         │
│                             │
│      EFFECTIVENESS AREAS    │
│                             │
└─────────────────────────────┘
```

IN SEARCH OF EFFECTIVENESS AREAS

The first step in performance planning is to identify Effectiveness Areas; the key output requirements of the job. This of course, requires thinking about the job in output terms, which may not be as easy as it first appears.

The problem is that too many jobs are described in terms of inputs; in terms of activities and not outputs at all. Consider for a moment the most common enquiry among strangers at, say, a party or on a plane trip. You are not likely to say to the person next to you "What are the key output requirements of your job?" Instead, you are very likely to ask "What do you **do** for a living?" The other person then replies with a list of **activities**.

One result of this activity orientation is the way in which many job descriptions are written. They are full of activity phrases such as: he administers .... she ensures .... he maintains records of .... he organises .... she schedules and arranges. Job descriptions like this are useful in conveying the nature of the job but they rarely describe the requirements for effectiveness. To find effectiveness we need to ask **why** these things need to be done — what is the **output**!

12

IN SEARCH OF EFFECTIVENESS AREAS

TRAINER EXAMPLE

INPUTS TO THIS JOB

TO DESIGN TRAINING PROGRAMS	WHY?
TO RUN TRAINING PROGRAMS	WHY?
TO TEACH PEOPLE	WHY?
TO INCREASE THEIR SKILLS OR KNOWLEDGE	WHY?

OUTPUTS OF THIS JOB

SKILL LEVEL/ KNOWLEDGE LEVEL

AWARENESS

SOMEONE ELSE'S JOB

TO IMPROVE THEIR JOB PERFORMANCE

WHY?

TO IMPROVE COMPANY PERFORMANCE

IN SEARCH OF EFFECTIVENESS AREAS

THE TRAINING OFFICER

Thinking in output terms can provide some valuable insights into the true nature of the job. For example, a training officer may go through the kind of process illustrated opposite.

Asked what his most important area is, he might reply — "to design training programs".

When asked "Why" he replies "To run training programs".

Again asked "Why" he says "To teach people, of course!"

We can almost see an output from here, and the next "Why?" takes us there. "To increase their skills and knowledge"

If we go any further we get into someone else's job. ("To improve their performance"). We cannot claim to be responsible for what someone else does. To go even further suggest that the training officer is a profit centre which is clearly incorrect. Activities and inputs are converted to outputs by asking "Why?" but we need to stay within the **personal responsibilities** and **authorities** of the job holder.

The real purpose of this job is not to design and run training courses but to increase people's skills and knowledge.

Expressed as Effectiveness Areas, this becomes SKILL LEVEL and KNOWLEDGE LEVEL.

This change in perspective is not simply different words for the same job. Effectiveness areas are the basis for performance planning and the two viewpoints will result in very different types of objective.

TO RUN TRAINING PROGRAMS
will result in objectives to do with the number of events, the number of student days and expense level i.e. **administration** effectiveness.

SKILL LEVEL
KNOWLEDGE LEVEL
will result in objectives which relate to what the pupils know and can do, i.e. **teaching** effectiveness.

We usually need both types of objectives. The point is that without scratching for the outputs we may never get beyond activities and to the real nature of the job.

14

CONVERTING INPUTS TO OUTPUTS

I AM RESPONSIBLE FOR

INPUT	OUTPUT
DEVELOPING AND TRAINING S.E.'s.	S.E. SKILL LEVEL
CONTROL OF EXPENSES TO BELOW BUDGET	EXPENSE LEVEL
ENSURING QUALITY IS HIGH	QUALITY LEVEL OR QUALITY AWARENESS
KEEPING MANAGEMENT INFORMED OF TECHNICAL ISSUES	MANAGER (TECHNICAL) AWARENESS
DEVELOPING MARKETING PROGRAMS	MARKETING PROGRAMS — AVAILABILITY — EFFECTIVENESS

CONVERTING INPUTS TO OUTPUTS

Because it is activity and busyness which fills our day, we can become distracted from the true purpose of the job, the key output requirements. Going back to basics, to EAs, almost always pays dividends in terms of enhanced understanding and focus.

Most inputs can be converted to outputs if the job is needed at all, as the examples opposite illustrate.

To discuss some of these —

EXPENSE LEVEL
  denotes that whatever the level of expense, I am responsible. We can define the expense target when we get to objectives.

This example also highlights a common stumbling block. Don't be concerned if EAs look somewhat passive or obvious. The action words, numbers and dates will come later when we expand each EA. Right now we are concerned with correct definition of responsibility.

I am responsible for the level of expense.

MANAGER (technical)
AWARENESS
  this helps to show the difference between busyness and effectiveness. The input statement invites us to set objectives in terms of preparation activities. The output statement will lead to objectives concerning manager awareness.

These examples also serve to show another useful aspect of EAs; they define the organisation in that they pinpoint the job responsibility.

For example,

QUALITY LEVEL
  I can only be responsible for the quality level of what I personally control.

  This denotes that I have line authority.

QUALITY AWARENESS
  This is a staff position and is concerned with programs which inform rather than personal accountability.

FOOTNOTE:
  Of course if there were no outputs for a given job you would wonder why it exists at all!

16

EXAMPLES OF EFFECTIVENESS AREAS

TOP MANAGER

Profitability

Return on Capital

Market Share

Reputation

SECRETARY

Document Availability

Administration Support

FINANCIAL PLANNER

Plan Soundness

Issue Management

CUSTOMER SUPPORT REP

Machine availability

Installs

Responsiveness

Customer Satisfaction

MARKET REP

Sales Level

Install Level

Customer Satisfaction

PLANT MANAGER

Production Level

Product Cost

Product Quality

EXAMPLES OF EAs

Opposite are some examples of EAs.

Remember that EAs are **general** output requirements. They contain no quantities, times or directional words, like increase, maximise, etc.

At first the EAs may appear to be bland and passive but they describe the organisation of work and the 'hardware' of standards and objectives comes later.

These are for example only and they are not intended to be complete nor to provide a "standard set".

While trying to maintain an outputs orientation, don't get so tied up in the wording that you lose the personal meaning or waste time in pedantics.

For example, a staff specialist whose job is to advise top management on industrial relations issues could concoct something like:

    EXECUTIVE MANAGEMENT
    INDUSTRIAL RELATIONS ADVICE
    SOUNDNESS/EFFECTIVENESS

When a simple statement would be better

    IR CONSULTANCY

even if it isn't quite so precise.

18

SIX TESTS FOR EFFECTIVENESS AREAS

1. REPRESENT OUTPUT, NOT INPUT

2. LEAD TO PERFORMANCE
   INDICATORS

3. BE AN IMPORTANT PART OF THE
   POSITION

4. WITHIN PERSONAL CONTROL

   AND, AS A WHOLE

5. REPRESENT ALL OF THE JOB

6. NOT TOO MANY

   HELPWORDS:

   SOUNDNESS   LEVEL

   AVAILABILITY   AWARENESS

HOW TO WRITE AND TEST EFFECTIVENESS AREAS

EAs are the key output requirements of a job; the major reasons why the job exists.

These are the sort of questions which will flush out EAs for a job.

All that the questions really ask is: "What is the job?" But they ask it in different ways.

What is this job's unique contribution? ....

What are my key responsibilities? ....

What are my key results? ....

What is my mission? ....

What would change if my job was eliminated? ....

What is the difference between my job and my boss' job or my subordinates? ....

What would I be most likely to concentrate on over two or three years if I wanted to make the greatest improvement in my unit? In the organisation as a whole? ....

When effectiveness areas are identified, they should satisfy six tests:

1. represent output, not input;

2. lead to associated objectives which are measurable; (Certain words will be found to be helpful in this regard. Words like availability, level, soundness, awareness lead readily to associated objectives).

3. be an important part of the position; and

4. be within the actual limits of authority and responsibility of the job holder.

Effectiveness areas as a whole should:

5. represent 100% of the outputs of the position; and

6. not be so many as to avoid dealing with the essence of the job or so few as to make planning difficult. Four to eight is usual.

20

PERFORMANCE PLANNING — OVERVIEW

PART 1
UNDERSTANDING EFFECTIVENESS

The idea of Effectiveness areas enables us to think about the job in terms of outputs and provides a sound basis for performance planning.

PART 2
A BASIS FOR ORGANISATION

Effectiveness Areas are required at individual level and at team level. We need to know what the team is here for and who is responsible for what.

Effectiveness Areas define the organisation and assist the delegation process by making it clear who is responsible for what.

The delegation matrix will show what is delegated to each team member and the difference between managerial responsibility and the manager's job.

22

THE LINKING PROCESS

EFFECTIVENESS AREAS ARE DEFINED AT THREE LEVELS

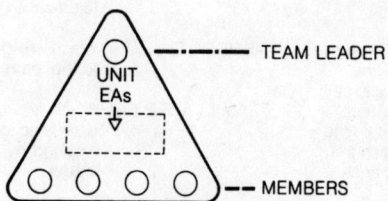

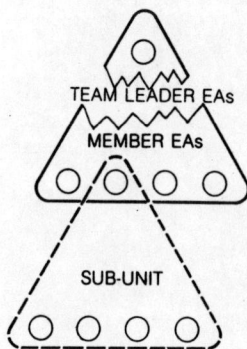

THE LINKING PROCESS

The most fundamental requirement of any team is to know "Why we are here and who is responsible for what". This requires teams to identify EAs at three levels.

The starting point is always Unit EAs, those Effectiveness Areas which apply to the entire team. Unit EAs provide focus for the team. They represent "why we are here" and the special role of the team within the larger organisation. Unit EAs are also the starting point for the Team Performance Plan.

The next step is to allocate these Eas, in whole or in part, to the members of the team, including the Team Leader, which is a special role within the team.

There are three levels of EAs within a team:

UNIT EAs — which apply to the team as an entire unit

MEMBER EAs — which are delegated to the team members

TEAM LEADER EAs — which are not delegated but are retained by the leader.

NOTE: Where team members are leaders of their own teams, their EAs become sub-unit EAs for those next level teams.

This is called the linking process because it links each team to the next level team.

24

THE DELEGATION MATRIX

UNIT EAs	MEMBER EAs				LEADER EAs PERSONAL
1					
2					
3					
4					
5					
LEADERSHIP					
RELATIONSHIPS					
TEAMWORK					

THE DELEGATION MATRIX

To show who is responsible for what in the team we use a simple spread sheet called The Delegation Matrix.

The first step in constructing a delegation matrix is for the team to agree Unit EAs.

The next step is to agree, for each EA, what (if any) part of it is delegated to each team member.

Finally we confirm this delegation by showing what remains to the team leader as a personal responsibility. There is an important piece of logic here. What is delegated cannot be retained. What is **not** delegated becomes the personal responsibility of the team leader. This logic provides the final check for completeness —

UNIT EAs = MEMBER EAs + LEADER PERSONAL EAs

Completing the delegation matrix represents a fundamental statement about the team:

• we know what the team is here for

• we have defined the organisation of the team

• we have made clear what is delegated and what is not

There is something else which is just as important. We have defined the leader's job within the team. The team leader is **responsible** (to the next level up) for it all, for the Unit EAs. The team leaders **job** (within the team) is shown in the last column.

If each plays his part as shown in the matrix, the Unit EAs will result.

The delegation matrix also illustrates and reinforces a fundamental truth of organisations: It is this:

MY FIRST JOB IS AS A MEMBER OF MY BOSS' TEAM.

MY SECOND JOB IS MY OWN JOB (or leader of my own team).

That's the way organisations work, top down!

26

MAKING DELEGATION WORK
(LINKING THE DELEGATION MATRIX)

UNIT EAs	SUB UNIT EAs				LEADER PERSONAL

UNIT EAs	SUB UNIT EAs				LEADER PERSONAL

UNIT EAs	SUB UNIT EAs				LEADER PERSONAL

MAKING DELEGATION WORK

The delegation matrix provides the machinery by which teams are linked throughout the organisation.

Starting at the top, the Unit EAs are the key outputs of the entire company. These EAs are spread across the "top team" providing the starting point of EAs for the various functions e.g. Marketing, Finance etc.

The Leader Personal column holds the EAs which are personal to the Chief Executive and here we can pause to illustrate the difference between the leader's responsibility and the leaders job. The Chief Executive is **responsible** for the achievement of the Unit results; profit, revenue, market share, reputation etc. However, his **job** is not to personally achieve all these things. That would be impossible and he has the entire company to do this work. The personal job is likely to concern matters which are pertinent to the role of the Chief Executive; strategy, organisation, morale, reputation etc.

Similarly, further down the organisation, a marketing manager will be **responsible** for that unit's quota achievement but may carry no personal quota. In this case, his or her **personal** job would not include quota achievement but the management job of quota allocation, key account planning etc.

These jobs are linked by a cascading series of delegation matrices, where each member's EAs provide the starting point for the next level team.

The result of this relatively simple and obvious linkage is of great importance to the organisation.

First, any person in the linkage can see how their individual job fits in the great order of things; one building brick in the whole edifice of organisation.

Second, it provides the machinery which links the tiller to the rudder, the channels along which can be communicated "what is important around here" and the channels for the response in terms of performance plans.

Constructing a delegation matrix and linking it to the next level teams (up and down) is a basic requirement of all teams.

28

COMMON EAs

FOR TEAMS	FOR INDIVIDUALS
LEADERSHIP	PEOPLE MANAGEMENT EMPLOYEE DEVELOPMENT SYSTEMS
RELATIONSHIPS	RELATIONSHIPS
TEAMWORK	TEAMWORK

COMMON EAs

The idea of common EAs simplifies the compilation of EAs for teams and individuals.

Actual experience in the development of EAs will quickly show that some EAs are shared by all jobs and all teams; they are **common**. For convenience we use three common EAs at team level.

LEADERSHIP
concerns how we get things done through people, through tasks, systems, procedures etc.
Leadership includes Security, Business Conduct Guidelines in fact the entire IBM Management System.

RELATIONSHIPS
all teams have relationships
e.g. with AFE/APG
with other departments and functions
with customers and suppliers
with government and the community
this EA is to cover these things.

TEAMWORK
includes how this team will work together and link to the next level teams, up or down the chain of command.

These three EAs are common to all teams.

When they are applied to individuals, we usually subdivide "Leadership into some major components.

PEOPLE MANAGEMENT
EMPLOYEE DEVELOPMENT
These apply only to people Managers.
SYSTEMS
This component applies to all and covers the individual's observance of established systems.
e.g. business practices, planning and expense control, information reporting, asset protection, quality
Once common EAs are understood, they help to broaden the basis for objective setting beyond "meeting the numbers".

30

UNIT EFFECTIVENESS AREAS

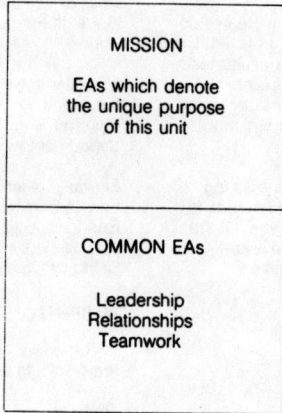

```
+-----------------------------+
|                             |
|          MISSION            |
|                             |
|    EAs which denote         |
|    the unique purpose       |
|    of this unit             |
|                             |
+-----------------------------+
|                             |
|        COMMON EAs           |
|                             |
|        Leadership           |
|        Relationships        |
|        Teamwork             |
|                             |
+-----------------------------+
```

MISSION EAs

The purpose of nominating common EAs is to save teams the time and effort involved in what amounts to re-inventing the wheel.

Common EAs are shared by all teams so let's treat them as 'given'. What is left is not common; is unique to that particular team. In other words, once we put common EAs aside we are left with the MISSION of the team, the unique purpose for which it exists.

The way to decide whether something belongs under Mission or Common is to ask "Is this why this team exists?" If the answer is "Yes!" it's part of Mission: if "No!" then it belongs to Common.

Take for example the output of "Plan Soundness". For most teams this belongs in Common, as part of the Leadership EA. After all, we aren't here **primarily** to make plans; this is part of how we get things done.

However, if we were part of the Planning function then "Plan Soundness" is a **mission** item, because a planning department was created to make plans.

Similarly, other items which are normally part of Common EAs can become Mission EAs for specialist departments whose main purpose in life concerns says Security or Hiring or Communication.

Summary:

Effectiveness areas are the key output requirements of a job.

There are two main types of Effectiveness Areas.

MISSION EAs — which are unique to this team or job

COMMON EAs — which are shared by all.

32

LINK TO PPC AND E

Delegation Matrix

Unit EAs	MEMBER EAs			LEADER PERSONAL EAs
1				
2				
3				
4				
5				
LEADERSHIP				
RELATIONSHIPS				
TEAMWORK				

▽ Individual PPC & E

Responsibilities	Objectives	Achievements
1		
2		
3		
4		
5		
LEADERSHIP		
RELATIONSHIPS		
TEAMWORK		

LINK TO PPC AND E

If we now turn to the PPC & E documentation, we can see that EAs provide the first column in the performance plan.

These are the areas in which the jobholder must be effective and where specific objectives will be agreed.

When we look at the delegation matrix it appears that the team leader has **two** sets of EAs, Unit and personal. Does this mean two performance plans?

Not quite! We need to look at the leader's EAs in two distinct roles.

First, as member of the next level team (the leaders **first** job). The leader is responsible and accountable to his or her own boss for the Unit EAs. This is PPC & E material between the leader and the next level manager.

Second, as leader of his own team, where his role is defined by leader personal EAs. This is entirely internal to his own team and not PPC & E material.

As part of this leader's performance evaluation, the reviewing manager will want to discuss the leaders effectiveness as a leader (did this team achieve the Unit EAs with the leader's help, because of the leader or in spite of him?) All of this is adequately covered under the common EA "Leadership", which includes an Effectiveness Standard "Fulfillment of Leader Personal EA's".

Each person on the team only has one set of EAs, mission and common which form the basis for performance evaluation.

The Manager's PPC & E documentation is specially adapted to the framework of mission and common EA's.

Summary:

Effectiveness Areas are defined at three levels:

UNIT EAs — outputs of the entire team.

MEMBER EAs — delegated to individual team members.

LEADER PERSONAL EAs — EAs not delegated and retained by the team leader.

34

PERFORMANCE PLANNING — OVERVIEW

PART 1
UNDERSTANDING EFFECTIVENESS

The idea of Effectiveness areas enables us to think about the job in terms of outputs and provides a sound basis for performance planning.

PART 2
BASIS FOR ORGANISATION

Effectiveness Areas define the organisation and assist the delegation process by making it clear who is responsible for what.

PART 3
PERFORMANCE PLANNING

Each EA is broken down to the key performance items where specific objectives will be required.

36

EFFECTIVENESS AREAS (EAs) the KEY OUTPUT REQUIREMENTS of a job or unit	EFFECTIVENESS STANDARDS (ESs) PERFORMANCE INDICATORS or criteria which apply to each EA
ASK	**ASK**
What are my important responsibilities?	How can I tell when I am doing this EA well? What will be reviewed or measured?
Can I express these as OUTPUTS (not activities)?	What criteria or requirements will indicate quality?
Is each expressed so that it leads to associated measures?	What will characterise performance?
Am I personally responsible and accountable for this EA?	What am I going to look at or review to determine effectiveness in this EA?
	Is this truly a measure for this EA?
	Do I own this ES? Is it what I, personally can control or contribute?
	Is it within my direct authority?

EFFECTIVENESS STANDARDS

Once the general output requirements (EAs) are established, we need to define how we are going to measure or recognise performance. Effectiveness Standards amplify each EA to indicate the Key performance requirements. We identify Effectiveness Standards by breaking down EAs into key components or requirements. There will usually be a number of ESs for each EA. For example, when breaking down the EA "Sales Level" we might say that, while the total number of points sold is important, there are other requirements for effectiveness in this area.

e.g. — the number of new customers;
— the level of outright sales;
— the number of competitive wins/losses.

Note that these are **not** objectives; there are no specifics as to dollars, time, etc. Effectiveness Standards define the criteria for effectiveness — which means that these are the areas where specific objectives will be required. ESs tend to change little year on year; they are converted regularly, usually annually, to objectives.

To identify ESs for a given area ask "How will I know if I am doing this well; what will I look at, measure or review to test for effectiveness? What expectations are held of me or this team?" What will characterise performance?

Check to make sure that each ES is within the personal control and authority of the jobholder. This check will frequently reveal that a person is being held accountable for an ES over which he or she has no real control. For instance, an expense planner cannot be accountable for the level of actual expenditure when this is entirely in the hands of line managers.

Summary

An Effectiveness Standard:

— breaks down an EA into key requirements;
— is a criterion or indicator of effectiveness in that EA;
— is within the direct control and authority of the jobholder;
— is converted regularly into a specific objective.

38

EXAMPLES OF EFFECTIVENESS STANDARDS

4

EFFECTIVENESS AREA	SOME ESs
MACHINE AVAILABILITY	• downtime • parts usage
CUSTOMER SATISFACTION	• level of complaints • survey results • repeat sales
EMPLOYEE MORALE	• EOS results • speak-ups • exec interviews
PLAN SOUNDNESS	• fit with APG plan • commitment of users • quality of communication
CREDIT MANAGEMENT	• days sales outstanding • overdue accounts • customer relationships
CANDIDATE AVAILABILITY	• number of candidates supplied • acceptance of the system • quality of hires

334   *The Output-Oriented Manager*

39

EXAMPLES OF EFFECTIVENESS STANDARDS

The examples opposite illustrate a cross section of ESs for some of the EAs shown in Part I. Some will be readily measurable and some will be very subjective and difficult to measure.

Note that many items could be EAs or ESs dependant on the level in the hierarchy we are addressing.

IDENTIFYING ES's

A good way to identify ES's is to ask "What will characterise performance? What indicators will denote excellence?"

Thus, for an EA like "Customer Satisfaction" you would ask "What characterises high customer satisfaction" and might come up with:

— few complaints
— high survey results
— self-sufficiency
— come back for more
This would result in ESs like
— level of complaints
— survey results
— repeat sales

ALL ESs APPLY, FEW ARE HIGHLIGHTED

This is an important point. The performance plan is not a job description; it does not detail every aspect of the job.

For each EA there are many performance requirements; there may be dozens of **potential** ESs AND THEY ALL APPLY. However, we only select a few to be highlighted in the performance plan. These are the really significant ESs where we intend to set specific objectives for achievement and to set up a feedback process to formally review results.

What is more, the ESs selected may change over time to meet changing circumstances or emphasis.

The result will usually be 1 to 3 ESs for each EA, enough to communicate the significant performance requirements and, (when turned into objectives) to provide a valid basis for performance evaluation.

40

REVIEWING EXPECTATIONS

5

EFFECTIVENESS AREAS	EXPECTATIONS				
	BOSS		CUSTOMERS		SUPPLIERS
1					
2					
3					
4					
5					

REVIEWING EXPECTATIONS

Another good way to identify Effectiveness Standards for a given EA is to ask "Who are my customers and what do they expect from me?" A worksheet like the example opposite will assist.

It allows you to show, in the left hand column, your EAs and then across the page to show the individuals and groups who have expectations of you. These are your customer requirements.

Once completed, this simple analysis can provide some valuable insights into the nature of quality for this job and may also have identified some extra requirements of the information system.

Clearly, such an exercise is also valuable for teams who want to identify ES's for Unit EAs.

42

EFFECTIVENESS STANDARDS FOR COMMON EAs

6

Because common EAs are shared by all teams, there is no need to develop ESs "from scratch".

Here are some suggested ESs for common EAs. They are intended as a guide rather than a check list and they will usually require amendment to suit particular individuals.

EFFECTIVENESS AREA — PEOPLE MANAGEMENT

So that subordinates are effective and achieve personal satisfaction.

EFFECTIVENESS STANDARDS

Delegation matrix is in place
Mutually agreed performance plans for all subordinates
Subordinates achieve their objectives
Fulfillment of Leader Personal EA's
Effective counselling, coaching, critique
Timely and appropriate evaluation
Timely and appropriate recognition
Salary administration, merit pay
Management of poor performance
Equal opportunity
Employee involvement and communication
Dept. meetings, timeliness and quality
Sensitive handling of personal issues
Establishment of high standards and sound team norms
Issue identification and resolution
Occupational health and safety

EFFECTIVENESS AREA — EMPLOYEE DEVELOPMENT

To meet individual potential and business needs.

EFFECTIVENESS STANDARDS

Hiring of quality people
Effective orientation, induction
Employee development plans in place
Development plans are achieved
Required skills are available
Replacement tables maintained
Contribution to X-functional training
Subordinate attendance at scheduled training events

Note: The Manager's Journal provides data relevant to these ES's.

EFFECTIVENESS STANDARDS FOR COMMON EAs

EFFECTIVENESS AREA — SYSTEMS
Support and improve the IBM management
and information system.

EFFECTIVENESS STANDARDS

Business practices observed
Sound planning and resource management
Control of headcount and expense
Timely reporting of required information
Protection of assets, security
Effectiveness of systems generated
Quality improvement, methodology in place

**EFFECTIVENESS AREA —
RELATIONSHIPS**

Where there is mutual support and respect.

EFFECTIVENESS STANDARDS

With other IBMA departments
With other IBM e.g. APG
With customers
    suppliers
    other non IBM

EFFECTIVENESS AREA — TEAMWORK

Team membership and linking to next level
teams.

EFFECTIVENESS STANDARDS

Personal observation of team norms,
standards
Contribution to sound team functioning, e.g.
in meetings
Contribution to team strategy and planning
Contribution to team results and reputation

44

MEASUREMENT PROCESS

EFFECTIVENESS AREAS (EAs) the KEY OUTPUT REQUIREMENTS of a job or unit.	EFFECTIVENESS STANDARDS (ESs) PERFORMANCE INDICATORS or criteria which apply to each EA.	MEASUREMENT PROCESS the FEEDBACK SYSTEM which will provide data relevant to each ES.
ASK	**ASK**	**ASK**
What are my important responsibilities?	How can I tell when I am doing this EA well? What will be reviewed or measured?	Where will I/my boss go to get the data?
Can I express these as OUTPUTS (not activities)?	What criteria or requirements will indicate quality?	What review process will determine if the ES is achieved or fulfilled?
Is each expressed so that it leads to associated measures?	What am I going to look at or review to determine effectiveness in this EA?	Where is the information?
Am I personally responsible and accountable for this EA?	Is this truly a measure for this EA?	Is this the right data for the EA/ES specified?
When complete, EAs should represent the *entire* job yet not be so many as to hide the essentials.	Do I own this ES? Is it what I, personally, can control or contribute?	Are all ESs covered?
	Is it within my direct authority?	If I can't get relevant data, if no review process is possible, what's the point of the ES or EA?

DEFINE THE ORGANISATION	DETERMINE WHERE OBJECTIVES WILL BE REQUIRED	SET UP THE MANAGEMENT INFORMATION SYSTEM

AT EACH STEP — CHECK — **do I own this, do I control it? is there logic EA-ES-Objective?**

MEASUREMENT PROCESS

Once an effectiveness area and associated effectiveness standards have been drafted, it is necessary to make a deliberate check on the MEASUREMENT PROCESS which will provide relevant performance data. For each ES we need to know what record, report or review process will provide information which will enable jobholder and manager to evaluate performance. If no such data or review exists it must be provided for, or objectives are likely to be no more than wishful thinking.

While most measurement problems can be solved with imagination, the cost of measurement problem may remain. To measure the impact of a training course may require many telephone calls or a questionnaire, and possibly a field survey. The outputs of a customer relations position are hard to measure without a formal survey of some kind. In these cases one has to ask whether the function is important enough to have even a rough measurement of its effectiveness. If so, then allocate part of the budget to measurement. If not, then question the validity of the chosen effectiveness standard or even the EA itself. There is too much conventional wisdom that a particular activity is a "good thing".

This does not mean that everything worthwhile must be measurable. Many important ES's can only be assessed subjectively.

The point is this: if an ES is truly a key performance requirement; if we intend to set performance objectives, then we should check out the feedback process. The information system is supposed to tell us how we are doing in important areas of performance, i.e. ES's. **If formal measurement is not possible we should at least discuss the basis on which a subjective assessment will be reached.**

8

46

EFFECTIVENESS AREAS (EAs) the KEY OUTPUT REQUIREMENTS of a job or unit.	EFFECTIVENESS STANDARDS (ESs) PERFORMANCE INDICATORS or criteria which apply to each EA.	MEASUREMENT PROCESS the FEEDBACK SYSTEM which will provide data relevant to each ES.	OBJECTIVES SPECIFIC & QUANTIFIED TARGETS which will apply to each ES
ASK What are my important responsibilities? Can I express these as OUTPUTS (not activities)? Is each expressed so that it leads to associated measures? Am I personally responsible and accountable for this EA? When complete, EAs should represent the *entire* job yet not be so many as to hide the essentials.	**ASK** How can I tell when I am doing this EA well? What will be reviewed or measured? What criteria or requirements will indicate quality? What am I going to look at or review to determine effectiveness in this EA? Is this truly a measure for this EA? Do I own this ES? Is it what I, personally, can control or contribute? Is it within my direct authority?	**ASK** Where will I/my boss go to get the data? What review process will determine if the ES is achieved or fulfilled? Where is the information? Is this the right data for the EA/ES specified? Are all ESs covered? If I can't get relevant data, if no review process is possible, what's the point of the ES or EA?	**ASK** What specific time bounded targets will apply for this time period? What meets requirements? If the objective cannot be quantified, can we agree subjective criteria for assessment - examples, benchmarks?

DEFINE THE ORGANISATION	DETERMINE WHERE OBJECTIVES WILL BE REQUIRED	SET UP THE MANAGEMENT INFORMATION SYSTEM	SET THE BAR

AT EACH STEP — CHECK — do I own this, do I control it? is there logic EA-ES-Objective?

OBJECTIVES

Objectives are the specific targets to be achieved in this review period (usually 6-12 months); they define where we "set the bar" for performance evaluation.

Effectiveness Standards show where we need to agree objectives and, while there may be more than one objective for any ES, try to avoid having too many. If there are many detailed objectives included in, for instance, a project schedule; then the appropriate objective will be "Achieve published schedule". Otherwise the performance plan becomes too detailed, a formalised "to do" list. *

There is another danger here. We can fall into the trap of thinking that, unless something is documented in our performance plan it doesn't apply or that we cannot be evaluated on that item. This would be nonsense. **All ES's apply** and we should not need to formally document every aspect of the job. After all, this is a performance plan and not a piece of tax legislation!

Also, while objectives should be as specific as possible concerning quantities and times; we need to accept that some will be subjective. In those cases, take time to discuss examples, benchmarks, some broad criteria for evaluation.

* Someone who is new to the job might need a substantial amount of guidance on the how to of the job. Early training might include detailed instructions but this training is a temporary phase and should not be a permanent feature of performance planning.

48

EFFECTIVENESS AND QUALITY

PERFORMANCE PLANNING

EFFECTIVENESS AREA	EFFECTIVENESS STANDARD	MEASUREMENT PROCESS	OBJECTIVE
WHAT IS THE KEY OUTPUT REQUIREMENT	WHAT ARE THE PERFORMANCE CRITERIA	WHAT IS THE RECORD OR REVIEW PROCESS	WHAT IS THE SPECIFIC TARGET FOR THIS REVIEW PERIOD

EFFECTIVENESS IS MEETING OUTPUT REQUIREMENTS

QUALITY

EFFECTIVENESS AREA	EFFECTIVENESS STANDARD	MEASUREMENT PROCESS	OBJECTIVE
WHAT IS THE KEY OUTPUT REQUIREMENT	WHAT ARE THE KEY QUALITY CHARACTERISTICS OR DIMENSIONS	WHAT DATA IS AVAILABLE TO MEASURE QUALITY WHEN, WHERE & HOW DO WE MEASURE	WHAT IS THE QUALITY REQUIREMENT OR SERVICE LEVEL

QUALITY IS CONFORMANCE TO CUSTOMER REQUIREMENTS

EFFECTIVENESS AND QUALITY

Effectiveness is common to performance planning and quality.

They are both concerned with defining the requirements for effectiveness. The chart opposite shows how, if we take the performance planning framework, the same ideas can readily serve quality.

Once we have defined *performance* requirements, we have defined the *quality* requirements. There is no need for additional EAs or objectives called 'Quality' because quality standards are built into the performance plan.

The quality movement has been instrumental in raising the sights of managers beyond cost and schedule to quality — meaning other requirements *as well as* cost and schedule. This influence has been good. We have learned that quality is not an 'either or' question, it's an 'and' issue. Not productivity *or* quality, but productivity and quality; not quota achievement *or* employee satisfaction, but quota achievement *and* employee satisfaction.

Similarly, in performance planning, especially as part of team building, we have learned to identify effectiveness standards over a wide range of job requirements — and beyond cost and schedule. We have sometimes called this "Common EAs" or "Culture" and many individuals and teams are developing specific performance plans for effectiveness areas like Relationships or Leadership.

Both approaches share an insistence on *data.*

Without data we can't get to grips with where we are now, where we want to be or how we will know when things improve or get worse. Without data, we are whistling in the dark.

Finally, just as measurement leads inevitably to objectives and standards, setting standards leads to appraisal: the essential step in the control cycle which compares actual results against the standard.

So we have two approaches to the same thing, the specifying of requirements and the systematic improvement of performance.

Neither the performance planning process, nor the quality process are, in themselves, complete. Together, however, they appear to provide a major breakthrough in the management of teamwork and excellence.

50

SUMMARY

While objectives are central to PPC & E,
they are not the starting point.

The starting point is performance planning,
which implies understanding of the job, it's
key output requirements and how it fits into
the bigger scheme of things.

The method described here provides a
logical and reliable process for delegation
and communication which can result in
some important insights into the true nature
of the job as well as a soundly based
performance plan.

It will also provide a comprehensive
understanding of quality requirements for
individuals and teams who might otherwise
believe "It isn't possible to be specific
about quality. If there are no outputs there
is no job!" The document which follows
contains a summary of this process.
Finally, it is well to remind ourselves that
the performance plan, the objectives and
measures are not *the job*, but a
representation of some of its key results.
The job is not simply to meet the numbers
but to manage the business, which
concerns the people we work with, our
customers and the community at large.

IBM

Case study — Performance planning for a hotel chef

The purpose of this case is to illustrate the logical flow of ideas from Unit Effectiveness Areas to Individual Performance Plan.

Organisation Chart

First, let's review the organisation of this very small establishment.

The hotel is run by a Manager, to whom report the Housekeeper, an Assistant Manager and the Chef (our subject).

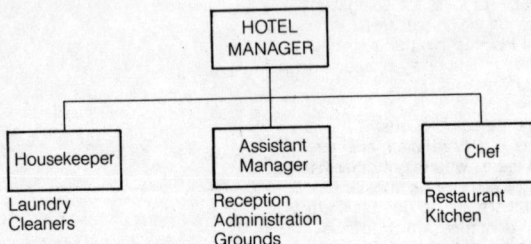

```
                    HOTEL
                   MANAGER
        ┌─────────────┼─────────────┐
   Housekeeper    Assistant        Chef
                   Manager
   Laundry        Reception      Restaurant
   Cleaners       Administration Kitchen
                  Grounds
```

We will now follow the *process* which produces the Chef's performance plan. The purpose is to show the flow and logic of each step and we will not construct a complete plan.

Step 1 — Unit Effectiveness Areas

The first step, as always, is to identify Unit EAs, the key output requirements of the Hotel as a whole enterprise. These include Profitability and Reputation.

UNIT EFFECTIVENESS AREAS
PROFITABILITY
REPUTATION

Step 2 — Personal EAs

The delegation matrix shows how the Unit EAs are broken down and delegated to individual team members. Constructing the matrix is basic to team building.

Delegation Matrix

Unit EAs	Member EAs			Manager
	Chef	Housekeeper	Asst. Mgr	
Profitability	Kitchen Efficiency			Revenue Expense level
Reputation	Meal Quality			Reputation

Part of the Motel Matrix is shown above

In this case, the Chef's contribution to the Unit EA "Reputation" is "Meal Quality". The Manager retains responsibility for overall reputation of the hotel.

We will now expand on the Chef's personal EA "Meal Quality".

Step 3 — Agree Effectiveness Standards for each EA

Once the EAs are agreed, the next step is to break down each EA to show the key performance indicators, ESs.

Taking the EA Meal Quality as an example, the Chef and his manager ask: "What will indicate performance in this area? What can we measure, review, look at?"

There will usually be more than one ES for any EA and they produce the list shown below:

E.G.

EA	EFFECTIVENESS STANDARDS
Meal quality	— quality and freshness of ingredients — variety — nutritional value — presentation — acceptability to diners

Note: these are not the quantified targets, nor are they action steps, they are the indications or requirements which can be examined to test for effectiveness in this EA (and, therefore, they indicate where objectives will be required).

Step 4 — Establish the Measurement Process for each ES

This is the feedback system which will provide data relevant to each ES. Ask: "Where will I go to get the information? What information record/system or review process will determine whether the ES is fulfilled?"

When the measurement process is 'manager review', discuss who is to review what, with whom and what the evaluation criteria will be.

E.G.

EA	ES	MEASUREMENT PROCESS
Meal quality	— quality & freshness of ingredients — variety — nutritional value — presentation — acceptability of diners	— sample inspection and taste — menu — ? ? — inspection by manager — relevant comments from guest evaluation returns

NEXT: Check that the chosen feedback process will provide data which is relevant to the ES and the EA. (It's surprisingly easy to find that something else entirely is being measured).

REALITY TEST: Check that relevant data is available for each ES. If, for a given ES it is not possible to check that it is being achieved (even by subjective judgement) then that ES does not, in reality, exist. In this example, although nutrition appeared to be a valid ES, there was no practical or convenient method of measuring it and it was deleted in favour of 'freshness' and 'variety'.

Step 5 — Establish the Objective for each ES

These are the specific, time bounded targets which will apply for this review period. They define quantities, times, deadlines, costs etc.

E.G.

ES	OBJECTIVE
Variety	at least 6 entrees/vegetarian and low-fat choices.

If it is not possible to establish a quantified objective, agree a subjective bases for assessment.

E.G.

ES	OBJECTIVE
Presentation	set a high standard of creativity and attractiveness which becomes a feature of this restaurant.

PART V

End Pieces

Introduction

These end-pieces are designed to provide you with yet more ways to get the best out of this book. It will be useful for you to look over the Glossary and check that you are familiar with all the terms and definitions. Should you want elaboration on any of the terms used then turn to the index to find the various pages where any term appears.

The examples of effectiveness areas are designed to provide some idea triggers. Some may look rather like inputs to you but the truth is that the output of a planner is in fact planning but that would obviously be an input for a production manager. It is useful to read over the list as a whole to see if you can lock into some ideas that will help you come to grips with aspects of your position.

The many examples of measurement areas provided show that the measurement area is an effectiveness area with the addition of the method of measurement. The important thing in the measurement area list is not so much the effectiveness areas on which they are based but rather the method of measurement used. The methods are comprehensive and range from ratios, absolute amounts, comparison with past period or per cent of something.

The examples of the objectives provided show that objectives are numbers added to measurement areas. As with the two prior sections it will be useful for you to read over all of them to see if they provide some idea triggers for you in thinking about your job and its objectives.

Glossary

accountability: The requirement to achieve outputs.

activity: A particular thing a manager actually does or intends to do.

activity network: A diagram of a particular combination of activities connected by arrows to show sequential relationships.

activity schedule: A visual arrangement of activities over a time period.

another's area: Effectiveness areas managers show as their own which are really those of other managers.

apparent effectiveness: The extent to which a manager gives the appearance of being effective.

areas alignment: When effectiveness areas for a set of related positions have to overlap or underlap.

authority (or, power): The influence over the actions of others or the utilization of things by the exercise of both formal authority and informal authority.

authority area: A short statement, prefixed with the word decide, identifying the authority associated with the position.

BO: Beginning of (usually a month but could be a year).

checkpoint meeting (CPM): A superior-manager meeting, usually held quarterly, at which the manager's progress towards objectives is reviewed.

command: Military term denoting the exercise of formal authority.

conventional job description: A written statement emphasizing the input requirements of a particular managerial position.

CPM: See *checkpoint meeting*

dedicated unit organization: A unit characterized by one unit member's outputs becoming another unit member's inputs with the top member inputs directed primarily to interfaces across unit members.

DUR: During (during a particular period).

EAs: See *effectiveness areas*

effective data: Quantified information which is relevant, timely, accurate and in an easily usable form.

effectiveness areas (EAs): General output requirements of a management position.

352

effectiveness areas errors: The five effectiveness areas errors defined in this glossary are: Input, Worry, Another's, Non-measurable and Time.

EO: End of (usually a month but could be a year).

formal authority: Influence over the actions of others or the utilization of things derived from the authority vested in the position one occupies.

horizontal alignment: When effectiveness areas for two or more positions at the same level have no overlap or underlap.

informal authority: Influence over the actions of others or the utilization of things derived from one's personal qualities.

input area: An incorrect statement of an effectiveness area which is based on an activity rather than a result.

inputs: What a manager does, or is to do, rather than what a manager achieves by doing it.

integrated unit organization: A unit characterized by a high level of interaction across unit members.

JED: See *job effectiveness description (JED)*

job description: see conventional job description.

job effectiveness description (JED):   A written statement specifying the effectiveness areas, measurement areas and authority of a particular management position.

leader: Someone exercising a high degree of informal authority.

leadership: The exercise of informal authority.

management information system (MIS):   The method by which managers are provided numerical measurement to evaluate their progress towards achieving objectives.

management: The exercise of formal authority.

manager: Someone exercising a high degree of formal authority.

managerial effectiveness: The extent to which a manager achieves the output requirements of the position.

managerial skills: Three skills required for managerial effectiveness: situational management, situational sensitivity, style flexibility.

measurement area: How an effectiveness area is measured.

member: See *unit member*

MIS: See *management information system*

non-measurable area: An unsuitable effectiveness area as the associated objective is not measurable.

objective planning form (OPF):   A form used to record a single objective of one measurement area together with priority, activities and plan.

objectives: Effectiveness areas which are as specific, as time-bounded, and as measurable as possible. Specific output requirements of a management position.

one-on-one meeting: The one-on-one meeting, usually lasting from four to eight hours, consists of the unit top member and each unit member in turn. The main outputs of the meeting are to review the unit member's JED, to agree unit member's objectives for a future period, to identify any blockages to achieving objectives that might exist and to identify help from the top member that will made available.

OPF: See *objective planning form*

organization output survey: A survey undertaken as part of an output orientation programme, to determine existing conditions in the organization.

outputs: What managers achieve, or are to achieve, rather than what they do.

overlap: When two positions are responsible for the same effectiveness area.

personal effectiveness: The extent to which managers achieve their own private objectives.

plan: A sequence of activities.

power: See *authority*

related unit organization: A unit characterized by a low level of interaction across unit members.

responsibilities: Outputs.

role clarification: A complete specification of effectiveness areas, measurement areas and authority.

sapiential authority: Presumed authority based on knowledge.

schedule: A plan with timings.

separated unit organization: A unit characterized by a low level of interaction across unit members except for top member inputs to unit members.

time area: An item on which a manager spends a great deal of time but which is not an effective area.

top member: See *unit top member*

underlap: When no position has been assigned an effectiveness area which is needed.

unit: A set of related positions including a unit top member and one or more unit members.

unit effectiveness description: A written statement specifying the effectiveness areas, measurement areas and authority of a unit taken as a whole.

unit member: A member, other than the top member of a unit, normally referred to as subordinate.

unit member outputs: The effectiveness areas of a unit member.

unit objectives meeting: A meeting usually lasting 1–1½ days, consists of the unit top member and all unit members. The main outputs of the meeting are to establish, for an agreed period, the objectives of the unit, the unit top member and unit team members.

unit outputs: The set of effectiveness areas for a unit which naturally include the outputs of the top member and all unit members summarized in some way.

unit outputs diagram: A diagram containing the four elements of unit member outputs, unit top member outputs, unit outputs and unit top member inputs.

unit outputs meeting: A meeting usually lasting two-three days, consisting of the unit top member and all unit members. The main outputs of the meeting are to establish the unit outputs diagram and to make changes as necessary in unit organization structure, policies and procedures.

unit review meeting: A meeting usually lasting one day, consists of the unit top member and all unit members. The main outputs of the meeting are to review the achievement of objectives of the unit as a whole, of the unit top member and all unit members.

unit top member: The head of a unit, often called the superior.

unit top member inputs: The activities of the top member to improve unit effectiveness.

unit top member outputs: The outputs of the unit top member having no overlap with unit top member inputs or with any unit member outputs.

vertical alignment: When effectiveness areas for two or more related positions at different levels have no overlap or underlap.

worry area: Effectiveness areas managers show as their own because they do not expect another manager whose area it is, to deal with it effectively without intervention.

Appendix A   Examples of effectiveness areas

You may find this appendix a further aid to establishing your effectiveness areas. It may give you some hints on alternative terms to use. Some managers will find it less useful and will prefer to work directly from their concept of the job rather than from a list such as this. It is simply a guide should you want to use it.

Some of the possible effectiveness areas listed here would be outputs for some jobs and inputs for others. The words themselves do not automatically indicate input or output. The authority must be known for the decision to be made.

These suggested effectiveness areas are quite deliberately not grouped by function. One of many reasons is that there is a strong temptation to simply look at one's own function and not realize that on looking at the job with a higher level of generality, that the concepts from other functions are equally ... or far better ... applicable. As an example a typical data processing manager need look no further than the outputs of the production function. That is exactly what the position calls for and the classic outputs of production function which include cost, timings, delivery and quantity apply better than a list that might be found under data processing.

This list could go on. It is provided to offer some ideas for you to think about: triggers.

Absenteeism
Accounting cost control
Accounts
   charge
   expense
   payable
   receivable
   slow pay and unsatisfactory
   uncollectable
Acquisitions
Administration

Advertising
   budget
   campaign
   direct mail
   institutional
   point of purchase
   production
   public relations
   sales promotion
   specialities
Applied research

Appraisal
Arbitration
Assets
  current
  fixed
  frozen
  liquid
  intangible
  utilization
Associations
Attitude survey
Attitudes
Auditing
Bad debt
Balance sheet
Banking
Basic research
Benefits
Bids quotations
Billing
Board of directors
Branches
Brand
  names
  national
  private
Budget
  account
  advertising
  calendar
  cash
  departments
  materials
  production
  sales
Budgetary control
Budgeted costs
Budgeting
Buying power
By-products
Capital
  appropriations
  circulating
  current

  fixed
  fluid
  gain
  goods
  stock
  structure
  quick
Capitalization
Cash
  availability
  budget
  disbursements
  discount
  flow
  journal
  petty
  receipts
Channels of distribution
Charge account
Charge-offs
Collection
Cash debt procedures
Collective bargaining
Commissions
Committee
  meetings
  organization
Common stock
Communication
Community relations
Company
  policies
  school
Compensation
Competition
Competitor
  relations
  surveys
Complaints
Computer
Conferences
Conferences and conventions
Confidential information
Construction

Public
  relations
  speeches
Publications
Purchasing
  costs
  schedule
Quality control
Quantity
Quotations
Raw materials
Receiving
Reciprocity
Recovery
Recreation
Recruitment
Redundancy
Relations
  community
  competitor
  customer
  employee
  government
  industrial
  labour
  political
  press
  public
  shareholder
  supplier
  union–management
  worker
Rejects
Release of information
Rentals
Reorganization
Research
  applied
  marketing
Reports financial
Reserves
Retail
  costs
  distribution

  sales
Retention
Retirement
Return of goods
Return on investment
Royalties
Safety
  programme
  security and
Salary
  administration
  levels
  survey
Sales
  budget
  contests
  convention
  force
  forecasting
  management
  programme
  promotion
  quota
  to employees
  volume
Scrap
Secrecy agreements
Securities
Security
Selection
Selection of projects
Selling expense
Seniority
Services
  customer, to
  technical
Shareholder relations
Shipments
Sickness
Spoilage
Standard costs
Standards
Stock
  capital

common
control
shipments
Storing
Strikes
Supplier relations
Supply
  costs
  schedule
Surplus property
Survey
  attitude
  competitor
  consumer
  customer
  employee
  opinion
  salary
Tax
  income
  sales
Technical development
  ideas
  papers published
  services
Termination
Terms
Territories
Testing
Time
  buying
  management
  studies
Tolerances
Tooling
Total cost
Tours
Trade
  discounts
  journals
  marks
  names
  secrets
  shows

Traffic
  control
  density
Training development
Transfer and relocation
Travel and transportation
Turnover
Union
  costs
  labour
  management relations
Unit costs
  hourly production
  labour cost
  overhead cost
  rejection rate
  scrap ratio
Utilities
Vacations
Valuation
Value engineering
Variance
Venture capital
Wage
  average
  guaranteed annual
  incentive
  money
  real
  time
Wages
  direct
  indirect
Warehousing
Welfare
Work hours
  in process
  stoppage
  study
Worker relations
Working capital
Working conditions
Written report

Appendix B Examples of measurement areas

Overhead costs levels as per cent of production costs
Money value of royalties received
Net profit as a percentage of sales
Ratio of direct to indirect labour
Ratio of scrap to output value
Reduction of clerical labour costs in three departments by the installation of a data-processing system whose leasing and operational costs are not to exceed a per cent of the projected savings
Sales cost levels in units
Average contract cost to be under plan
Deviations from standard costs
Accounts receivable trends in per cent compared to month prior year
Excess costs charged to department
Inventory to sales levels ratio
Percentage of performance variance against budgets
Transmit quality requirements for products to Marketing and Manufacturing management
Cost of transportation as a percentage of sales
Back order ratio with inventory levels
Percentage of projects completed against forecasts
Percentage increase in dividends year on year
Techniques in work simplification mastered, as related to machine-shop operations through a cost-reduction meeting for machine-shop supervisors
Validation of standards of qualifications for new hourly employees
Percentage of unit cost in material handling
Ratio of inventory to assets
Amount of lost time owing to out-of-stock condition
Inventory-sales ratio reduction
Percentage of return on investments
Current assets to current liabilities ratio
Percentage of utilization of available floor space
Frequency of missed delivery dates
Job-time completion rates in per cent variance from standard time

Overtime to normal time ratios

Customer complaints percentage reduction

Late deliveries less than percentage of total sales volume

All warehouse shipments to be made as scheduled

Meet client quality, cost and time standards as established in each contract

Reduce drawing revisions percentage of original submissions

Completion of design and development of new prototype without subcontracting

Improve research know-how in section B by increasing PhD hirings

Profit to total assets ratio

Debt to total assets ratio

Number of patents lodged this year

Percentage of delivery dates met

Percentage of error in filling orders

Ratio of absentee to worked time

Per cent change in accounts overdue by 60 days by quarter

Cost of employee recruitment

Direct to indirect labour ratios

Absolute machine hours per product

Percentage share of actual markets

Percentage share of potential market

Number of conferences attended by middle management

Late deliveries less than percentage of orders

Percentage reduction in the cost of outside legal services

Service costs within established budgets . . . % of all orders to arrive at the customers' plants at the scheduled time

Establish quality standards for major products

Paint vehicles with company insignia

Completion of product design specification for product M

Approval obtained from three departments of production plans for customer, costs, and schedule

Reduction of cost of pump and engine repairs per year per mechanic

A new horizontal boring mill acquired

Gross profit margin percentage increased

Attain gross profit as percentage of sales

Reduction of secretarial staff by end of year

Acceptance of company policies by all employees

Reduction in cost of recruiting each engineer

Results of a sampling survey of the organization's hiring image in three adjacent labour markets

Number of uncollectable accounts per year

Value of assets sold annually

Ratio of technical ideas generated to accepted/rejected per annum

Damage claims as a percentage of sales orders
Demand time to supply time ratios
Number of branches under budget
Number of branches 10 per cent above budget/profit/turnover
Ratio of experienced production employees to new employees
Number of leavers quarter by quarter
Labour utilization as percentage of production costs
Sales per employee ratios
Advertising responses per annum
Average number of participants per conference
Average cost per conference
Increase the percentage of outside correspondence answered
Reduction of quality control labour costs by introducing centralized
    rather than decentralized inspection
Reduction of plant operating costs per 100 units produced
Capital value increase year on year
Value of capital written-off last year
Collections made each day
Complaints made to suppliers
Average per cent commission earned per sale
Computer usage in hours per day
Total suggestions submitted and percentage implemented
Inventory turnover per annum
Number of branches opened per month
Number of branches closed per month
Collected cost-reduction ideas from operating managers
Completion of literature and patent search for five patentable ideas
    useful in entering new markets K, L, and M
Reduction in weld rejects of XYZ steels of all plates in assembly S
Cash flow amounts
Cash levels at end of each day/week/month
Complaints received from each sales region
Copyrights applied for in each year
Employee transfer requests made each quarter
Annual average lateness per division
Set-up and preparation time as percentage of production time
Programme initiated to perfect production process and formulate
    programme to design Product A
Quality control costs not exceeding percentage of sales
Achieve a return on investment increase quarter by quarter
Reduction of current debt to tangible net worth position to a
    percentage for proposed creditor account
Depreciation value written-off per annum
Value of discounts allowed/received per month

Number of disciplinary cases reported per month
Number of customer complaints product by product
Number of new distributors established in quarter
Number of published papers accepted or published in professional journals
Completion for distribution a 20-page, 10-topic industrial relations policy manual for newly hired employees
All organization charts audited and, as necessary, updated
Performance appraisals and salary reviews conducted for all subordinates
Funds available per period
Warehousing cubic space used each quarter
Number of promotions made from within per annum
Introduction of stock option plan for managers
Decrease in termination rate of clerical employees
Read new management books at a rate of one per month
Organization plans showing replacements for each key position prepared
Percentage increase in share of market
Income tax paid per tax year
Amount of down time per hour/day/week
Completion of an attitude survey of labour–management relations among all employees
Completion of the planning, organization, and installation of an employee suggestion system
The process of managing by objectives implemented one level lower in the organization
Maintenance of total heat losses as a percentage of total heat-transferred when changing from system A to system B
Number of new class 'A' accounts obtained
Percentage pensions growth year on year
Amount of down time per machine section/department/plant
Number of contracts from new clients obtained
Percentage share of the wholesale market gained
Ratio of sales calls to orders at or under 6 to 1
New to old product ratios
Amount of incentives earned per sale made
Volume of Product C developed three fold
Sales costs and sales expense ratios maintained within established budgets
Number of locations visited per trip
Scrap increase/decrease in percentage terms month by month
Trained replacements available for some of my subordinates
Have available trained replacements for each management position

in marketing
New to old sales ratios
Training completed of replacements for key positions in accounting
section

Appendix C   Examples of objectives

Here is a comprehensive list of objectives. All are quantified specific and measurable. It will be useful to look over all of them and select some which after some work on may be suitable for your position. Many are deliberately worded in a general way so they could be applied to many different positions. Time bounds are omitted, in most cases, but must be included for a complete statement of an objective.

Ratio of direct to indirect labour over 3 to 1

Increase inventory turnover to 20 months

Complete study and construct index of expense trends for all departments for the past five years and project forward

No lost time owing to out-of-stock condition

Inventory–sales ratio reduced by 18 per cent

All warehouse shipments to be made within four days of receiving order

Meet client quality, cost and time standards as established in each contract

Complete write-up and acceptance of organization cost-reduction manual and distribute to all members of management within two months

Complete design and development of new prototype in five months within cost of 1000 money units without subcontracting

Before mid-summer acquire a new horizontal boring mill

Gross profit margin increased 1.3 per cent

Obtain gross profit of 260 money units per month for each consultant on staff

Capital expenditure projects to 5 per cent of actual, of estimates of savings anticipated

Lost time accidents take less than one per cent of total time worked this year

Not more than two grievances past second stage in any one month

Reduce cost of recruiting each engineer next year from 800 to 600 money units while meeting requisition totals and dates

Complete, for distribution at the end of next month, a 20-page, 10-topic industrial relations policy manual for newly hired employees

Conduct performance appraisals and salary reviews for all subordinates within six months

Floor space utilization for production to be a minimum of 85 per cent this budget year

Overtime time not more than 8 per cent of regular hours worked

Maintain total heat losses at 17 per cent of total heat-transferred when changing from system A to system B

Share of market increased two per cent by end of year

Obtain 20 new class 'A' accounts this quarter .

Increase sales revenues of new products by 50 per cent

Increase occupancy ratio in hotel rooms from a yearly mean of 65 to 75 per cent while maintaining rate structure

Develop volume of Product C threefold in one year

Trained replacements to be available by end of year for four of my eight subordinates

All operators with eight months' service capable of assuming at least 90 per cent efficiency on at least four different assembly operations

Obtain at least 25 per cent of gross income from project management services

Average contract cost to be 5 per cent under plan

Obtain 3 per cent reduction from projected expense trends in next year

Customer complaints reduced by 6 per cent

Raw material inventory maintained between 500 to 600 value per 100,000 tons of monthly output

Late deliveries less than 1 per cent of total sales volume

Warehouse inventories will meet 95 per cent of sales requirements and provide a 6.3 per cent turnover every six months

Reduce drawing revisions to 35 per cent of time of original submissions

No mill shutdowns owing to inadequate water supply

Complete product design specification for product M within budgetary period

Reduce cost of pump and engine repairs from 67 to 52 money units per year per mechanic

Complete construction of 50,000 square feet, two-storey approved addition to existing plan within cost of five units per square foot by spring of next year

Attain gross profit of 12 per cent of sales

To increase earnings from two money units per share last year to 3.20 units per share in four years time

Submit by 13 March 199– . . . a capital appropriation request for the addition of 25,000 square feet to the plant

Reduce secretarial staff by 24 per cent by end of financial year

Acceptance of company policies by all employees within six months of engagement

Decrease termination rate of clerical employees from 13 per cent to nine per cent

Read 12 new books in management by the end of a year, at a rate of one per month

All organization charts will be audited and, as necessary, updated every 12 months

Organization plans showing replacements for each key position will be prepared annually

Each new employee will receive at least three hours of first-day induction and orientation

Reduce indirect labour costs by 35 per cent this financial year

Monthly overtime hours not to exceed hours lost due to absenteeism

Increase average order size to 8000 money units before 31 DEC

Increase total annual sales by 18 per cent

Complete 90 per cent follow-up calls of new inquiries within three days of initial inquiry

Develop new product by JUL and determine commercial acceptability by DEC

Initiate market development of new product to be piloted by mid-199–

Have available at least one trained replacement for each management position in marketing

Complete training of three replacements for key positions in accounting section by next JUN

Complete training programme A for all district representatives to assure readiness for distributing product Y at the first of the year

Consultant paid time to be average of 3.2 days per week

Excess costs charged to department not above 5.5 per cent

Reduce clerical labour costs in three departments by 35 per cent with the installation of a data-processing system whose leasing and operational costs are not to exceed 50 per cent of the projected savings

Late deliveries less than 1 per cent of orders

Seventy per cent productive utilization of warehouse space

Keep service costs this year within established budgets

Treated water costs at or below budget estimate

Accidents down 14 per cent on last year

Supply three new products to market within the coming financial year, with forecasted sales not less than 10 million

Reduce weld rejects of XYZ steels from 3.2 per cent to 2.3 per cent of all plates in assembly S

Achieve for the machine-shop a process layout by end of year to reduce material-handling costs to 2.2 per cent of manufactured costs

To divest ourselves of retail division within three years at, at least 40 per cent above book value.

Reduce by 10 per cent the working cash required in bank deposits

Four published papers accepted or published in professional journals

Lateness reduced to one occurrence per two months per employee

Complete within three months an attitude survey of labour–management relations among all employees within budget cost

No new employees to be hired for a position for which there is no job description or set salary range

Increase the production capacity for Unit A from 70 units per day in 199– to 74 units in 199– and to 80 units in 199–

Obtain six contracts from new clients totalling at least 110,000 money units by 30 SEP

Obtain contracts from at least 10 per cent of customers with whom no contracts have been completed in the past two years.

Increase Product A volume by holding our share of the expected market growth

Complete strategic plans for pricing and distribution of Product A and Product C in face of competition from other products within three months

Master ten techniques in work simplification as related to machine-shop operations through a six-month-by-month cost-reduction meeting for machine-shop supervisors

Complete course in statistics within the next term with a grade of B or better

Excess costs charge to department not above 5.5 per cent

Maximum bonus earnings not more than 120 per cent

Ratio of direct to indirect labour not exceed 3.2

Complete master schedule of sales and inventories for next financial year to reduce stock-out frequency rate to two per week

Reduce by 30 per cent the cost of outside legal services

Hold city direct mail promotion costs to 0.05 money units per item

Eighty-five per cent of all orders to arrive at the customers' plants at the scheduled time

Five per cent reduction in standard labour content in product 'A'

Establish quality standards for 46 major products

All vehicles painted with company insignia

Complete network layout for contract B within the pre-budgetary planning schedule

Complete value analysis job plan for three engineering sections during operating quarter

Quality control costs will not exceed 0.5 per cent of sales in any quarter

Achieve a 13 per cent return on investment within five operating quarters

Maintain current asset to current debt ratio not less than 5 to 1 for the next financial year

Secretarial labour to be not more than 20 per cent of total clerical staff

Complete planning, organization, and installation of an employee suggestion system at the start of next year's cost-reduction programme

During 199– carry the process of managing by objectives one level lower in the organization

Maintain overtime hours at the level of 10 per cent of scheduled hours while completing emergency work programme A

Increase our share of the wholesale market this year from 12 per cent to 21 per cent

Ratio of sales calls to orders at or under 6 to 1

Broaden market for Product C by achieving at least one new volume programme in product line or end-use market

Set up and validate five standards of qualifications for new hourly employees

Complete training by December 199– of all supervisors in two-day seminars on managing by objectives

Reduce clerical accounting labour by 50,000 money units per installation of electronic data-processing equipment

Transmit each month quality requirements for products to marketing and manufacturing management

Reduce average handling time of customer complaints by 6 per cent

Reduce number of customer complaints on commercial business from 3 per cent to 1.5 per cent of orders involved

Money settlement on returns should not exceed 5 per cent of total invoices

During next year raw materials inventories not to exceed a ratio of 2 to 1 to the next quarter's forecast volume

Complete construction and equipping of approved addition to new plant within cost of 40,000 money units

Reduce quality control labour costs by 10 per cent by introducing centralized rather than decentralized inspection

Increase diversification programme with development and introduction of five new products within the small product line

Achieve a net profit average of at least 15 per cent of sales and 9 per cent of net assets

Complete an operating and financial strategy statement for each objective within three months for presentation to the board of directors

Introduce a stock option plan for managers by end of calendar year

During 199– have each plant establish a customer liaison representative to act as host when a customer visits the plant

Maintain a once-a-day contact with all subordinates at their work stations and hold a once-a-month work appraisal meeting in office with all subordinates

Obtain 20 per cent of sales from new accounts next period

Reduce accounts receivable from average of 70 days in 199– to 60 days in 199– and 55 days in 199–

Achieve an average age of accounts receivable below 60 days

Reduce inventory lead time from 13 weeks to 10 weeks

Reduce obsolete items and all adjustments to inventory to 12 per cent of commercial sales

Obtain from research efforts two accepted improvements

Reduce plant operating costs to 13 money units per 100 units produced

Complete literature and patent search by end of year for five patentable ideas useful in entering new markets K, L, and M

Reduce research investment pay-out time from five years to three years

Reduce capital expenditures, class B from 17 to 15 during the next two years

Increase by 25 per cent the working cash required in each of seven banks at the end of the year by holding inventory levels at 80 per cent capacity

Maintain sales promotion expenses at last year's levels

Reduce turnover of salespeople to less than 16 per cent per year

Restrict bad debt losses to less than 3 per cent on non-defence sales

Improve margin by 4 per cent with same revenues but with reduced costs of three per cent

Develop technological capability to introduce two new products in market sector BB by end of three-year profit plan

Collect ten suggested cost-reduction ideas per month from each of six operating managers

Index